Wills and Probate

About the author

Paul Elmhirst is a practising solicitor of many years' experience in the area of wills and probate, and has written for other publications on the subject.

Other contributors

Ewan Kennedy, author of the chapter on Scotland, studied and taught law at Glasgow University. He has been in general practice in Glasgow for over 35 years.

Alastair Rankin, who wrote the chapter on Northern Ireland, is in a firm of Belfast solicitors. He has contributed to a number of publications in the area of succession law, and is a part-time lecturer in Belfast.

Wills and Probate

Paul Elmhirst

which

?

Which? books are commissioned by
Consumers' Association and published by
Which? Ltd, 2 Marylebone Road, London NW1 4DF
Email: books@which.co.uk

Distributed by The Penguin Group:
Penguin Books Ltd, 80 Strand, London WC2R 0RL

First edition 1967
Many new editions including 1988, 1991, 1994, 1995, 1997, 1998, 1999, 2001
This edition March 2004
Reprinted November 2004

British Library Cataloguing in Publication Data
A catalogue record for *Wills and Probate* is available from the British Library

ISBN 0 85202 971 3

For a full list of Which? books, please call 0800 252100, access our website at www.which.co.uk, or write to Which? Books, Freepost, PO Box 44, Hertford SG14 1SH.

Editorial and production: Robert Gray, Nithya Rae, Barbara Toft
Index: Marie Lorimer
Original cover concept by Sarah Harmer
Cover photograph by ESB – Esbin-Anderson/A1Pix

Crown copyright material on page 155 is reproduced with the permission of the Controller of HMSO and the DCA.

Typeset by Saxon Graphics Ltd, Derby
Printed and bound in Wales by Creative Print and Design

For information on the latest Budget go to www.which.co.uk, click on 'Bookshop' and follow the links.

Contents

Introduction   7

1   Why you should make a will   9
2   The basics of making a will   18
3   Inheritance tax   35
4   What to put in your will   47
5   Examples of wills   68
6   Alterations to your will   81
7   Applying for probate   87
8   The administration   156
9   Problems and disputes   186
10 Intestacy   193
11 Wills and confirmation in Scotland   205
12 Wills and probate in Northern Ireland   230
Glossary   247
Useful addresses   249
Index   253

★ An asterisk next to the name of an organisation in the text indicates that the address can be found in this section

Whether you are writing your own will or sorting out someone else's will, please note that it is important to consult a legal adviser if the situation is at all complex.

Introduction

Death comes to all of us in the end – whether we make a will, think about making a will but never get round to it, or never let it cross our minds.

This book is intended to help at two separate stages. First, it explains why you should make a will, how to make a valid will and, by use of examples, how to give effect to your wishes. Second, it describes what has to be done after someone has died in order to administer his or her estate. The example used is a relatively straightforward case but it is hoped that it will give you a reasonable understanding of what has to be done when someone applies for probate. The book also explains what happens when someone dies without having made a will.

Married couples sometimes assume, wrongly, that they do not need to make a will because if they die everything will go to the surviving spouse. However, this will not be the case if the person who dies has more than £125,000, and even if he or she does not have assets worth that much his or her failure to make a will may create an unnecessary inheritance tax liability when the surviving spouse dies. So for married couples, a will is essential.

While most people who write their own wills or administer the estates of others are able to do so quite successfully without any deep knowledge of the law, it is as well to be aware that there are some 30 Acts of Parliament which provide the framework and rules for making wills and administering estates and trusts. Some of the rules are very strict but others can be modified. The Trustee Act 1925, the Administration of Estates Act 1925 and the Trustee Act 2000 are just three of the more important Acts. This book provides only an outline of the law of wills and probate, and cannot provide all the answers, so you may have to use other references or take advice if the issues are complicated.

It has been said that the one thing worse than not making a will is making a mess of a will. Common errors in home-made wills include not getting it properly witnessed and not clearly identifying the bequest or the person for whom it is intended. One man said in his will 'All to Mother', no doubt clear in his own mind where his estate was going. Unfortunately, he had always called his wife 'mother', so his will was ambiguous.

When it comes to applying for probate or letters of administration the Probate Registry (district registries are to be found in most large cities) provides a special procedure for those who wish to apply without using a solicitor. This book should help such people by explaining the procedure for obtaining probate as well as covering what must be done to administer the estate after probate has been granted.

This book does not try to explain all the complexities of inheritance tax or tax-avoidance schemes but you should be aware of the principles if you are going to make a will or administer an estate. It does explain how substantial savings of inheritance tax can be made by a fairly simple course of action, and should give an understanding that will enable readers to discuss more complicated tax-avoidance proposals with solicitors, accountants and financial advisers.

Wills and Probate explains the basic law and procedure in England and Wales. There are separate chapters to explain how the law and procedure differ in Scotland and Northern Ireland.

Chapter 1

Why you should make a will

For most people, what happens to their property and family when they die is a matter of importance, but others fear making a will as if to do so would somehow tempt providence. More commonly, people die without having made a will because they have just not got around to it.

What happens if you do not make a will

If a person dies without having made a will – or 'intestate' – the law (or more accurately, the Administration of Estates Act 1925) sets out who is to administer the person's estate and who is to benefit and in what proportions. It is possible that the intestacy rules would match exactly your own thoughts about the division of your property on your death, but that is not a common occurrence (see Chapter 10 for more details).

However, even if, under the intestacy rules, the property you own today would go to the people you would wish, it is impossible to guess in which order the death of your spouse or children will occur, and what gap there will be between them. It is therefore quite possible that, without a will, the property may not go to the people whom you might have assumed would automatically benefit. Also, your financial position could alter substantially between now and the time when you die. You may become wealthier or worse off, and in either case you should make a will. The value of your property might increase merely because of inflation, so that property worth under £125,000 (see page 10 for why this is a significant figure) now could be worth considerably more than £125,000 in a few years' time.

A will can also deal with things such as funeral wishes, appointments of guardians for children, and the passing down of specific items, such as family heirlooms and small gifts to express gratitude for friendship or other kindness during your life. It can be used to express a number of other provisions and wishes. Some of these may not be binding on the people concerned but they are a useful way of recording your views and wishes. See Chapters 2 and 4 for details.

If you make a will, you can also dictate who will be your executors, that is, the people responsible for administering your estate and looking after all your affairs after your death. If there is no will, the law dictates that your nearest relatives should take on the task of managing your estate (in this case they are called administrators). You may prefer to specify someone else to look after all your concerns – a relative or friend or, say, your solicitor – but to do this, it is essential that you make a will.

Your administrators are determined by law. If you have a spouse (estranged or not), he or she would be your administrator. If you have no spouse but you do have children, they will be eligible to be your administrators if they are over 18. The priority list continues working its way through the chain of family relationships. The administrator must obtain letters of administration, collect all the assets of the deceased, pay all the debts and then divide what is left among family members according to the rules laid down by the Administration of Estates Act 1925 (see Chapter 10 for distribution on intestacy). To leave the division of your estate to the intestacy laws may well cause trouble within the family as well as incurring unnecessary inheritance tax (IHT) – see Chapter 3.

The need to make a will in particular cases

Married couples

When there is a husband and wife and all the assets of the one who has died come to less than £125,000, everything goes to the surviving spouse, irrespective of whether there are any children. If the deceased's estate is worth more than £125,000 and there are children, the position becomes more complicated. However, if the deceased owned a house jointly with the surviving spouse as 'joint tenants', his or her share of the house would pass automatically to the surviving spouse irrespective of the rules of intestacy.

If there are children, the surviving spouse gets the first £125,000 and the chattels (see *Glossary*). If the surviving spouse is not a joint tenant of the matrimonial home, he or she is not entitled to get the house (unless its value is under £125,000 and he or she elects to have the house as part of his or her £125,000). The rest of the estate, in excess of £125,000, is then divided into two equal parts. One part is divided between the children (they have to wait till they are 18 to claim it) and the other half will be placed in a trust in which the surviving spouse will have a life interest. The surviving spouse is entitled to the income for life from that trust but, when he or she dies, the trust capital is then divided equally between the children.

The trust income paid to the surviving spouse might take the form of bank interest, share dividends or rent from property. What the surviving spouse cannot touch is the capital.

If there are no children, but the deceased leaves a surviving spouse as well as brothers and sisters, the rules provide that the surviving spouse gets the first £200,000 and the chattels plus one-half of the remainder. The other half of the remainder will be divided between the brothers and sisters (if there is no living parent).

As is evident, the rules can be harsh if the matrimonial home is worth more than £125,000. It could mean that the surviving spouse will be short of cash or, worse still, one of the grown-up children might try to force a sale of the matrimonial home to get at his or her share of the estate.

Unmarried couples

The intestacy rules which apply to a husband or wife do not apply to an unmarried couple, even if they have lived together for ten years, have six children and call themselves Mr and Mrs Smith. In such a case, when an unmarried parent dies, the whole of the estate will be divided between the children as if they had no surviving parents. If there are no children, the estate will pass to the parents of the deceased, and if there are no living parents, the siblings of the deceased will benefit. It is therefore essential for cohabiting couples to make wills to provide for one another as the intestacy rules will not help them at all.

A cohabitee in a relationship which has lasted for more than two years immediately prior to the death of a partner may be able to claim a share of the estate through the courts (see Chapter 9) but his or her own children could oppose him or her. A divorced person is treated as having no spouse.

Second marriages

If you are in a second marriage, the lack of a will may land your administrators with a very difficult problem. Whatever your intentions, the law of intestacy provides that your chattels go to your spouse along with the first £125,000 of your estate. If you have children by both marriages they will all be eligible to share in the remainder of your estate in accordance with the intestacy provisions. Uncle Arthur's gold watch and your sports car could well end up in the hands of your second wife and then your stepchildren even if you had intended giving them to your son from your first marriage. See Chapter 2 for more details.

Alternatively, your second wife might be faced with having to sell the house if it is worth substantially more than the £125,000 allocated to her under the intestacy rules.

Divorce and separation

Following your divorce, even if you do not remarry, the issue of a decree absolute renders void any gift to your ex-wife in an existing will. If you die intestate after your divorce, your ex-spouse gets nothing under the intestacy provisions although it is possible that he or she could mount a successful claim for part of your estate under the Inheritance (Provision for Family and Dependants) Act 1975 if that right has not been relinquished in a divorce settlement. See Chapter 2 for more details.

Death of parents with young children

If a single parent with young children dies (or if both parents die together in an accident) the intestacy rules provide that the estate is to be held in trust for the children until they reach 18. The rules say nothing about guardianship of the children, which could mean that the children are taken into care or that there is a dispute over who should care for them.

The Probate Registry would require two testamentary guardians to be appointed to obtain letters of administration and to supervise the money being held in trust for the children. These people may not be the ones you would have chosen to carry out that task.

A man (or a woman in similar circumstances) also has to consider the position which could arise after his death if, under the rules of intestacy, his widow is entitled only to a life interest in part of his estate. This means that she is not entitled to have the use of the capital which might be necessary simply to maintain her standard of living if the income from the capital is not enough or if, through inflation or reduced interest rates, the income becomes too small for her to live on.

In an intestacy, there are restrictions on the kind of investments that can be selected, and they may not necessarily be the investments which would be advised for the best management of the funds. In a will, these restrictions can be removed or modified so that a man can give his widow a chance of a better income, and *vice versa*.

A greater problem can arise if a husband and wife are killed together, in a common accident, leaving the children behind. The children would be able to receive the capital to which they were entitled only when they become 18. Until that time, it would have to be held in trust for them and be invested on their behalf. The restrictions on the kind of investments that can be selected might prevent the property being dealt with as flexibly and advantageously for the benefit of the children as might have been wished. Making a will can give greater freedom regarding investments, and the children could be better off.

Do-it-yourself or use a solicitor?

There is no legal requirement that a will should be drawn up or witnessed by a solicitor. Many people successfully write their own wills.

Intestacy rules

The intestacy rules go through a particular sequence of family members who are to benefit as a result of a death. If there are no children and no parents, the brothers and sisters benefit. If there are no brothers or sisters, the grandparents benefit. (For the complete sequence, see Chapter 10.) If there are no living grandparents and no living descendants of those grandparents, the Crown will be entitled to the estate. Stepchildren do not count as children of the deceased under the intestacy rules, although legitimate children, illegitimate children and adopted children do.

If you are thinking of using a printed form bought in a stationer's shop, it is essential that you understand what makes a valid will and that you can recognise when the printed form is not appropriate for your particular circumstances. It is easy to fill in the boxes of a printed will form thinking that the printed form is somehow 'right'. In your case it may be wrong or not quite what you had in mind. It may be better to avoid the forms altogether and to prepare the document yourself, but if your circumstances are straightforward and you feel happy with a printed form you will find a selection of very simple wills in *Make Your Own Will* from Which? Books.

Unfortunately, the one thing worse than not making a will at all is making a mess of writing a will. Many lawyers say that they make more money out of sorting out poor home-made wills than they do out of drawing up wills for clients, and there is probably some truth in this. There are many ways in which people who prepare their own wills can go wrong. This can lead to long and expensive court cases to resolve the problems, with enormous fees for the lawyers, which can reduce by a staggering amount the size of the estate over which the beneficiaries are arguing.

A will is a legal document but, if you understand the basic elements of will-making, there is no reason why you should not be able to make a straightforward will unaided. This book sets out to explain the steps you need to take in order to make a valid will. It also highlights the areas where problems arise in order to help you recognise when DIY is not appropriate.

As in all DIY, some amateurs are highly competent and capable of producing a professional job. Others, less competent, end up with a botched job and have to call in the professionals to put it right. This book attempts to flag up the legal rocks and sandbanks which might otherwise wreck your attempts to write your own will.

Will writers

There are various companies and individuals who advertise will-writing services. These offers can look attractive because the cost is usually (but not always) less than what a solicitor would charge. Some state that the preparation of the wills is supervised by solicitors. Don't assume that a will-writing service will also sort out your tax planning for you.

It is hard to generalise about the quality of service you will get from these companies but, if you decide to use one you would be wise to check the qualification of the person who is to prepare your will and what comeback your executors would have if they found the will to be defective after your death, some 20 years later. If you decide to use a will-writing company, make sure that it belongs to the Society of Will Writers* or the Institute of Professional Will Writers*. Ask for evidence of indemnity insurance. Some professional indemnity insurance policies cover theft of clients' money. Check with the regulatory body what minimum cover it requires.

When to use a solicitor

A solicitor is likely to charge anything from £50 to £250 for preparing a will in a normal case, depending on the time he or she spends discussing your circumstances and wishes, the complexity of your financial affairs, the extent to which IHT mitigation is required and whether it becomes necessary to involve an accountant or independent financial adviser in the tax planning. In complicated cases the cost of the advice given will be much higher than the cost of preparing a straightforward will but, in such cases, the stakes will be high and may well involve tax savings in excess of £100,000.

Whatever your circumstances, you should always be able to obtain an estimate of the likely costs from a solicitor before you instruct him or her to prepare your will.

Apart from actually having the will prepared for you, there is one other significant advantage in having a complicated will written by a solicitor. He or she will be covered by indemnity insurance if he or she is negligent and makes a mistake in preparing the will or in giving advice. If you mess up your own will there will be no insurance protection for your beneficiaries, who will be stuck with the consequences.

You should seriously consider taking legal advice from a solicitor if you are intending to make a will in any of the following circumstances:

- you are receiving an income from a family trust under which you have the right to determine, by your own will, who should benefit from that trust property on your death (this is called 'a power of appointment')
- your permanent home is in a foreign country, or you are resident in England or Wales but you own a foreign property
- you have made or are intending to make any large gifts during your lifetime
- your estate is likely to exceed £255,000
- the combined value of your own and your spouse's estate exceeds £255,000.

You should also consult a solicitor if what you own includes any particularly complicated types of property, for example:

- a business which you are carrying on either on your own or in partnership with other people
- a farm
- shares in a private family company
- involvement in any Lloyd's underwriting syndicate
- a share in a property with someone who is not your spouse.

Great care is required if there are any particular complications in your own personal situation, such as being separated but not divorced from your wife or husband, or in any case where you intend to benefit other people to the exclusion of your spouse or children.

You should also seek advice if, rather than making an outright gift to someone, you wish to create a life interest by specifying that a person should be entitled to benefit from your property only during his or her life and to whom the property should go when that person has died.

Advice can also be useful where the estate is large and there are IHT complications, or for picking up ideas which might help save tax and therefore pass more benefit from your estate to members of your family. In smaller estates of less than £200,000 there is unlikely to be any IHT unless you also benefit from a trust or inherit from someone else (see Chapter 3).

Legal Help scheme

If your disposable income is below a certain level, or you receive income support or family credit and your savings are within certain limits, you will be entitled to receive free legal advice under the Legal Help scheme. Unfortunately, the Legal Help scheme does not cover the making of wills unless, as well as being eligible under the scheme, you fall into one of the following categories:

- you are over 70 years old
- you are seriously handicapped, deaf, blind or dumb
- you are the parent of a child who fits into the above category
- you are a single parent wanting to appoint a guardian for your child.

Chapter 2

The basics of making a will

This chapter covers preliminary issues to do with making a will (Chapter 4 goes into them in more detail). It first sets out the criteria for a valid will, and then explores some situations in which special care should be taken in the preparation of a will. Some frequently asked questions about the making of wills are answered at the end.

What is a valid will?

For a will to be valid, it must be:

- in writing (either handwritten or typed)
- signed by you (see below for what is required for those unable to read or write)
- signed in such a way as to make absolutely clear your intention to give effect to the will. In other words, rather than signing it on the back or on the side of the will, sign it at the end of the writing on the final page
- signed in the presence of two witnesses (who must not be beneficiaries or potential beneficiaries under the will). They must both be present when you sign and must then 'attest' and sign the will themselves. It is also advisable for you and your witnesses to sign at the bottom of each page of the will. Note that if the will does not include an attestation clause (such as 'signed by the testator in our presence and attested by us in the presence of the testator and each other') in it, your witnesses will be asked, on your death, to sign an affidavit confirming that

they were both present when you signed the will. See Chapter 4 for more details.

If a testator (that is, the person making the will) is blind, the attestation clause must say that the will was read to him or her and that, having stated that he understood it, he signed it or, alternatively, it was signed on his behalf. Appropriate variations have to be made for illiterate testators (who cannot read) or physically disabled testators (who may not be able to read or write).

Mental capacity

In order to make a valid will, a testator must understand what he or she owns, understand the effect of the will and recognise individuals to whom he or she might have responsibilities – for example, a wife with young children. If you are an executor and you believe that the testator lacked this mental capacity (known as testamentary capacity – see pages 30–1) when making the will, you should proceed with caution. You should seek medical evidence and legal advice. It can be very difficult to distinguish the will of a person lacking testamentary capacity from the will of a deeply eccentric person.

Undue influence

Anyone wishing to challenge the will on the grounds that the testator was threatened or improperly influenced must show that the testator was induced to make the will by force, fear or fraud or that in some other way the will was not made voluntarily. Legal advice should be taken before attempting to challenge a will on these grounds. Your will should contain your own wishes, not someone else's.

Ambiguity

The way to avoid ambiguity is to be very clear in the language you use in your will. As a first step you should be clear in your own mind about your wishes. People often have conflicting wishes which have to be resolved or compromised before they start making their will.

Is tax avoidance your overriding objective or is the provision for your spouse more important even if there is more tax to pay on her death? Do you want to help your children get established or do you think they should have to make their own way? You will have to decide where you stand on these issues before making your will.

Vague or ambiguous words

It may seem obvious to say so, but you must watch for ambiguous language if you are making your own will. The following are examples of the sorts of thing you should avoid.

- *'I give £1,000 to my nephews.'* Do you mean £1,000 each or £1,000 to be divided between them?
- *'I give my house to my daughter and the adjoining barn to my son.'* You may know where the dividing line is to be and who should own the driveway, but do they?
- *'I give all my money to my friend Jack.'* Do you mean the cash in the house, all your investments apart from your house, or everything you own when it has been sold?

Defects

There are numerous reasons why a will can be defective. Some of these defects are serious, such as the lack of witnesses, undue influence or lack of testamentary capacity. Other defects, however, though not serious, can cause problems at the Probate Registry. These include amended wills, the lack of an attestation clause, the lack of a date, unexplained marks or pinholes on the will, or the lack of a legible name or full address for the witnesses.

The rules for special cases

Farms and businesses

Farms and businesses can be run as private companies, partnerships or by a sole proprietor. In all cases special inheritance tax (IHT) rules apply which give tax relief (the details are set out in leaflet IHT17, which can be downloaded from the Inland Revenue's website★). The IHT relief can be 100 per cent, and even when the relief is less there may still be concessions which allow the tax to be paid by instalments.

If you wish to bequeath shares in a private company it would be sensible to establish how these shares would be valued on your death. If you have a controlling interest in the company the Capital Taxes Office will look at the value of the controlling interest, not just the value of the individual shares. You should also find out whether the shares can be left to anyone you wish or whether they have to be offered for sale to existing shareholders first.

Where the business or farm is run as a partnership it is important to understand what the partnership agreement says in the event of the death of a partner. It may give the surviving partner the right to buy the deceased partner's share but it may also set down other arrangements which would have to be observed by the executors of the deceased partner. In exceptional cases it may even give the deceased partner the right to introduce another partner as his or her successor. If there is no written partnership agreement the matter will be determined under the provisions of the Partnership Act 1890.

If you are in a partnership it is sensible to look carefully at the arrangements in place should one of you die. If the surviving partner hopes to carry on the business it would be sensible to agree terms now and to consider insuring each other's lives in order to pay out the claims of a deceased partner's spouse or children.

Jointly owned property and assets

Joint ownership of a house can be set up in one of two ways. 'Joint tenancy' means that on the death of one joint owner the deceased person's share passes automatically to the survivor. This is the usual arrangement for married couples, although you should be aware that it bypasses anything you might say in your will about your share of the house.

A 'tenancy in common' means that, on the death of one joint owner, the deceased person's share passes according to his or her will. If no restrictions apply, the person who inherits the half-share can compel the owner of the other half-share to join in a sale of the property so they can both realise their asset. If you wish to 'sever the joint tenancy' in order to create a tenancy in common you should write a notice to the other joint tenant giving him or her notice that you are severing the joint tenancy.

These arrangements do not affect IHT, which may be charged on a half-share passing to the surviving joint tenant – unless the estate, including the value of the half-share, is under the nil-rate band (see Chapter 3) or the half-share is exempt because it is passing to the surviving spouse.

Foreign property and domicile

It is now quite common for British nationals to own foreign property. If you do own foreign property, you must establish what happens to the property on your death under the laws of the country in which the property is located. In some cases your wife and children get a fixed share whatever your will says. Generally speaking, you should have a will prepared by a local lawyer to dispose of the foreign property on your death, but remember to modify any clause in your English will which revokes earlier wills. The Law Society★ can help with the names of such lawyers.

Your domicile is also an issue if it is not in England or Wales, as the law of your country of domicile may overrule some or all of the provisions of your English will. If you have made your will abroad you should take local advice.

Nominations

It is unusual to come across this method of gifting property now. Previously, some kinds of property, such as National Savings Investments, could be nominated to a particular person so that he or she received the investment on your death whether you made a will or not, but that arrangement is no longer possible.

Trusts

A trust can be created by will or lifetime gift. In the latter case, the terms of a trust are set out in the trust document and the trust begins on a chosen date. In the case of a trust created by will, the trust begins on the date of the testator's death.

What is a trust?

Trusts can be created by will or by deed. Where money or other assets are held by trustees on behalf of a person or group of people this is a trust, providing the following conditions apply:

- the person creating the trust must make his or her intention clear
- the money or assets to be held on trust must be clearly defined
- the person or group of people who are to benefit from the trust must be clear.

You might, for instance, use your will to create a trust for your infant children. The executors and trustees of your will would be the legal owners of the property or investments and, under the terms of the will, would be obliged to look after the property or investments on behalf of the infant children until the children reached 18 (or 21), at which time the investments would be transferred to the children.

Another common type of trust established by will is where the executors and trustees of the will hold property or investments in trust and pay the income to a beneficiary for his or her lifetime, after which the capital is to be paid to other beneficiaries (the remaindermen).

Remember that a trust puts the legal ownership of property into the hands of – and under the control of – trustees, who act on behalf of the beneficiaries of the trust and on the terms set out in the will or deed creating the trust. They are totally responsible for the administration of the property.

So if you are creating a trust by deed or by will, you must think carefully about the choice of trustees and any replacement. You must also give careful consideration to the powers to be given to the trustees and the duties imposed upon them. Perhaps most important of all, as each type of trust has its own taxation consequences, you must be aware of those that relate to the trust you have decided to establish. A variety of trusts can be created by a lifetime gift of assets or money which, if without reservation of benefit for the giver, become potentially exempt transfers (PETs) and a possible way of avoiding IHT. It is worth looking at any insurance or pensions policy you hold to see what happens to it if you die. There can be substantial IHT benefits if the money from the policy is paid into a discretionary trust rather than to your estate.

The powers and obligations of trustees have, over the years, been carefully defined by law in order to protect the interests of the beneficiaries, but these can be varied by the deed or will.

Fixed trusts

These trusts set out, in fixed proportions, who gets what. Some flexibility can be introduced by giving the trustees wider powers but the main advantage of such trusts is their simplicity. They are easy to understand and relatively easy to administer.

Discretionary trusts

These set out who the beneficiaries may be (for example, wife, children and grandchildren) but give the trustees the discretion to decide what proportion of income and capital each beneficiary should receive each year. The trustees do not have to pay anything out if they choose not to. Although the person creating the trust, the 'settlor', can tell the trustees how he or she would like them to exercise their discretion, the trustees are not legally bound by those wishes. The benefit of these trusts is in their flexibility but the taxation provisions are somewhat complicated.

Accumulation and maintenance trusts

These trusts are usually established to benefit children and grandchildren. Tax concessions are available for them but care must be taken not to extend the period of accumulation beyond the 25th birthday of the beneficiary or the tax concessions are lost. The tax regime applying to accumulation or maintenance trusts is more complicated than for other trusts, so professional advice should be taken.

Protective trusts

These trusts are used to provide for beneficiaries who may be profligate or are liable to be made bankrupt. Often what happens is that the beneficiary receives the income from the trust, but the payment of capital is subject to the discretion of the trustees.

Trusts for disabled beneficiaries

Special arrangements are permitted under the provisions of Section 89 of the Inheritance Tax Act 1984 which give favourable tax treatment to what are, in essence, discretionary trusts if the beneficiaries are, according to the act, disabled, i.e. incapable of managing their affairs or in receipt of attendance allowance or disability living allowance.

Taxation of trusts

The taxation of trusts is a subject in itself. If you are contemplating the creation of a lifetime trust, you should seek advice on the consequences of both IHT and capital gains tax. You should also investigate the income tax consequences of creating such a trust.

Children

People who have children must watch out for the following when making their wills. First, if a parent leaves property to his or her children (without being specific) he or she is by default including any illegitimate children he or she may have, children of a previous marriage and any adopted children (who lose the right to inherit from their natural parents). Stepchildren are not included unless they are specifically mentioned.

Second, a child will receive his or her benefit at the age of 18 unless the will requires him or her to be older – say 21. If the child is under 18 when the testator dies it is the job of the executors to look after the money for him or her until he or she reaches the age at which the money can be paid to him or her. However, this rule is modified by the provisions of the Trustee Act 1925 which allows a proportion of the gift to be applied by the trustees, before the child is 18, for his or her maintenance, education or benefit.

Third, there is an area of confusion which arises when a beneficiary with children dies before the testator. If that beneficiary is unrelated to the testator the gift becomes void and the children get nothing, but if the beneficiary is a child of the testator the 'statutory trusts' (see below) apply unless any subsequent beneficiary is excluded by the will.

The statutory trusts (see page 195) apply to both wills and intestacies where a beneficiary, who is a child of the testator, has died before the testator, leaving children. In the event of such a death, these children (grandchildren of the testator) will share the money which their parent would have inherited had the parent survived the testator (but only if the surviving children are natural or adopted children of the testator – stepchildren would not benefit).

Charities

If you are intending to leave money to a charity you should check to make sure that it still exists as a registered charity and that you have the correct name and address in your will. Some charities have quite similar names so confusion could easily occur.

If you are intending to leave something quite substantial, such as a house, you should check with the charity first because it may be able to suggest a suitable clause.

One benefit which is common to all charitable gifts is that they are free of IHT, but the way in which an estate is divided between an ordinary beneficiary and a charity can increase or decrease the amount received by the charity. If the individual gets a legacy to bear its own tax and the charity gets the residue, the residue can be greater than if the charity got the legacy and the individual got the residue, subject to IHT.

For example, if your estate is worth £360,000 and you make a gift of £60,000 to a charity and leave the balance to an individual, he or she will get £282,000 after paying IHT of £18,000.

If, however, you make a specific gift of £282,000 to an individual (to bear its own tax) with the residue going to a charity, the individual will get £271,000 (£282,000 less IHT of £10,800). The charity will get £78,000. IHT is reduced by £7,200 when compared with the first example.

Particular problems to watch out for

Care of the elderly and mentally disabled

If you wish to leave something to a person who is being cared for in a residential home and who is in receipt of means-tested benefits you should be aware that a gift of capital or income to such a person could result in benefits being withdrawn. The creation of a discretionary trust (see page 24) in which the beneficiary has no absolute right to benefit may be the best solution for this problem, but it is wise to take advice in such circumstances.

Pets and animals

If you have a dog or some other pet which might outlive you it would be sensible to think what you would want to happen to it in the event of your death. You should be realistic about your wishes and what it will cost to carry them out. If you own cattle or horses you should have a contingency plan known to others before your death.

Divorce and maintenance

If you wish to make a gift by your will to a person who is involved in divorce proceedings you may find that your gift is being claimed as a financial resource by the opposing spouse. In such cases the creation of a discretionary trust may protect your estate from such claims. Alternatively you might decide to make your gift to the children of the divorcing beneficiary.

If you are the person embroiled in a divorce you may be comforted by the thought that the issue of the decree absolute automatically deletes from your will any benefit directed to your ex-spouse. Unfortunately, that may not be the end of the story. If you have agreed to pay maintenance to your ex-spouse, or if the financial settlement is not finally resolved at your death, your ex-spouse may decide to issue proceedings under the Inheritance (Provision for Family and Dependants) Act 1975 in order to claim some or all of your estate (see Chapter 9).

Debts, mortgages and connected life policies

If you are making a will you should be aware that your debts do not disappear when you die. An exception to this rule occurs when your debts are greater than your assets – what happens then is that the assets you have will be shared among your creditors (after your funeral expenses have been deducted) and your estate will be declared insolvent. Where the assets are greater than the liabilities your estate will have to meet all these liabilities before anything can be paid to the beneficiaries.

You should look closely at any mortgage debt. If you are leaving a mortgaged house to a particular beneficiary, that person will become responsible for paying off the mortgage unless your will sets out a contrary intention. Matters can be made worse if there is an insurance policy which you are assuming will be used to pay off the mortgage. Unless the policy or the will makes your intention clear you may find that the insurance money ends up in the residue of your estate going to one person while the house, subject to a mortgage, goes to another person.

Most debts will be notified to, and paid by, your executors from the assets of your estate, but the situation can be much more complicated if you are paying maintenance to an ex-spouse under a court order. In such cases the ex-spouse will be able to make a claim against your estate unless a reasonable provision for the ex-spouse is made in your will (see above).

Profligate children

If you are concerned, say, that your child is too young at 18 to receive a substantial inheritance in the event of your death, or if your child is a drug addict who will use any bequest to stock up with more drugs, you need to take care when drawing up your will.

If you are concerned by the youth of your beneficiary you can create a trust according to which the trustees can be instructed to delay payment until the beneficiary shows signs of financial wisdom. If the problems are more intractable you may wish to consider creating a trust which can provide accommodation and medical treatment for the beneficiary without giving him or her access to large sums of money.

If the beneficiary is insolvent and on the road to bankruptcy it would be sensible to create a trust such that the trustees can wait and see before making any payment to the beneficiary. A discretionary trust would provide such flexibility.

Beneficiary dying before you

You should think about this when writing your will even if the beneficiary is much younger than you. If the beneficiary dies before you and is not your descendant, your gift will lapse. If you want the gift to go to his or her spouse or child in the event of his or her death before yours, you should say so in your will.

However, if a son or daughter of yours who is destined to receive something under your will dies before you, leaving a child, the gift you had intended to leave to the son or daughter will automatically go to that son or daughter's child unless you make specific provision that it should not do so.

In the case of a cash legacy such as '£100 to John Brown' or a specific bequest such as 'my diamond brooch to Jane Smith' no problem arises – if John Brown or Jane Smith is dead, the gift will simply become part of the residue and swell the amount that will go to the person who is to receive your residuary estate.

If the person who is to receive the residue of your estate dies before you, that would leave part of your property undisposed of. This is called partial intestacy. It is therefore wise to name an alternative if your will provides for only one residuary beneficiary.

In a situation of partial intestacy, the important question is: who was alive when the testator died? It does not matter whether a beneficiary dies before actually receiving the benefit from the estate if he or she was alive when the testator died. For example, if a friend is given a legacy of £250 in a will and then dies after the testator but before the £250 is actually paid to him, the beneficiary's estate will receive that money – it does not go into the residuary estate of the original testator.

Husband and wife

Married couples whose combined assets exceed the nil-rate band (the threshold below which no IHT is charged – see Chapter 3) of £255,000 and who leave everything to the survivor will not have to pay IHT on the first death but, because they have failed to use both the nil-rate bands, their beneficiaries will have to pay unnecessary IHT on the second death. See Chapter 3 for details.

A change in circumstances can arise if one spouse has to go into a residential or nursing home. In such a case the fit spouse may decide to leave his or her assets, including his or her share of the house, to the children rather than it being used to reduce the means-tested benefits received by the spouse who is resident in a home (see page 32 for details).

Commonly, a husband would give the main part of his estate to his wife so that the wife becomes the residuary beneficiary. If the wife were to die first, the husband would make a fresh will, making provision for the children instead. If there are no children, he could dispose of his estate elsewhere, according to the circumstances. But it might happen that the husband and wife are both victims of the same road accident, the wife being killed outright and the husband surviving for a few days but then dying without having had a chance to make a new will. In this case the husband's intention of leaving everything to his wife would have been defeated because she would have died first. When this happens the property which his will left to her is distributed according to the rules of intestacy (although there are special rules that apply when husband and wife die intestate and it is not known who died first). The intestacy rules might well not accord with his wishes. It would therefore be better for the husband to make specific provision for this possibility in his will stating who the property should go to if his wife does not survive him (and his wife should also make this provision in her will). In many cases, this would be the children.

To cover the case of such a joint accident in which it is impossible to know who will survive whom and by how long, a will can contain a provision that the wife (or husband) will inherit the property provided that she (or he) survives for a given number of days and, if that does not happen, that the property goes to a named person or class of persons or 'another beneficiary'. Be careful of the IHT consequences if you include such a clause in your will.

Frequently asked questions

What if the testator is elderly and forgetful?

Unfortunately, there is no clear line between being capable of making a will and being incapable of doing so. The definition of testamentary capacity requires that the testator understands that he is making a will, knows what he owns and that the will distributes his property on his death. He must also be aware of those who might have claims or an expectation of inheriting on his death.

It is one thing to remind an elderly parent that he or she should be making a will but the whole process could be jeopardised if the will was written out by a main beneficiary even if the witnesses were independent.

If the testator has good days and bad days, it is not always obvious whether some member of the family has been left out deliberately or as a result of forgetfulness.

If there are doubts about the mental capacity of the testator the only safe way to proceed is for the matter to be discussed with the testator's medical advisor and for that advisor to be one of the witnesses when the will is signed. In practice it may not be as easy as that, especially where the testator is eccentric or mischievous.

Where a will divides a testator's property, say, equally between his three children it is unlikely, but not impossible, that there will be a dispute. However, where the testator attempts to vary the distribution of benefit, for example based on the number of visits each child makes to the care home where he resides, there can be a bitter legacy for that family.

What if the testator is being influenced?

It is one thing to have suspicions that a testator is being influenced to make a will benefiting one person at the expense of another, but it is much harder to produce solid evidence.

Undue influence could come in the form of gentle suggestions to a vulnerable testator or by physical threat. A common, and difficult, situation can arise when one member of the family living close to an elderly parent suggests that he or she should make a will. The elderly parent then makes a will but, in gratitude for the care being provided, gives everything to the person providing the care. To avoid suggestions of undue influence it is probably wise to persuade the person making the will to visit a solicitor alone so that instructions can be given to an independent person.

What if I end up in a home?

If you are already in a home it is not too late to make a will but, unless your fees are being paid from income, it is unlikely that your assets will survive more than a few years of nursing home fees.

If you have significant assets which you hope to leave to your family you should be considering IHT mitigation. As it happens, such mitigation can have the effect of taking assets out of the estate of a testator, thus removing them from the claims of others such as the Benefits Agency.

One simple step for a couple who are joint owners of a house is to sever the joint tenancy (see *Jointly owned property and assets*, above) and then to make wills leaving their respective shares in the house to trustees or to other members of the family. The consequences and risks need to be carefully examined, but this can protect the assets of one spouse from claims by the Benefits Agency in respect of the other.

What if my wife marries again?

This is a common occurrence. Where a marriage comes to an end either by death or divorce there may be children who could be excluded from benefit under their parents' will or intestacy because of a subsequent marriage.

For example, Mr Johnson dies, leaving Mrs Johnson and 25-year-old twins called Robert and William. Mrs Johnson then marries Mr Forbes two years later, but forgets to make a new will. Mrs Forbes is then tragically killed in a car accident, leaving an estate of £120,000 which passes on her intestacy to Mr Forbes. Mr Forbes eventually gets over his grief and marries his doctor, Liz Adams, but sadly dies of a heart attack on his honeymoon. Mr Forbes has made a will in consideration of marriage to and in favour of his wife to the exclusion of his two stepsons. The result is not what the first Mr or Mrs Johnson would have expected or wanted.

One solution is based on trust. If, in the example above, Mr and Mrs Johnson had agreed that, in the event of one of them dying the survivor would make a will (whether remarried or not) that would ensure that their estate passed eventually to the twins. The agreement would be defeated if the survivor failed to make the will unless the parties had entered into a legally binding agreement.

Another course of action would have been for Mr and Mrs Johnson to make wills leaving each other a life interest in part of their capital assets but ensuring that, on the death of the survivor, the assets would pass to the twins.

Similarly, they could have made wills containing a discretionary trust in which the surviving spouse and the twins would be potential beneficiaries. In that case a letter of wishes could be placed with the will explaining to the trustees how they would like the assets eventually to be passed on to the twins.

What if my daughter divorces?

This thought might cross the mind of parents whose daughter, in their view, has chosen a husband unwisely. The parents could be afraid that, in the event of their death, their untrustworthy son-in-law would divorce their daughter and lay claim to her inheritance to set himself up in a manner that his personal efforts could not achieve. Of course, if the parents are thinking about making a will now, or if they are considering making a lifetime gift to their daughter, they could leave her out altogether, but that could be too drastic.

They could wait and see what happens to their daughter and son-in-law and delay making the will but that would not help as the intestacy rules might give her a share anyway. If they sought advice they might be advised to create a discretionary trust by their will making their daughter a potential beneficiary but expressing the wish, to carefully chosen trustees, that the state of the daughter's marriage be noted before any payments were made to her.

What if I remarry?

An earlier example (see *What if my wife marries again?*, above) examined a number of possibilities to do with remarriage. If you are intending to remarry, and have children from your first marriage, it is essential that you discuss the subject of wills with your spouse-to-be. If he or she already has children, he or she will have the same concerns as you.

If you want your estate eventually to go to the children of your first marriage you should look carefully at the financial consequences of your death shortly after your remarriage. A common decision is for one spouse to sell his or her present house and to purchase a half-share in the other's house. This should be done as tenants in common so that the wills can provide for the survivor to live there for life, or for a specific period after which the children of the deceased spouse could recover their parent's share in the house.

Where one party has children and the other does not, the final decision will depend upon the wealth of the parties, the length of time they have been together and the strength (or otherwise) of the relationship between the surviving spouse and the stepchildren. The important thing is to bring this issue into the open before the second marriage so you both know what the deal is to be, and then put it all in writing.

What if my child is a drug addict?

Parents who have a child with an addiction may wish to exclude him or her from all benefits on the grounds that their hard-earned savings will otherwise be frittered away. Those who want to help their child back into more sober ways may wish to create a discretionary trust which can provide benefits for him or her without putting too much cash in his or her pocket (see *Profligate children* above).

Chapter 3

Inheritance tax

Inheritance tax (IHT) is the only form of tax or duty imposed on the death of a person whose domicile is in England and Wales. For many years the tax was known as estate duty. In 1975 this was changed to capital transfer tax to reflect the fact that it affected not only the property which passed from one person to another on the former's death but was also a tax on the larger gifts that people made in their own lifetimes.

The Inheritance Tax Act 1984 (originally known as the Capital Transfer Tax Act 1984) states in s.1 that IHT shall be charged on the value transferred by a chargeable event. This tax relates mainly to property passing on death but also affects lifetime gifts unless they fall into an exempt category (see *Small gifts and other exemptions*, below).

One of the reasons for making a will is to reduce the IHT which might be charged on your death or later on the death of your spouse. Although the basic principles are easy to understand, the devil is in the detail. Nevertheless, it is important that you understand the tax well enough to know if you are going to be affected by it.

This book also suggests a number of ways to reduce the incidence of IHT so that you can discuss the matter thoroughly with your solicitor or your independent financial adviser if you decide not to tackle the job yourself. *The Which? Guide to Giving and Inheriting* is another invaluable source of information on this topic.

IHT on death

On a person's death, IHT is charged on the value of his or her net estate – that is, all his or her property and assets less all his or her liabilities and debts. (The funeral costs can also be deducted.) The value on which IHT is charged includes the capital value of any trust in which the deceased had a life interest or from which he had any benefit or was entitled to the income. The amount of any gift made by the deceased up to seven years prior to the death is also added back to give the total value upon which IHT will be levied.

Before 15 March 1988, the rate of IHT varied from 30 per cent to 60 per cent depending on the size of the estate. Since 15 March 1988 the rate of IHT has remained at 40 per cent, but the nil-rate band (the threshold below which no IHT is charged) has gradually gone up since 1990 from £128,000 to £255,000 in April 2003.

Usually a new set of tables is published each year, increasing the nil-rate band. Even if the standard rate of IHT (40 per cent) does not change, there is generally an annual increase in the nil-rate band in keeping with inflation. It is essential to realise that the appropriate table for the rate in force at the date of death must be used for calculations. In some circumstances, if the deceased person has made substantial lifetime gifts of property within seven years of his death (or longer if he retained an interest in that property), then some or all of the nil-rate band may have been used up. Even worse, there may be tax to pay on some of the gifted property if the gift exceeded the nil-rate band. In this case a solicitor should be consulted because tax may have to be recovered from the recipient of the gift. A gift of shares in a private company can also have complicated tax consequences which are beyond the scope of this book.

Lifetime gifts

IHT affects most transfers of property on death and certain transfers made within seven years before the date of death. The taxation rules of lifetime gifts between people are quite complicated but offer certain advantageous tax exemptions. This should be an incentive to make use of the provisions for tax-free lifetime gifts while they exist, as the rules could be changed at any time.

Most lifetime gifts by individuals to other individuals or to certain trusts are either entirely free from IHT (but watch out for capital gains tax, CGT) or, where there is potential IHT, the charge is avoided if the person making the gift survives for seven years after making the gift (and does not reserve any benefit from the gift).

There are, however, certain exceptions, which include lifetime gifts to companies or to discretionary trusts. In such cases the tax is payable at the reduced lifetime rate of 20 per cent where the gift is made, unless it falls within the nil-rate band. If the person making the gift survives for seven years no further tax will be payable but the tax already paid cannot be recovered.

In most cases, however, the gift will either fall into one of the exempt categories or it will become a potentially exempt transfer (PET).

The seven-year rule

IHT is a tax on the value of a person's estate and certain other assets at the date of his or her death. To prevent people giving away all their property immediately before they die in a bid to avoid the tax, the rules provide that tax is calculated not only on the value of the property which a deceased person has when he or she dies but also on the value of the gifts which the person made in the last seven years before his or her death. If the deceased person has retained an interest in the gifted property, he or she will lose the benefit of the seven-year rule.

If a PET has been made in excess of the nil-rate band and the donor then dies within seven years, the beneficiary will have to pay the tax which is due on the amount by which the gift exceeds the nil-rate band. If significant amounts are involved it would certainly be wise for the beneficiary to consider taking out a form of term life insurance payable to the beneficiary so that, if the donor dies within the seven-year period, the policy will provide an amount equal to the tax which may become payable. If the gift is under the nil-rate band (currently £255,000) there will be that much less of the nil-rate band to set against the value of the deceased's estate.

Tapered relief

This relief (not to be confused with CGT taper relief) applies where a person makes a PET *in excess* of the nil-rate band but then dies after at least three years. In such a case the IHT due on the value of the gift will be reduced by 20% if the death occurs in the fourth year, by 40% in the fifth year, by 60% in the sixth year and by 80% in the seventh year. It is important to realise that this relief applies only to the amount by which the gift exceeds the nil-rate band. If the gift was equal to the nil-rate band there will be no tapered relief.

Small gifts and other exemptions

No IHT is payable on the following gifts nor do they use up the nil-rate band:

- **£3,000 per annum,** which can be carried forward for one year if unused (every individual has this allowance)
- **small presents** – any number of individual gifts of up to £250 per recipient can be made each year in addition to the annual allowance of £3,000. Note that the same person cannot receive £3,000 as well as £250 under these provisions
- **gifts to a spouse** – all property passing between husband and wife. Husband and wife are regarded as entirely separate people for IHT purposes but any property which passes from one to the other by gift or to the survivor on the death of one of them is wholly exempt from IHT. This provision does not apply to unmarried couples
- **gifts to children in consideration of their marriage,** up to £5,000 per parent, £2,500 per grandparent and £1,000 from anyone else
- **normal expenditure out of income** – what is normal expenditure depends on the income and spending habits of the giver but this can be a valuable exception
- **charities** – all gifts by will to charity are wholly exempt from IHT
- **political parties** – gifts by a will to the main established political parties are exempt
- **gifts to the nation or of public benefit** – gifts to certain national museums or collections and some objects or property of national importance are exempt if accepted.

There are also a number of variable exemptions or 'reliefs' affecting such types of property as Lloyd's underwriting accounts, farmland, forestry and timber, partnership businesses and family company shares. You should get advice from a solicitor or accountant if you are involved with any of these. The qualification rules for these reliefs are complicated and so is the calculation of the figures involved.

Example

In this example it has been assumed that the person who has died ('the deceased') has made no lifetime gifts other than the usual birthday, Christmas and similar 'small' (that is, under £250) gifts and other sums coming to less than £3,000 a year.

For these calculations, the IHT rate operative at the date of death must be used.

Harold (H) and Winifred (W) are married. On 1 June 2002 H dies, leaving all his property to his wife, W. His total estate is valued at £255,000. The size of his estate is irrelevant because all the property passes to W and is exempt because she is his spouse.

On 1 October 2003 W dies. Her estate is worth £510,000 (she had approximately £255,000 of her own property in addition to the £255,000 she received from H's estate when he died). Under her will, all of the property passes equally to their two children, Sam (S) and Diana (D), apart from a legacy of £10,000, which was given specifically by W's will to 'The Gentle Home', a registered charity.

On H's death no IHT is payable because of the spouse exemption (it is also below the IHT threshold).

On W's death the calculation is as follows:

Amount	Tax payable
£10,000 to charity	n/a (exempt)
£255,000	nil (nil-rate band)
£245,000 (the balance)	£98,000 (40% of £245,000)

However, this tax could have been reduced significantly if H and W had taken the following steps.

If, when H had died on 1 June 2002, he had left all his property to his children S and D, only the excess of £5,000 (above the nil-rate band, which at the time was £250,000) would have been taxed, which would have been £2,000.

Subsequently, when W died on 1 October 2003, leaving £10,000 to charity and the balance of £245,000 to the children, there would have been no tax to pay. So the total tax payable on the joint estates of the husband and wife (of which almost all passes to the children S and D), is £2,000 rather than £98,000. The reason for this is that the aggregation of the husband's and wife's estates is avoided and therefore the nil-rate tax band in both estates is utilised (£250,000 on the first death and £255,000 on the last death).

The important principle to grasp is that the maximum saving is achieved when the nil-rate band has been fully utilised by both husband and wife.

In cases of death close together

A husband will usually want to make sure that his wife benefits from his estate on his death so that she will be comfortable for the rest of her life. It is possible, however, for a husband and wife to die as a result of some joint accident so that one of them survives the other for only a few days or weeks. He or she will then have inherited the property without any opportunity to enjoy it.

For that reason a husband and wife may wish to leave their property to the other with the proviso that, in order to inherit, the survivor survives for at least, say, 30 days. If the survivor dies within that period, the property does not go to the survivor but will pass directly to the children.

The stipulated survival time could be some other number of days: 30 is usually chosen because if the survivor survives for more than 30 days, the chances are that he or she will have some independent life after the deceased and should therefore benefit from the property. In cases where IHT is payable such a clause may not be a good idea. For example, assume H has an estate of £430,000; W has a nil estate. H's will leaves £255,000 to the children and the residue (£175,000) to W, provided she survives him by 30 days. H and W die in a common accident, W surviving it by (say) 20 days. The whole of H's estate passes to the children, and IHT is payable on £175,000 at 40%, which is £70,000.

Without the survivorship clause, £255,000 would have passed to the children, using H's nil-rate band, and the residue of £175,000 to W free of tax. On W's death her estate of £175,000 would have passed to the children with no IHT due on it because of it was below the nil-rate band. H's estate of £430,000 would thus have passed to the children tax-free. However, the decision to include or exclude a survivorship clause must depend on the tax-planning of each person's estate. Tread carefully where there is a possible liability to IHT.

Example

For the purposes of this example, it is assumed that the rates of IHT will remain the same throughout (although they can be changed as the Chancellor directs). Neither is consideration given to the complexities of the rules in relation to business assets, agricultural property, timber and the like, for which professional advice must be sought.

In June 2000 G makes a gift of £2,000 to his son, S. This is wholly exempt, being under the £3,000 annual limit (and there is also £1,000 of unused annual exemption that can be carried over).

In June 2001 G makes a gift of £1,750 to each of his daughters, D and E, so that the total gift in the tax year 6 April 2001 to 5 April 2002 is £3,500. Of this, £3,000 is exempt because it is under the annual limit for that year. The rest is exempt because of the £1,000 of unused annual exemption brought forward from the previous year. Of course, only £500 of that £1,000 is being used, but the other £500 cannot be carried forward for another year because of the rule that the unused annual exemption can be carried forward for one year only and the current year's annual exemption must always be used first.

In June 2002 G makes other gifts as follows. He gives to S and D £150,000 each and to E he gives his second home, a cottage in the country worth £150,000. (This might, however, incur a potential charge of CGT).

The total gift is therefore £450,000. Of this, £3,000 is exempt under the annual exemption. None of the remainder (£447,000) is immediately taxable under the IHT rules which abolished tax on certain lifetime gifts. However, the gifts could become taxable if G dies within seven years, depending on the value of his estate. S, D and E could therefore find that on G's death they receive a demand for IHT payable on the gifts they have received. (They should either set aside a sum to cover this, or take out insurance to provide an amount to cover the tax payable on G's possible death within seven years.)

If G does die within seven years, tax will be payable on the gifts he has made in June 2002, assessed at the rates shown by the IHT table that is current at the date of G's death.

G fails to survive for seven years: he dies in March 2006. Since the gifts he made in June 2002 he has made no more taxable gifts (only some wholly exempt ones within the annual allowance or usual presents).

His estate is worth £300,000. In his will, he gives his wife, W, his main house, which is worth £150,000 and is in his sole name, and he also gives her a legacy of £100,000. He directs that the rest of his property should go to each of his three children equally.

The tax payable is calculated on the lifetime gifts and on the estate as follows.

On the lifetime gifts to the children

Tax payable at 'death rates' (that is, IHT tax rates) on the chargeable gifts of £447,000 is:

on the first £255,000   nil
on the balance of £192,000 at 40%   £76,800

(The above figures assume a nil-rate band of £255,000 in 2006.)

However, as death occurred between three and four years after the original gifts were made in June 2002, under the tapered relief provisions the tax will be reduced by 20% to £61,440. That divided between the three children works out at £20,480 each.

On the estate of G

The gifts to W of £250,000 are exempt because there is no IHT on property passing between husband and wife.

The taxable estate is therefore £50,000 (that is, G's total estate of £300,000 less the gifts to W), which is the residue passing to the three children equally. In the last seven years, the only chargeable gifts made by G were those of June 2002 (which came to £447,000).

As you will recall, the nil-rate band of £255,000 has already been used up on the lifetime taxable gifts of £447,000. There is therefore no nil-rate band available to set against that part of the estate which passes to the children.

IHT payable on the £50,000 passing to the children at 40% is £20,000. The total tax payable is therefore £20,000 on the estate plus the £61,440 (£76,800 less 20% relief) on the lifetime gifts.

In the above example, we have assumed that the tax rates remain constant for the whole period. It is most likely that new figures will be published each year, and when dealing with the lifetime gifts it is the rate current at the date of death that is used to calculate the tax. On the other hand, the value of the house given during the donor's life is assessed at the date of the original gift even if it has gone up in value. This could result in a large saving of IHT if appreciating assets are chosen.

So, there can be an advantage in giving away property even if it turns out that the gift was made within four years of the donor's death, providing the property is likely to increase in value during that time. If the gift is not cash it is wise to have the property or item valued at the date of the gift in case the value is disputed later. It is also important to remember that a lifetime gift of property or other assets may incur CGT.

Who gets the residue?

In the above example, the wife was given a particular sum of money and the house by G's will, and the children were given the residue of the estate. What would have been the position if the children had been given a legacy and the wife had been given the residue of the estate? This is in fact more usual, but the calculations required are much more complicated. This is because the wife's entitlement to the residue can be calculated only after the tax has been calculated on the gift to the children.

Who pays the tax?

In our example, if G had given the sum of £50,000 to be divided equally between his children subject to the payment of any IHT attributable to it, the calculation would have been exactly the same. It is more usual that a legacy is given 'free of inheritance tax' (and this is implied if it is not specified in the will). This means that the children would have to receive £50,000 after the tax has been calculated, but the tax rules state that the tax payable on the legacy counts as part of the legacy itself, for tax purposes. This means that one would have to gross up the legacy of £50,000, and the question therefore becomes: 'What total amount of taxable legacy will leave £50,000 after the tax on that legacy has been paid?'. The Inland Revenue publishes 'grossing up' tables from which the answer can be calculated. In G's particular case, the amount of legacy to be given to the three children after the tax has been paid would reduce the residue available to pay to W.

If there have been taxable gifts of amounts exceeding the nil-rate band of IHT within (what may turn out to be) the last seven years before death, it is important that the widow should be given an absolute legacy rather than a share in residue, and that the children's interest should be a share in residue and not a legacy.

The alternative is to say in the will that any legacy given to the children must bear its own tax. In this way, the person making the will knows that the amount by which the estate will be decreased by the legacy is limited to the amount specified and will not need to be 'grossed up' for IHT purposes so that the amount which the widow will receive from the estate will not be put at risk, even if the net amount of the other legacies will be decreased. Another option would be to limit the children's legacy to the amount that could be given without IHT becoming chargeable.

Deeds of variation

There are rules which allow the adult beneficiaries of an estate to vary the provisions of the will or the distribution upon an intestacy within a period of two years from the date of the deceased's death so that the property may pass to them in a more tax-efficient manner than would have been the case had the provisions of the deceased's will been put into operation. These are called deeds of variation or deeds of family arrangement and can enable effective tax-planning after a death.

This is a very useful concession from the Inland Revenue. It can be used to achieve substantial tax savings, in particular where the nil-rate band has not been fully utilised on the first death. (See Chapter 6 for further details.)

The house

A lifetime gift of a parent's own main residence to a son or daughter would not be an effective gift for saving IHT if there were any understanding that the parent would be allowed to go on living there free of charge, because that amounts to 'reserving an interest'. However, giving away a house unconditionally, or perhaps even a second home where the question of the giver remaining there would not even arise, could lead to considerable tax saving (but watch out for CGT if you are thinking of giving away a second home).

Jointly owned property and tax-saving

As mentioned previously, there are two forms of joint ownership of a house: a joint tenancy (where the share of one owner passes automatically to the other on death) and a tenancy in common (where each owner is able to dispose of his or her share by will as he or she wishes). In the case of a joint tenancy, the surviving owner will become entitled to the house automatically – irrespective of the provisions of the deceased's will or the rules of intestacy. In the case of a tenancy in common, the deceased's share of the house will pass under the terms of his or her will (or in accordance with the rules of intestacy governing the deceased's estate). Where the owners are husband and wife there will be no IHT liability but in any other case, whether joint tenancy or tenancy in common, the value of the half-share will be included in the estate for IHT purposes.

In order to change a joint tenancy to a tenancy in common one owner must notify the other that he or she wishes to sever the joint tenancy by a written notice, and the step should then be notified to the Land Registry★ by completing form RX1.

An IHT saving can be effected in circumstances where a married couple severs the joint tenancy of the matrimonial home in order to create a tenancy in common. Each spouse then makes a will giving his or her half-share in the matrimonial home to the children or to a discretionary trust, thus taking advantage of the nil-rate band of £255,000 on the first death without having to hand over cash. However, this is a tricky area on which legal advice should be sought.

Other ways of saving IHT

There are other ways in which tax may be saved, but these are more elaborate and beyond the scope of this book. They are mentioned here so that you can give them consideration with your advisers. Also, see *The Which? Guide to Giving and Inheriting* for details.

For instance, it is possible to include a provision in a will whereby, for a period of two years after a person's death, the estate is held on trust for a class of people – usually 'my husband/wife and children', or 'my brothers and sisters' – and where the executors may, at their discretion, pay out the capital to any member of the class at any time within that period. This is called a 'two-year discretionary trust' and is very flexible because the decision as to who will get what part of the property can be left for up to two years after the death, and it can therefore be used to obtain efficient tax treatment of a person's property at death. In this way (even though it may not be as efficient a distribution of property for IHT purposes as leaving it all to the children) the wife can get the capital, or part of it, from the estate if or when she needs it, and the decision to pay it to her can be made at the last moment, thus preserving the possibility of at least reducing the tax burden.

Deeds of variation and family arrangements (see Chapter 6) which can be entered into within two years of the deceased's death can be made to effect substantial savings of IHT where there are, for example, business assets or Lloyd's underwriting accounts, farming or woodland property, or family company shares.

The government may revise these rules from time to time and may pass legislation which would severely restrict these possibilities. It is essential, therefore, to be up to date with legislation and any case law which may affect tax-avoidance schemes.

Chapter 4

What to put in your will

Chapter 2 gave a basic overview of what a will is and how it is to be written. This chapter covers in detail what needs to be in a will and explains some of the terms used in the writing of a will.

The essentials

Definition

As pointed out in Chapter 2, anyone can make a will provided that he or she is at least 18 years old and has testamentary capacity (that is, being able to appreciate the nature of the document he or she is signing, and its effect). If there is a dispute later, medical evidence would be required to prove that this was the case (or not) at the time the will was made. The will can therefore be made and signed in a lucid period during a psychiatric illness, although you may find that some hospitals and residential care homes have rules preventing nurses from witnessing the wills of patients. It is even possible for a person who is a patient under the Court of Protection (see pages 65–6) to make a will (with the approval of the Court of Protection).

Layout

There are no formal rules here but a will usually has four distinct sections. The first deals with the appointment of executors (the people responsible for dealing with all your affairs after your death) and guardians if you have young children.

The second section deals with the distribution of your property (that is, who is to have what after your death) and upon what terms. Legacies are usually fixed amounts, but the residue, where there are several beneficiaries, is distributed as a percentage or fraction of the whole.

The third section contains any powers that the executors will need in order to carry out their duties properly, although many powers are supplied by existing Acts of Parliament, such as the Trustee Act 1925 and the Trustee Act 2000.

The fourth section contains directions, such as arrangements for the funeral or the terms on which a person can live in a house.

Use simple language and avoid any expressions which are vague and ambiguous or which you do not fully understand.

Revocation clauses

There is one clause which should always be included in a will (unless you have made a foreign will disposing of property abroad), namely one saying that any previous wills are revoked. A later will does not automatically revoke an earlier one. If a person leaves two wills and parts of them are not inconsistent with each other, they stand together; where the wills are inconsistent the later one prevails; but having two wills is almost always likely to cause problems.

Even if you have not in fact made a will before, it is a good idea to include a statement that previous wills are revoked because your executors might wonder, after your death, whether perhaps you left an earlier will. Having a revocation clause in your will saves your executors a fruitless search for any earlier will by showing that it is revoked anyway. There is, however, one exception: when you make a will before you get married you can provide that the will should remain valid after your marriage even though marriage normally invalidates an existing will (see Chapter 6 for more on revocation by marriage).

Executors and trustees

Executors

Executors should always be appointed by will. If the will does not appoint an executor your next of kin will usually be appointed by the intestacy rules for administering your estate; they are then called the administrators. Executors and administrators are both personal representatives but executors have power to deal with the affairs of the testator (the person making the will) from the moment of death whereas administrators have no such authority and must theoretically wait for the court to grant them letters of administration before taking any action at all. This can present problems if there is a dispute about who is to make the funeral arrangements or if certain members of the family start going through the possessions of the deceased without the agreement of others equally entitled to them.

Trustees

Trustees are persons who legally own and administer property for the benefit of someone else (called the beneficiary). They are not usually allowed to benefit from that property themselves in their capacity as trustees but they can be both trustee and beneficiary within the same trust. Their job is to manage the property for the benefit of the beneficiaries under the terms of the trust and in accordance with the law. For example, a trust arises where property is given to children under the age of 18. The trustees of the will or deed then hold the property for the benefit of the children until they reach the age of 18. The terms on which the property is held in trust are set out either in the document setting up the trust (which can be a will) or by various Acts of Parliament.

An executor is a special kind of trustee because he is responsible for administering all the affairs of the testator when he dies. People are sometimes puzzled to find one person who is both trustee and beneficiary. It might be explained as the wearing of two hats – there is the trustee hat, under which you must observe all the obligations placed on you as a trustee by the will and by statute; and the beneficiary hat, under which you are entitled to a certain share of the estate of the deceased.

If the beneficiaries are of full age and absolutely entitled to all the property held on their behalf by a trustee, they can compel the retirement of that trustee. An executor, so long as he is not guilty of any misconduct, cannot be forced to renounce or retire. It could therefore be difficult but not impossible to persuade a bank to relinquish its executorship even if one or more members of the family are joint executors with the bank and could act quite satisfactorily without the bank.

Once the administration of an estate has been completed by realising the assets, paying the debts and distributing the residue, the executor's job is finished. He or she may, however, continue to work as a trustee if, for instance, some of the money has to be retained for minors until they reach 18.

What executors do

Executors' duties are no mere formalities; there is a great deal of work involved and much responsibility. They will be responsible first for collecting in all the assets of the estate, dealing with the paperwork and calculations, and paying all the debts, liabilities and taxes and the various expenses such as funeral costs and administration costs. Ultimately they are responsible for distributing all the property that remains in the estate in accordance with the terms of the will. (Administrators have to observe the rules of intestacy.) They will have to pay the legacies, transfer particular items of property to the beneficiary, pay out the residue of the estate to one or more specified beneficiaries, or hold the property 'in trust' on the terms specified in the testator's will. If they misinterpret the will or a specific tax law, they can become personally liable for someone else's loss. (See also Chapter 7.)

Who to appoint

You cannot force someone to take on the duties of being your executor, so it is much better to ask the people you have in mind first if they agree to be appointed. An executor may not really wish to act but may feel duty-bound to do so when the time comes, because he or she has been appointed. You should therefore try to find someone who you know would be willing to act and capable of doing so.

In normal circumstances, a husband will appoint his wife to be his executor and *vice versa*, especially where they do not have grown-up children. This is a good idea, as a rule, because the surviving partner will usually be receiving most of the estate, so it is sensible that he or she should have a hand in its administration.

It is perhaps as well, though, that a wife/husband should not be the only executor. She (let us say) will have enough to cope with at the time of her husband's death without this. Alternatively there may, of course, be some common accident. Who to choose as the other executor should depend largely on the circumstances of the people concerned. If there are infant children it may be sensible to have a professional person, for example, a solicitor or an accountant, to act because the property will subsequently have to be held in trust for the children, although there is no reason why the trustee should not be a trusted friend of the family. If the children have attained their majority, one or other of the children can be a joint executor. Often the grown-up children are the only executors.

It is sensible to appoint two executors. This is particularly so where the burden needs to be shared, and is essential where the will creates a continuing trust, for example for children. If the executor is not a member of the immediate family and not someone who is a professional, and is therefore undertaking the duties as a trusted friend, it is sometimes thought appropriate to leave him a legacy – £1,000 say – for undertaking the office of executor. Otherwise, executors are entitled to recover expenses but nothing for the time they have spent on the job.

If you own a business or are perhaps a writer with literary assets, it will be wise to appoint executors who have the knowledge to run the business while it is being sold or to dispose of your literary assets to the best advantage. The will should also give appropriate powers to enable executors to carry out these tasks and to compensate them for doing so.

When a solicitor or other professional is appointed to be an executor it is normal to include a clause in your will enabling him to charge normal professional fees for his legal work in administering the estate, although the Trustee Act 2000 allows a professional trustee to charge reasonable fees if his co-executors agree. There is no obligation or presumption that a solicitor should be given a legacy for acting as an executor.

Appointing a bank

A bank can act as an executor of your will. You may wish to consider appointing a bank if there is no one individual to whom you feel you could entrust this task, maybe because there are family arguments. However, the disadvantages of having a bank as an executor include the fact that the costs of administration of the estate will usually be considerably more than those of professional trustees and executors such as accountants and solicitors. Also, banks do not always have the personal knowledge of the family that an individual appointed by you would usually have. There are likely to be some tasks which require the personal touch, such as sorting out the personal belongings of the person who has died, for instance. Banks may employ competent and sympathetic staff, but they are no substitute for the right friend or relation.

Sometimes a bank is appointed to be an executor jointly with an individual, perhaps a member of the family or a close friend. When the time comes to administer the estate, the individual executor may feel quite capable of doing so himself without the assistance of the bank, but if the estate is large it is very unlikely that the bank would agree to renounce its role and therefore its fee. If you are going to appoint a bank to be the executor of your will, you should use the appointment clause supplied by the bank.

If you are considering appointing any commercial organisation, including a bank, as your executor, examine its own literature and publicity, and in particular the rates of charging for administering the estate, including additional items such as acceptance fees, arrangement fees, annual management fees and withdrawal fees. Work out how much it will cost, especially if the administration is likely to be straightforward. If you are leaving everything to your wife and adult children, it may not be necessary to use the bank at all. Some banks charge a fee of 4 per cent on the first £250,000 of the estate (and some 4 per cent on the first £500,000) with a decreasing scale for the remainder.

In straightforward cases it is probably better to appoint individuals to be your executors if suitable candidates are willing to act. It is usually preferable to select as an executor a person who is younger than you. It is also sensible to provide in your will for a substitute executor in case the first people you appoint are unwilling or unable to act, or in case they die before you do.

Guardians

You can state in your will who you wish to take on the obligations and liabilities of bringing up your children if they were orphaned, rather than leaving it to the court to decide who is the most suitable person. For anyone with young children it is sensible to appoint a guardian (or guardians). Under the provisions of the Children Act

1989, a person must have parental responsibility before he or she can appoint a guardian for a child. The father of an illegitimate child could not appoint a guardian unless he already has parental responsibility. If he does have parental responsibility, he should seek legal advice if he wishes to make a will appointing a guardian.

If either the father or mother of a child dies, the survivor will usually be responsible for bringing up the children although unmarried fathers should ensure they have been granted parental responsibility or they may have problems. However, on the death of the survivor or following some common accident in which the husband and wife or unmarried parents die within a short time of each other, the appointment of guardians will become necessary. Generally, guardianship issues would arise only after the death of both parents.

The choice of guardians requires careful consideration. The main issues are to do with the personal qualities of the friends or relatives you wish your children to be brought up by, and also their ability in financial matters. Potential guardians will obviously want to know if any money will be available to meet the cost of maintaining the children, otherwise they might not be able to afford to take on the responsibility. Sometimes the testator will set down a formula for calculating how much money should be paid to a guardian for looking after the children, for instance by linking it to the local authority payments to foster parents. If the appointment of guardians takes effect, the estate of the deceased person will almost always be held in trust for the children and its income can be used for their maintenance. It is worth considering, therefore, whether to make the guardians executors and trustees as well. It may not be a good idea to make them the only executors and trustees. Perhaps a professional (for example, a solicitor or accountant) should join them as a trustee to intervene if there is any risk of a conflict of interest. He or she can also help with the formalities of the administration and investment of the money if the guardians are kept busy by the day-to-day care of the children.

Who gets what

Before deciding who you wish to benefit from your will, it is a good idea to set down a rough calculation of your estate and what it is worth. You need not be too exact about this, because it is bound to change by the time you die. The assets you have at the present time will change in value – you will acquire new ones and dispose of some of those that you have. There will also be debts and liabilities and mortgages and such things, all of which can alter between the time you make your will and the time you die. Nevertheless, it is a good idea to know roughly how much your estate is worth and, if you are married or in a stable partnership, to involve your spouse or partner so that you can make an assessment of what tax will be payable and who will get what. Do not forget any lifetime gifts or shared property passing to the co-owner outside the provisions of the will.

Legacies

Legacies are usually particular items or fixed sums of money. If you are giving a house to someone, decide what should happen to any mortgage which is outstanding. Is the gift subject to it or is the mortgage debt to be cleared from the residue of your estate? It may be that the mortgage debt is covered by an insurance policy so that the mortgage would automatically be repaid on your death. Be careful to check whether the insurance policy will be paid direct to the mortgage company or, as part of the residue, to your executors. If your will does not make the situation crystal clear you may find that your will has left a house subject to a mortgage to one beneficiary while the proceeds of the endowment policy (intended to pay off the mortgage) actually pass to someone else. Remember to take into account your car, your personal possessions and any other benefits which are payable on your death by reason of other life policies or pension fund payments.

Then make a note of the people to whom you wish to give any legacies, including, possibly, a friend who has agreed to act as executor. List any particular items you want to leave to special people – for example, your wedding ring to your granddaughter, or the piano to your nephew. If the gifts are valuable, make a note of their likely value. You may wish to give money to a few of your friends, relations, godchildren or people who have been especially helpful to you in some way or other (for example, £100 to the child of an old friend).

You can also give a sum of money to a class of people, for example '£500 to each of my brothers and sisters living at my death' or one particular sum of money, for example '£2,000 to be divided equally between all my grandchildren living at my death'. Avoid gifts to a class of people which may not be known for many years, for example, 'to all my grandchildren'. You may have a son aged 30 who fathers a child when he is 60. If you die soon after making your will, your executors would have to wait at least 30 years to be sure that all the grandchildren had been born. It is important to specify carefully the class of people whom you wish to benefit and to specify, for example, whether it excluded illegitimate children or includes stepchildren and whether your husband's brother's sons are covered by the word 'nephew'. (For these purposes, there is now no legal distinction between children born in wedlock and adopted children.) Are the husbands of aunts included in the word 'uncles' or does it mean the brothers of parents only? Does the term 'nephew' include illegitimate nephews? If there is any doubt at all, it is better to list people by their names.

Remember that the will is operative only from the date of your death. If you leave someone a particular item of jewellery or any other property by will but then you dispose of it before your death, the beneficiary will not receive that item of property.

You may wish to give a sum to charity. Often people leave a sum of money to a particular charity with which they have been concerned in their life. A particular friend or relative may have benefited from a heart research foundation or leukaemia fund, for example, so you might wish to make a donation to that particular charity. It is very important to get the name and address of the charity correct, otherwise the gift could be invalidated. It is also wise to give an alternative, in case the charity no longer exists at the date of your death. It is unwise to leave the money in a specific account to a beneficiary as the account may have changed or the bank may have been taken over by another bank before your death.

The rest of your estate (the residue)

It is impossible to specify the amount of money which will go to the residuary beneficiary. Even if this could be calculated at today's date, it would certainly not be correct on your death in, say, ten years' time. All you can do, therefore, is to specify who is to receive the rest of your estate and, if more than one person, in what proportions. The lawyers call it 'residue'; the term 'residuary estate' is everything that is left after all the debts, liabilities, taxes, costs and legacies have been paid or transferred. The residue can go to one person, or to a number of people in equal or unequal shares. It is usual to include a term in the will stating that all debts, testamentary expenses and inheritance tax (IHT) are to be paid from the residue. If you are making a will you should be clear about your debts and set down how they are to be paid in the event of your death.

Life interest or absolute gift

When disposing of the residue of your estate you will have to decide if you wish the main beneficiaries of your estate to have the property (meaning the capital of your estate) outright (or 'absolutely') – that is, without any condition whatever. Alternatively, you might wish them to receive the income, but not the capital, for the rest of their lives so that the capital can then pass on their death to someone else you have chosen. If this is the case, bear in mind that the beneficiary with the life interest will only be entitled to the income from the property during his (or her) life. He will be entitled to the interest and/or dividends on the money or investments, and will be able to have the use of any property which does not earn income, such as a house. In such a case the beneficiary could rent out the house and receive the rent. (There can be complications as to repair, maintenance and outgoings of a house where the interest is limited in this way.) The right wording is extremely important as you may establish either (a) a right to reside in a house with no continuing benefits if the beneficiary moves out or (b) a life interest where you are giving the beneficiary the right to use the house or to sell it and enjoy the income generated by the resulting capital for the rest of that person's life. After your death, during the period of the life interest there will be the costs of administering the estate, completing income tax returns and trust accounts, so you may wish to appoint a professional executor.

If you have provided that the residue should be invested and only the income paid to someone (your wife, perhaps, during her life), the capital would have to be protected by your trustees until the death of the life tenant, when it would be divided between the 'remainder men' who share the property when the life tenant dies. These matters can be important where you wish to guarantee that the capital passes the way you want it to rather than allowing your spouse to make that decision. It may be even more important where, for example, you have children from a previous marriage, or if you are living with a partner to whom you are not married and you wish him or her to be provided for, for life, but also to guarantee that any of your children benefit from your property after the death of your present partner.

Usually, however, most people will wish to give the property outright, that is, to make an absolute gift.

Powers of trustees

The law provides automatic powers for the trustees of your will to enable them to carry out their duties. The main ones are the following.

- **The power of advancement** This allows trustees to advance capital to an infant beneficiary who has not yet reached the age when he or she becomes absolutely entitled. The advancement is limited to one-half of the beneficiary's expected share.
- **The powers of appropriation** This enables the trustees to pass over shares or property in order to satisfy a legacy or bequest without selling them and handing over the cash.
- **The power to run the testator's business** This enables the trustees, while they try to sell the business as a going concern, to run it for up to a year.
- **The power of trustees to charge** Under the Trustee Act 2000, 'trust corporations' and professional trustees with the consent of the other executors may charge for work done, even where the will does not contain a charging clause. Generally speaking, a trustee cannot charge for work done as a trustee but can recover expenses.
- **The power to delegate** Trustees may delegate their administrative powers but not their powers of distribution. A recent change in the law (the Trustee Act 2000) has greatly expanded and clarified the position.
- **Insurance** The trustees have power to insure the trust property.

- **Investment** While the Trustee Act 2000 gives wide powers of investment to the trustees, it also places them under a duty to obtain and consider proper investment advice and to review their investments each year. The adviser must be suitably qualified with appropriate expertise and subject to a professional code of conduct. In particular circumstances, you may feel that further powers are needed by your trustees including the extension of some of the statutory powers.

Any other powers you want to give to your executors and trustees should be set out in your will. The following additional trustee powers are often found in wills:

- the power to postpone the sale of property held on trust
- the power to advance all the capital to benefit beneficiaries in satisfaction of their 'contingent' interest – for example, where someone is entitled to payment at the age of 21 this power enables the trustees to make the payment at any time from 18 onwards if they think fit (perhaps to pay university fees)
- wide powers of investment including the right to invest in non-income-producing assets such as insurance policies
- the specific power to carry on your business for longer than a year
- additional power to borrow or lend (with or without charging interest)
- the power to use income or capital to improve trust property
- the power to sell assets to beneficiaries who are also trustees.

Directions to your executors

This is a bit of a 'catch all' section. Some typical directions are set out below:

- **Advance payments** You can state: 'If any beneficiary in my will has received a gift or advance payment from me, no account of that gift or advance shall be taken when ascertaining the entitlement of that beneficiary'. Or, conversely, 'If any beneficiary in my will has received a gift or advance from me, that gift or advance shall be taken into account with/without interest when ascertaining the entitlement of that beneficiary'.

- **Foreign property** If you have made a foreign will disposing of foreign property, make clear in your UK will what property is covered by the foreign will and remember not to revoke all earlier wills
- **Funeral arrangements** If these are complicated, write out detailed instructions so your executors know what you want. The will can then state your preference for burial or cremation
- **Donation of your body for medical research** If you wish to donate your body, contact your chosen medical school or teaching hospital, which can give guidance and information on the best way to make the donation effective (see *Living Wills*, below).

Trying to disinherit a dependant

When deciding who should benefit, most people naturally favour the members of their own immediate family, and this is a notion that the law encourages. Although you are free to give all your assets to anyone you specify in your will, certain people who are closely related to you in one way or another and whom you have supported can, regardless of the terms of your will, make an application to the court for a share in your estate. If for any reason you decide that your spouse or any of your children or anyone else financially dependent on you should inherit little or nothing under your will after your death, any one of them could apply to the court for reasonable provision to be made for them out of what you have left. The same rules apply if someone has been left out because of the intestacy rules (a cohabitee, for example). See Chapter 9 for details.

There are circumstances in which such people can properly be excluded from benefiting from your estate, for example because a wife has already been given a house and large sum during the husband's lifetime, or is financially wholly independent.

To prevent people from making successful claims against your will, make sure the wording is clear and well thought out. Alternatively, you might consider making a bequest to people who might make such a claim as they might be less likely to claim if they have been given something rather than nothing at all.

A checklist

If you are about to make your will it might be helpful to make a list of your assets and liabilities as well as any other points you wish to cover in your will. These are the common and important matters you must bear in mind.

- **Executors** Do you know who they will be? Are they willing to act for you? Are they younger than you?
- **Guardians** If you have infant children and you die, who will look after them? Would your chosen guardian have enough money to care for them as you would like? How much do you think they should be paid for looking after your children (who might be 3 or 17 at the time)?
- **Beneficiaries** Who are they? Are they under 18? If so, do you want to give the executors power to release money to them before they reach 18 (or 21)?
- **Foreign property** Do you own any? If so, you should make a will in that country to deal with it. If you have already done so, do not negate that will accidentally by using the normal revocation clause in your UK will.
- **Trusts** Are there any existing trusts which might affect IHT on your estate? In any case it may be sensible to create a trust yourself through your will.
- **Gifts** Have you made any gifts in your lifetime which qualify as potentially exempt transfers (PETs)? Have you made any gifts which do not qualify as PETs because you have retained an interest or benefit?
- **IHT** If your estate is likely to be subject to IHT, is there any way to avoid or reduce it?
- **Claims against your estate** Is there a chance of any claims being made if you leave someone out? Should you include an explanation for any exclusion?
- **Automatic transfer of property** What property automatically changes hands irrespective of what your will says? For example, do you own your house as a joint tenant? Do you have insurance policies written in trust for your spouse and children?
- **Specific items** Are there any you want to leave to a particular person?

- **Specific sums of money** Are there any you want to leave to a particular person?
- **Residue of your estate** What do you want to happen to it?
- **Your body** Do you have any specific wishes? Do you want it buried, cremated or given for medical research?
- **Pets** If you have any, what is to happen to them?

Finishing off your will

Once you have decided on the contents of your will you can type it out but you must observe the strict rules which apply to the signing of a will. The attestation clause is a helpful and necessary reminder.

Attestation clause

The will should contain an attestation clause, that is, a clause explaining the process of signing and witnessing. If the clause were missing, then, after the testator's death, when it comes to proving the will, it would be necessary to have an affidavit – a sworn statement – from one of the witnesses to explain what happened when the will was signed and witnessed. This could cause great difficulties if the witnesses could not be traced, or were dead. So a properly worded attestation clause should be included in the will.

The Principal Probate Registry★ and the District Registries★ will accept the following attestation clause: 'Signed by the testator in our presence and attested by us in his/her presence and in the presence of each other'.

It is not strictly necessary for the witnesses to write their addresses on the will. Their signature is all that is legally required. But it is much better if they do add their addresses, and perhaps their occupations as well, so that if there were any questions raised later about what happened at the time, they could more easily be traced. For the same reason, it is a good idea to write the witnesses' name in block letters underneath their signatures, especially where the signature is hard to read.

Signing, formalities and witnesses

A will does not have to state the date on which it was signed but there will be a problem obtaining probate if it does not; the date can appear at the beginning or at the end. There is no need to set out the date in an extravagant way. To say 'in the year of Our Lord...' is unnecessary: you could simply put '27 November 2003', provided it is written legibly in the space on the will meant for it. The date should be put in when the will is finally signed in the presence of the witnesses.

No one who is left anything in the will (or their husband or wife) should be a witness. Where this happens, the will is still legally valid – in other words, these witnesses are perfectly all right as witnesses – but they lose their legacies or benefits; the will is interpreted as if the gift to the witness, or the spouse of the witness, were cut out of it. Similarly, a person appointed as executor should not really be a witness. If he is, the will is valid and so is the appointment, but any legacy or gift to the executor would not be.

A blind person cannot be a witness. Also it is probably more sensible to avoid having someone under the age of 18 to be a witness though there is nothing in law to prevent it.

The will must be signed first by the testator (the person whose will it is) within the sight of two witnesses who should both be present together when the testator actually signs. The witnesses should then both sign in the presence of the testator and of each other.

If a testator is blind, the attestation clause should say that the will was read to him or her and that, having stated that he or she understood it, the testator signed it or, alternatively, it was signed on his or her behalf. Appropriate variations have to be made for illiterate testators (who cannot read) or physically disabled testators (who may not be able to read or write). The testator must sign first and the witnesses afterwards; the other way around will not do.

To sum up:

- the person making the will must be there all the time while anybody is signing
- both the witnesses must be there when the testator signs
- each witness is then to sign in the presence of the testator and to be present when the other witness signs
- the will should be dated.

When the will is long

If your will runs to more than one page, sign each page at the bottom immediately after the last line of writing, without leaving any gap and ask the witnesses to do the same. This is not a legal requirement, but it does help to prevent any forgery of your will.

It is better not to leave blank the back page of any sheet of paper on which your will is written. Either continue with the clauses on to the back of each page, or draw a line right across the blank space and put your initials at the top and bottom of the line. Ask the witnesses to do the same. The aim should be to make any tampering with your will as difficult as possible and to make it obvious which are the sheets of paper which comprise your will, each sheet of which should bear your signature at the bottom. Make sure that each page of your will is numbered so that no one can craftily slip in a couple of extra pages containing benefits to him- or herself. Finally, do not pin or clip anything to your will and make sure that no pin holes appear in it. Such holes, or marks where a paper clip has been attached, may give the impression that a sheet of paper forming part of your will was at one time attached to it but has now disappeared.

Where to keep your will

From the moment the will is signed and witnessed and dated it is valid. There is no law in England and Wales requiring that wills must be registered before death. It is up to the testator him- or herself to find a safe place for his will, to put it there and to let his or her executors know where it is. Tell them when the will has been made, where it is and confirm that the will appoints them as executors. Don't forget to tell them if you move it or destroy it.

Quite a few people lodge their wills in their bank but this often leads to problems or delay with the release of the will following death. If you have a safe place at home this is the obvious place in which to put your will. Failing that, perhaps the best place for your will is wherever you keep your other important documents – marriage and birth certificates, savings certificates, title deeds of the house, and so on. Put the will in an envelope and seal it, and write on the outside your full name, the word 'WILL' in large letters and the date. No further formalities are required before putting the will away safely.

If the will is lodged at the bank it may be helpful to make the executor known to the bank, perhaps even introduce him or her personally to the manager so that there will be no difficulty about handing the will to the executor. If the will is locked away in your house or your office, your executor will need to know how to get a key on your death.

If you have appointed guardians for any children, your guardians should know in advance the measure of the job they are being asked to take on. As time goes by and your situation develops and changes, you should keep your list of assets and liabilities up to date (as well as your will). Your objective should be to make things as easy as possible for your executors and family when you die. Any tendency to be secretive about your assets is likely to make life more difficult for your executors unless there is comprehensive information with your will.

You should also keep your list up to date as to where the essential documents are to be found. The logical course, obviously, is to keep things such as share certificates, building society accounts books, savings certificates, insurance policies, title deeds and all similar documents in one place – a family safe, for instance, or a locked drawer. This may be the same place where you keep your will. If you keep your affairs tidy and orderly so far as possible, when the time comes for your executors to act, they will not find that they have taken on an investigation instead of an administration. Age Concern England* has published a useful four-page form, *Instructions for my next-of-kin and executors*, on which to fill in a host of details including a 'where to find things' list (including the will) and personal/financial information that will be useful to executors when the time comes for them to act.

If you want to, you can deposit your will at Somerset House. If you write to the record-keeper at the Principal Registry of the Family Division*, you will be sent a large envelope and instructions about completing all the details requested on it, signing and witnessing, and where it should be taken or sent. A small fee is payable. You will be given a deposit certificate which has to be produced if the will is to be withdrawn. The Administration of Justice Act 1982 may eventually establish a new system for the deposit and registration of wills.

There is no special advantage in depositing a will in this formal manner (rather than, say, putting it in a safe or depositing it with your bank). It does not prevent future wills or codicils being made.

Reviewing your will

You should review your will every few years and more frequently if there are big events in your life such as a marriage or children. It is possible to make small changes by codicil but, even then, it may be better to make a completely new will if circumstances require any changes.

Other issues

Enduring powers of attorney and Court of Protection

Although your will says what should happen to your estate on your death it is worth considering what would happen to your property if you became incapable, through age or infirmity, of managing your own affairs. Until 1985 your spouse or some other person would have had to apply to the Court of Protection for an order authorising him or her to deal with your financial affairs under the supervision of that Court.

Since 1985 it has been possible to give another person the authority to look after your financial affairs without the expense of making a full application to the Court of Protection. You may appoint one or two such people (who will be called your attorneys) if you wish. If you are elderly, you may want to put arrangements in place so that, should you at some point become unable to handle your own affairs, the power to deal with them on your behalf will pass to someone you know and trust.

The authority for someone to act on another's behalf is established by the signing of an 'Enduring Power of Attorney', available as a printed form with explanatory notes, from law stationers, including Oyez Straker*. In the event of the need to invoke this authority, following mental incapacity, the attorney must pay £220 (of your money) to register the power of attorney at the Court of Protection and may be required to produce a medical certificate confirming your incapacity. The attorney will then be able to manage your affairs under the Court of Protection's supervision. This is a lot cheaper and quicker than making an application to the Court of Protection for an order.

Joint ownership

As has been pointed out earlier, if two people own a house as joint tenants and one dies, the deceased's share passes automatically to the survivor. But if they own the house as tenants in common and one dies, the share becomes part of the estate. If the survivor does not wish to sell the house and agreement cannot be reached for the survivor to buy out the estate of the deceased person, the executors have to apply to the court for an order for sale. This can be tricky if the children of the deceased are living in the house. Seek legal advice if this becomes a problem.

Burial, cremation or medical research

These matters are covered in detail in *What to Do When Someone Dies*, published by Which? Books. If any particular arrangements are required – your wishes for burial in a particular plot or for your ashes to be scattered in a specific place – they should be set out in the will. If you want to leave your body for medical research or donate your organs for transplantation, you should make arrangements with your chosen medical school or hospital. These organisations provide the necessary documentation and a contact address for your executors. It is always wise to tell your executors of the arrangements so they can act quickly in the event of your death.

Living wills

If you want to avoid a situation where you are incurably ill or severely incapacitated and are not able to refuse treatment that is keeping you alive, you can make a 'living will' which will express your wishes in the event of this happening.

In particular, the living will can express your views on receiving treatment which might ease your suffering even though it would not prolong your life. It might also request your doctors to withhold or withdraw certain treatments which could keep you alive. It would be sensible to discuss such a will with your doctor before completing it.

A number of organisations, including the Law Society★ and the Terence Higgins Trust★, can provide further information on living wills.

Chapter 5

Examples of wills

Here are some examples of wills designed to suit different circumstances, some of which may be similar to your own.

Will of a man with wife and young children

This example happens to be that of a husband. It could equally well be the will of a wife with similar assets.

Matthew Seaton is in his mid-thirties, married with two children aged two and four. He owns the matrimonial home, which is in his sole name, but he has a repayment mortgage on it with a mortgage lender. The mortgage is covered by an insurance policy should he die before the mortgage has been repaid.

He has about £10,000 invested in a building society, his own car worth about £5,000 and a bank account into which his salary is paid. He just manages to keep in credit and tries to avoid credit-card debts lasting for more than a few months. His salary is £30,000 a year, which he hopes to increase by promotion within the firm he works for.

He is lucky in that his employer still runs a contributory pension scheme. If he left to work elsewhere he would lose that benefit.

Matthew is in good health. His wife, Emma, has temporarily given up her job until the children are both at school, but she does receive rental income from a holiday cottage which she inherited from her aunt and which is worth about £80,000.

Matthew started by making some notes about his circumstances, which he will destroy once the will is made in case they are mistaken for the will itself. He soon realised that it would make sense for Emma to make a will at the same time, especially as their combined assets are likely to exceed the nil-rate band for inheritance tax (IHT) of £255,000. Matthew and Emma then sat down together to discuss how, on the one hand, they would like to avoid paying IHT but, on the other, how they would not want the survivor to be short of money while being responsible for young children.

They then agreed to transfer both properties into one another's joint names as tenants in common so each could leave their shares by will. They also decided to take out a term insurance policy which would run for 20 years which would protect the family if either of them should die in that period. If the policy was written in trust for the survivor it would not form part of the estate of the deceased.

Finally, they realised that it would be sensible to discuss their financial affairs with an independent financial adviser who might see some gaps in their plans.

The notes were set out like this:

What Matthew owns:

the house, 14, Twintree Avenue, valued at £200,000 subject to a mortgage to Forthright Building Society still owing about £80,000 so net value of house about	£120,000
savings in Halifax plc	£10,000
car	£5,000
bank account estimate	£150
half-share of contents of house	£6,000
	£141,150

What Emma owns:

the holiday cottage, value	£80,000
pension fund	£30,000
various ISAs	£20,000
half share of contents of house	£6,000
	£136,000

Notes for will:
1) Revoke previous wills
2) Executors – Emma and brother David for Matthew, and Matthew and Emma's sister Janet for Emma, with Andrew Robinson as a reserve for both wills.
3) Guardians for children if they are both killed in an accident – Janet and her husband Nicholas.

4) Cremation and wishes for a secular funeral to be arranged by the executors (consider setting down wishes in more detail in a side letter).

5) Specific bequests:

Matthew's golf clubs to brother David

Emma's cello to niece Charlotte

6) Legacies:

£500 each to the executors

£500 to cancer research on second death

£500 each to all nephews and nieces on second death

7) Residue to Emma

8) If Emma dies before Matthew the residue be held for the children by the executors (as trustees) until they reach 21.

9) Consider transferring a half-share in each property to one another which will then be held equally as tenants in common. In the case of 14 Twintree Avenue the mortgage lender would have to be consulted.

10) Remember to check the mortgage protection policy to ensure that it will be held on trust for the survivors and will not form part of the estate of the deceased.

Having carefully thought out how he would like to frame his will, Matthew turned his attention to the precise wording. He wrote it out in draft form first, and then made a few amendments to tidy up the wording. Traditionally, lawyers did not use punctuation in legal documents but, if used as an aid towards clarity, there is no reason why a will should not be punctuated.

Then he typed out the will itself (the engrossment, as lawyers call it). He could have written it out by hand, but word-processing or typing is better in order to make it legible.

He used single spacing, mainly because the whole will would then fit on to two sides of one sheet of paper, leaving sufficient room at the bottom for the signatures of himself and the witnesses. (Apart from looking slightly absurd, there could be legal problems if the signatures appeared on a page by themselves. If a will extends to more than one sheet of paper, it is best to leave one full clause for the next page to make any tampering with your will as difficult as possible. Also, if the continuation is on a fresh sheet, the first sheet should be signed by the testator and his or her witnesses.)

After typing the will, Matthew noticed a couple of typing errors. He therefore produced a clean copy without mistakes. (This is important, because alterations appearing in the will are assumed – unless the contrary is proved – to have been made after the will was signed, and so to form no part of it.) If there had been any errors in preparing the engrossment, he and the witnesses would have had to authenticate the alterations by writing their initials in the margin beside each alteration.

This is what he typed:

This will dated .....2003 is made by me Matthew John Seaton of 14, Twintree Avenue, Minford, Surrey

1. I revoke all earlier wills and codicils.
2. a) I appoint as my executors and trustees my wife Emma and my brother David Gordon Seaton.
   b) If my wife Emma or my brother David are unwilling or unable to act or if they die before me I appoint Andrew Robinson in their place.
3. If my wife Emma dies before me I appoint Janet Saunders and Nicholas Saunders to be the guardians of my infant children.
4. I give to my brother David Gordon Seaton my golf clubs and bag and trolley free of all taxes.
5. I give the following legacies free from all taxes:
   a) To my brother David Gordon Seaton the sum of £500 if he proves my will.
   b) To my friend Andrew Robinson the sum of £500 if he proves my will.
   c) If my wife has died before me I leave £500 to each of my nephews and nieces who are living at my death.
   d) If my wife has died before me I give to the Imperial Cancer Research Fund of (address) the sum of £500 and confirm that the receipt of a person who appears to be a proper officer of the charity shall be a discharge to my trustees.
6. I give the residue of my estate (after payment of my debts, funeral expenses and any inheritance tax) as follows:
   a) To my wife Emma absolutely if she survives me.
   b) If she does not survive me my trustees shall hold the residue on trust to divide it equally between my children providing they attain 21 but if either of them should die before me leaving children those children shall on attaining 21 take equally between them the share which my deceased child would have taken if he or she had survived me.
7 My trustees shall have the following powers:
   a) To pay income to which a beneficiary who is under 21 is entitled to his or her guardian for his benefit or to the beneficiary him- or herself upon reaching 16.

b) To apply capital for the benefit of any beneficiary who is under 21 as if the Trustee Act 1925 section 32 applied to the whole (and not just half) of the beneficiary's interest in that capital.

c) If the house of the guardians of my children is too small to accommodate their family and my children my trustees may lend money to the guardians in order to improve the house or to purchase a new house upon terms which in the opinion of the trustees will not cause the guardians to lose money.

8. I wish my body to be cremated and my ashes scattered at a place to be chosen by my executors but I would like it to be accompanied by a non-religious ceremony, the form of which I leave to my executors although I may leave guidance in the form of a letter.

Signed by Matthew John Seaton
in our presence and attested by us in
his presence and in the presence
of each other:

}

M. J. Seaton

Witness 1: signed.....Margery Abrahams.....................................
    Full name......MARGERY ABRAHAMS
    address.. .22 Twintree Avenue, Minford, Surrey
    occupation....Sales Manager

Witness 2: signature.....M. Roberts...
    Full name...........MICHAEL ROBERTS
    address.......The Reddings, Park Avenue, Little Minford, Surrey
    occupation.........Schoolmaster

Matthew Seaton's will was ready to be signed. It would not all fit on one side so he carried over to the other side of the sheet.

Comments on Matthew Seaton's will

Clause 1 Remember that the will takes effect on your death so you can revoke it at any time before then. It is possible to amend a will by signing a codicil without revoking the will in full. When making a will it is important to revoke any previous will and codicil so that there can be no confusion about the provisions which govern your estate on your death.

Clause 2 The main beneficiary (in Matthew's case, his wife) is appointed to be executor. Quite apart from saying what should happen if she did not survive, he decides to appoint a substitute executor in case either executor is unable or unwilling to deal with the administration of the estate when the time comes. Any executor can renounce the appointment, although no one, not even a spouse or other co-executor, can force another executor to renounce.

Clause 3 This clause appoints guardians but Clause 7 makes financial provision for them in case Matthew and Emma die before their children are grown up.

Clause 4 It may seem far-fetched to allow for taxes arising on the gift of a set of golf clubs. Where IHT is payable, it is usual for this to be paid out of the residue of the estate before the residuary beneficiaries get their share. In fact, the law automatically implies this but a change in the law is always possible. The phrase 'free from all taxes...' also avoids complications if there have been sizeable gifts by the testator in the seven years immediately prior to death using up all the nil-rate tax band. Any gift in a will can, however, be made to carry its own tax (which would be a pro-rata share of the total tax payable). It is therefore proper for the will to state whether any gift should be free of tax or that the beneficiary will have to pay the relevant proportion of the tax on the estate.

Remember also that if any of these items is not owned by the testator at the date of death, the beneficiary will not receive that item and the clause in the will becomes void.

Clause 5(d) In relation to the gift to the Imperial Cancer Research Fund, the clause providing for the proper discharge of the executors if they get a receipt from an officer at the Fund means that the executors cannot be blamed for paying the money to the wrong people. Give the full name and address, as some charities have very similar names.

Clause 6 This deals with the residuary estate: Matthew leaves all the rest of the property to his wife. If an estate is likely to be liable for IHT think carefully before you insert a condition that the beneficiary must survive 30 days to inherit. It can have bad consequences if a nil-rate band is not utilised (see Chapter 3).

Clause 6(b) This directs what happens to the property if his wife has died before him. Executors are a type of trustee. Where there is any land or houses or any leasehold interest in the estate, it is essential to have what is called a 'trust for sale' to avoid complicated legal pitfalls. The wording of clause 6(b) creates such a trust by saying that the trustees are to hold the residue on trust.

In a will, there is always a 'trust for sale' (even if the words are not actually used) so that the executors can administer the estate properly. They have to have sufficient cash to pay all the taxes, debts and liabilities so assets must be sold to realise cash. However, so that the executors can keep the particular gifts given by the clause 4, for example, and also keep anything they think might be a good investment, they are given a discretion to postpone the sale of anything for as long as they think fit, provided they raise sufficient cash to pay all the debts and liabilities and taxes. They are also given the power to invest or apply the money as if it were their own. This means the executors do not have to stick to the limited list of investments to which trustees would normally be restricted, but the executors will have to take proper advice as to the investments, not only because it is the sensible thing to do but also because the law says so. The clause does not mean they can help themselves to the cash.

The children will be entitled to the property when they become 21. Matthew thought 21 was the proper age because he felt they would have a little more maturity. Nevertheless, children become legally entitled to inherit at the age of 18 unless your will says otherwise.

If you want to postpone the age at which a child will become entitled to inherit to a greater age than 21 you should take legal advice as there are a number of taxation complications to watch.

Matthew also thought that the age of the grandchildren should be 21 if circumstances arose in which they became entitled.

Clause 7 (a) and (b) Where infant children are entitled to property under a trust such as this, the law automatically imposes provisions (by virtue of Sections 31 and 32 of the Trustee Act 1925) which allow the trustees to use any part of the income for the children's benefit and up to one-half of the capital to which they will become entitled on attaining the given age. The children might miss an opportunity if their trustees were to be restricted to using only one-half of the children's interest for their benefit. For instance, the children might be showing a particular aptitude for some profession or activity and require more capital than one-half of their prospective interest to be trained in that profession. Such a provision is particularly relevant where children do not become entitled until the age of 21, or even older. Matthew therefore widened the provisions of the Trustee Act by saying that any part of the capital (not just up to one-half) could be so used. He was quite happy to rely on the trustees' judgement.

Clause 7 (c) Even if the guardians are the same people as the trustees they have to keep separate the two different functions. They should keep proper accounts of all financial payments, receipts and transactions. Matthew also realised that the guardians might require a larger house but did not want to make an outright payment shortly before his children reached 18 because then his children might have more need of money for themselves. It is important to be clear what payment (if any) will be made to the guardians from the estate so that they are not out of pocket but it is equally important not to waste capital on them especially if the children are nearly independent when their parents die. Great care should be taken when deciding whether (and, if so, how) guardians should be paid.

Executors' and trustees' powers of investment

This is now largely governed by the provisions of the Trustee Act 2000. This Act describes the duty of care which a trustee must exercise together with his or her powers of investment, his or her power to employ agents and his or her right to recover expenses and, in certain cases, the trustees' right to remuneration.

The provisions set out in a will may enlarge the powers and extend the rights of trustees, but in all cases the trustees must normally obtain and consider proper advice when making or reviewing the investments of their trust.

Will of a wife with young children

A wife and husband, particularly those with children, will usually each make a will in largely similar terms at the same time because they cannot know which of them is going to die first and how long there will be between their two deaths. Both of them should make provision for what is to happen if the other dies first. The wills should, therefore, be largely in the same form, although thought should be given to what should happen if both die together, for example, in an accident.

In our example, Emma's will would take the same form as Matthew's: they agreed, in particular, about the appointment of the guardians. For clause 2, however, Emma wished her sister Janet to be the other executor instead of her brother-in-law David Gordon Seaton.

Emma directed that she wished her body to be buried; she had no particular wishes in relation to donating organs by transplant.

She left her cello to her niece Charlotte, in addition to which she bequeathed her diamond earrings to her niece Louisa Forbes, left £250 to her potential executors and left legacies of £50 each to Sally and Martina Saunders, who had been her bridesmaids.

Except for substituting 'my husband Matthew John Seaton' where appropriate, the important clauses in her will were the same as in his.

Matthew and Emma have provided for a number of situations which may or may not arise over the next few years. They can revoke or alter the will at any time before their death. Although Matthew should be aware of the tax consequences of his will, he should not allow the desire for tax avoidance to prevent a proper provision for Emma, and *vice versa*.

Will of a single elderly person

An elderly person who is single, divorced or widowed (and who perhaps has few relatives) might wish to leave all his or her property to one or two people without any complications. To avoid the risk of intestacy, the executors should be younger than the testator and there should be provisions for what should happen to the property if the chosen beneficiaries die before the testator.

Take, for example, the very simple will of John Ryder who is 78 years old. He is a widower and his only living relative is his son, David Ryder, who is unmarried and 40 years old.

His will might read like this:

This will of John Ryder of 142 Chiltern Court, Thoden Gardens, Hastings, Sussex is made the.....day of..... 2003.

1) I revoke all previous wills and codicils.

2) I appoint my son David Ryder of 15 West Wind Way, Hastings, Sussex, to be the sole executor of my will, but if he is unable to act or if he dies before me I appoint X of ....and Y of .... as my executors and trustees.

3a) If my son David survives me I give my whole estate to him.

b) If he dies before me I give my whole estate to the World Wide Fund for Nature (address) and the Musicians' Benevolent Fund (address) in equal shares and I declare that the receipt of the persons professing to be the proper officers of those institutions shall be a full and sufficient discharge for my trustees.

Signed by John Ryder in our presence and then by us in his presence and in the presence of each other:

Signed: John Ryder

Witness 1: (signature, address, occupation)

Witness 2: (signature, address, occupation)

If David Ryder dies before his father, the two charities will benefit in equal shares from the whole estate. It is very important to put in executors who can arrange your funeral and secure your house at short notice, especially if you have no spouse or close relatives.

Such a will can also be the pattern for that of a husband and wife who have no children or other relatives; the first beneficiary and executor would usually therefore be the other spouse unless the mitigation of IHT is a consideration. John Ryder could provide in his will for the possibility of David having children who would inherit if David died before him.

Will of a divorced/separated person

If the testator wishes to avoid any benefit going to a previous or separated spouse, legal advice should be sought because there can be complications; the former spouse might make an application to the court for a share in the estate regardless of the terms of the will, particularly if the division of the matrimonial property has not been finalised or if the testator was still paying maintenance at the time of his or her death. Show your adviser any order of the divorce court dealing with matrimonial assets or maintenance. Clean-break divorce settlements usually preclude the parties from claiming against one another's estates, but the situation is different if there is a continuing obligation to pay maintenance.

If the testator has a new partner who he or she wishes to benefit for the rest of his or her life, but then wants the property to go back to his or her children by a first marriage it would be necessary to create a trust giving a life interest to the new partner, who would live in the property and/or enjoy the income for the rest of his or her life. After the partner's death the property would revert to the testator's children.

Will of a husband/wife with grown-up children

Where there are adult children and the total family assets exceed £255,000, a will requires some consideration to reduce the effect of tax. If you are certain that your spouse does not need the whole of your estate to maintain him or her for the rest of his or her life, you should consider giving some of your property direct to your children in order to avoid the aggregation of your own estate with your spouse's on the death of the survivor and in order to utilise your own nil-rate band.

If you have made substantial gifts within the last seven years, you could, however, consider leaving your spouse a specific sum of money or property which will not be taxed, even if that would dispose of most of your estate. The remainder, your residuary estate out of which IHT will be paid, could then pass to your children.

The will could take a similar form to the others considered above, but the clause dealing with the distribution of the assets might run something like this:

"To my wife Marion I give the sum of £150,000 and all my interest in property known as 5 High Street, Hughtown, or any other property which is our main residence at the date of my death.

I give the rest of my estate to my trustees on trust for sale as follows:

a) To pay my debts and testamentary expenses as well as any inheritance tax on my estate

b) To divide what is left equally between my children Frank and Diana but if either should die before me leaving children those children should take the share which their deceased parent would have inherited.

If your estate is worth more than £255,000 you may hit a problem if you make a large, tax-free bequest to, say, a daughter and then give what is left to your spouse (who is exempt from IHT). The law states that the value of the tax-free gift must then be 'grossed up' to include the tax payable as well as the gift. Seek advice if this looks likely.

If there have been no gifts during the last seven years, and provided you are happy that your spouse would have sufficient to maintain him or her for the rest of his or her life, then substantial savings of IHT can still be made by giving legacies to the value of the nil-rate band before leaving the residue to your spouse. Your spouse would do the same, although it might be necessary to equalise your estates in order to make the most of this action. The legacies to be given, which could therefore total up to £255,000, need not necessarily be given to your children but could be given to any beneficiary other than your spouse (for whom all your gifts are tax exempt). It is increasingly common to give a sum equal to the nil-rate band to a discretionary trust which can then be used to distribute that money to a variety of beneficiaries (see Chapter 2).

Will of an unmarried couple with no children

As mentioned earlier, a will is usually revoked on marriage. If an unmarried couple are contemplating marriage and wish to avoid this problem, they should insert a revocation clause at the beginning of their respective wills which might read as follows:

1) This will shall not be revoked by my intended marriage to [partner's name]

If no time limit is inserted, the will remains valid even if the relationship breaks up.

If the couple want their wills to take effect only on their wedding then the clause could read:

1) This will is made in contemplation of and is conditional upon my marriage to [partner's name].

In the latter case, however, it should be borne in mind that until the wedding the partners will be intestate. It is therefore much better to use the first alternative unless there is some special reason for the latter.

If, on the other hand, an unmarried couple have no intention of getting married then they should simply make their wills as soon as possible in the usual way without either of the above clauses. They should remember, however, there is no IHT exemption for transfers between cohabiting couples and that other benefits such as widow's pension will not be available.

Unmarried couples may want their property to revert to their own family rather than go to the family of the survivor or perhaps to the family of someone else whom the survivor may marry or live with in the future and who would then benefit through the survivor's will.

There are a number of ways of dealing with this. Bear in mind that it cannot be known in advance which partner will die first, nor the period of time between the two deaths. It may be five minutes, five days or 50 years. Some couples feel that, provided it is likely that the survivor will have a long life after the death of the first person to die, then it is right and proper for the survivor to benefit absolutely from all the property. To make sure, the survivorship period may be extended to three or even six months in the case of some common accident, so that the property will pass to the survivor unless the deaths are close together.

Another way in which the first partner to die can be certain that his property will revert to his own family on the death of the survivor is to limit the benefit of the survivor to a 'life interest only', allowing the survivor the use of the property for her life and then dictating who benefits from that property on her death, for example, his own family. This, however, requires the creation of a trust so it would be sensible to take legal advice.

Chapter 6

Alterations to your will

If you have made a will you can change it at any time. You may want to alter it because of a change in your circumstances, such as a birth or a death, or a change of heart following a difference of opinion, for instance. Alternatively, you may want to change your will for tax reasons, perhaps because you have just made a very large gift (and there is, of course, no guarantee that you will live another seven years – see Chapter 3), or because seven years have elapsed since you made any large gifts, or because there have been changes in tax law.

You must not cross out bits of your will, or write bits in, or make any alterations whatsoever on it. The will is valid in the form in which it stood on the day it was signed. Any obvious alterations made on the face of a will are presumed – until the contrary is proved – to have been made after the original signing and witnessing took place and so do not form part of the legally valid will. Furthermore, any legacy which appears underneath your signature is not valid.

In theory, you could make subsequent alterations on the will itself by signing the altered will and having that new signature witnessed again as was done when the will was first signed. But this is messy and unsatisfactory, and quite the wrong way to go about making alterations to a will.

Codicils

If all you want to do is make a simple alteration to your will as it stands, either by revoking a provision or by adding something, you could do this by making a codicil. This is really nothing more than a supplement to a will which makes some alteration to it but leaves the rest of it standing. For instance, you may wish to increase a cash legacy to take account of inflation since you made the will, or re-allocate a bequest because the intended recipient has died.

A codicil can also be useful for changing the executors or guardians in a will. The guardians you have chosen may become separated or divorced, or they may now not wish to be your executor. A codicil can include a provision revoking the appointment and substituting others. It can also be used to specify that a will previously made should be 'in anticipation of marriage' (see *Not always revoked by marriage*, below). In this way the subsequent marriage will not revoke the will.

To be valid, a codicil must be signed and witnessed in exactly the same way as a will. It has to be signed by the testator in the presence of two witnesses and they must both sign it in the presence of the testator. These witnesses do not have to be the same two who witnessed the original will. Here is an example:

I, Matthew John Seaton of 14 Twintree Avenue, Minford, Surrey declare this to be a first codicil to my will dated 27th November 1999.

1) I revoke the bequest of my golf clubs and trolley to my brother David Gordon Seaton.
2) I give £250 to my brother David Gordon Seaton.
3) In all other respects I confirm my will.

Date: 20 December 2003

Signed by Matthew John Seaton as the first codicil to his will in our presence and then signed by us in his presence and in the presence of each other } Signed M. J. Seaton

Signed: Ivy Gurney
IVY GURNEY
The Larches
Greta Grove
Eastbourne, Sussex
Bookseller

Signed: P.G. Ambrose
P.G. AMBROSE
36a Wolf Street
Halford, Surrey
Concert Artist

Provided it contains a clause in the terms of clause 3 in the example above, a codicil acts as a confirmation of everything contained in the will that has not been expressly revoked by it, and the will has to be construed as at the date of the codicil. To find out the whole of the testator's wishes, both the will and the codicil have to be considered.

There is no limit on how many codicils you may make. Some people make quite a few, but a codicil is suitable only for a straightforward alteration to a will. For anything more than that it is better to make a completely new will anyway and not bother making a codicil.

Deed of variation

The provisions of a will or the rules of distribution on an intestacy can be varied after the death and, providing certain conditions are observed, the variations will be accepted as though they had been set out in the original will or intestacy.

The executors should be looking for the tax benefits which could result from a post death variation, but if a beneficiary thinks that tax could be reduced in this way he should bring it to the attention of the executors straight away.

A typical example might arise in the following way.

Mr H dies in October 2002, leaving £400,000, of which £150,000 is left to his children and the balance of £250,000 to his wife (no IHT to pay).

In March 2004 Mrs H dies, leaving £350,000 to her children less £38,000 IHT (£350,000 − £255,000 = £95,000 x 40% = £38,000).

If the variation of Mr H's will increases the amount left to the children from £150,000 to £250,000 there is still no IHT to pay, but the amount passing to Mrs H is reduced from £250,000 to £150,000. The estate of Mrs H is thus reduced by £100,000 to £250,000, on which there is no IHT to pay. The total saving for the children is £38,000.

It is easy to spot IHT savings where the second death takes place within two years of the first death. It can be more difficult to spot a tax-saving opportunity on the first death but it is always worth looking at ways to use the whole of the nil-rate band. A rewritten will can also be used to bypass a generation by transferring assets from grandparents to grandchildren thus saving IHT on the estate of grown-up children.

A deed of variation is an extremely useful document which can save large sums of inheritance tax (IHT). If you are administering an estate on which IHT is payable you should consider whether a deed of variation could be used to reduce tax.

The following conditions apply to any deed of variation:

- the variation must be in writing
- the variation must be made within two years of the death
- the beneficiaries must agree (if the beneficiaries are under 18 or subject to a Court of Protection order, consent will have to be obtained from the court if the deed is to be made on their behalf)
- the executors' agreement must be obtained if the variation results in more IHT becoming payable.

Substantial savings can be achieved for couples where variation ensures that the nil-rate band is utilised in both estates. If a variation of a deceased spouse's will is being considered during the lifetime of the surviving spouse, it is important to make sure that the surviving spouse retains enough capital for the rest of her life and to support her children while they are still young. It can also be a very useful way of utilising both nil-rate bands where husband and wife have died within two years of one another.

Revoking a will

If you make a will it should normally contain a clause which revokes any previous will and codicil. There are, however, other ways of revoking a will apart from including a specific clause of this sort – destroying it or getting married.

Revoking by destruction

If you deliberately burn, tear up or in some other way destroy your will, it is revoked. It must be a deliberate act. If your will were to be accidentally burned, whether by you or by someone else, it would not be revoked. There have, in fact, been cases where a will has been declared valid after the testator's death, the original having been accidentally destroyed. In one case, for instance, the torn-up pieces were assembled and proved as a valid will when it was shown that it was torn up in mistake for an old letter.

The testator himself must burn the will, or tear it up in order for it to be effectively revoked. Alternatively, it may be done by someone at his direction and in his presence. However, his will would not necessarily be revoked, for example, if he were to write to the bank manager who kept it, telling him to destroy it, even if the manager did so. The destruction has to take place in the testator's presence – otherwise it will not reverse the will. (There will be serious problems to overcome if no one knows for sure what was in a will which has been destroyed but not revoked.)

Revocation by marriage

The other way of revoking a will is surprising and is not always remembered: getting married. The law supposes that a man or a woman who has made a will and later gets married does not want that will to stand. As a result, merely to get married without saying anything about an existing will revokes the will. The whole will is revoked, including any legacies to people wholly independent of the new husband or wife.

This can lead to some curious results. Imagine that a widow with young children has made a will leaving her property to the children. Some years later she marries again. She must make a new will just before the marriage and with a clause stating that it is in anticipation of marriage to the second husband, otherwise she would die intestate and her second husband would inherit the first £125,000 of her estate with her children getting a share of what was left, if anything. If she waits until after the marriage to make a new will it is possible that she could die just after the marriage and before she has made a new will.

Another unusual situation could arise if a long-established cohabiting couple (who have made wills) get married. Their wills immediately become void even though the new wills contain exactly the same provisions as the old ones.

Not always revoked by marriage

It is, however, possible to make a will which says that it is made in contemplation of a forthcoming marriage.

The will must state that it is made in contemplation of marriage to a particular person who must be named, and also that the testator intends that the will shall not be revoked by his or her marriage to that person. Such a will is not revoked by that marriage but, should that marriage not happen and, instead, the testator marries someone else, the will is then revoked. If no marriage whatever takes place, the will, of course, remains effective – unless it was made conditional on the particular contemplated marriage taking place within a certain period of time.

The effect of divorce

Divorce does not automatically revoke all the provisions of a will. The effect of divorce is that any appointment of the former spouse as an executor will be invalid, and any gift in the will to the former spouse will be treated as if the former spouse had died on the date of the divorce. Where the gift is a specific one – for example, of a house or £10,000 – such property will go to whoever is entitled to the residue of the estate. But where, under the terms of the will, the former spouse was given the residue of the estate without further provision, it will instead be dealt with in accordance with the intestacy rules.

If Matthew and Emma (of the examples in Chapter 5) had divorced and no alterations were made to the wills, then the executors of Matthew's will would have been David Gordon Seaton and Andrew Robinson and Clause 6 (a) would have had no effect.

If you are contemplating divorce, it is possible to cover this situation by executing a short codicil before the decree is pronounced, amending the circumstances in which the children will benefit to include the divorce. This would read along the lines of:

'In the clause of my will after the words "does not survive me for the period of thirty days" shall be inserted the words "or we are divorced at the time of my death"'. But it is best to make a new will on divorce.

Chapter 7

Applying for probate

Earlier chapters in this book have examined why it is advisable to make a will and how to make a valid will. The following chapters explain what must be done when someone dies.

If the deceased has made a will, there will be executors, who will usually have to apply to the Probate Registry for a document called 'probate of the will'. If the deceased has not made a will, the next of kin will usually have to apply to the Probate Registry for a document called 'letters of administration'. The flow chart later in this chapter sets out the essential steps of an administration.

Probate and letters of administration

Probate of the will is a single-sheet document which bears the seal of the Probate Registry and carries the following words:

Be it known that (name and address of testator)
Died on (date of death)
Domiciled in England and Wales
And be it further known that the last Will and Testament of the said deceased (a copy of which is annexed) was proved and registered in the High Court of Justice and that Administration of all the estate which by law devolves to and vests in the personal representative of the said deceased was granted by the said Court on this date to the Executors (name and address of executors)

The gross and net value of the estate is shown and the document is dated.

Letters of administration have a similar format but instead of referring to the will the main clause reads as follows:

And be it further known that Administration of all the estate which by law devolves to and vests in the personal representative of the said deceased was granted by the High Court of Justice on this date to (name and address of administrator)

When you apply for probate of the will or letters of administration you must establish that you are legally entitled to do so. Once granted, that document is legal proof that you are entitled to claim the assets of the deceased, not for yourself but in your capacity as personal representative. You must then administer the estate according to the law – either following the will or the rules of intestacy.

Do I need to apply for probate?

If the estate consists of assets which, individually, are less than £5,000 in value, or jointly owned assets where the surviving joint owner automatically inherits the deceased's share, it may be possible to administer the estate without obtaining probate of the will. If, for instance, the estate consists of a house held in joint ownership as joint tenants and if the only other asset is a small building society account or a bank account, the house passes automatically to the survivor. You can then complete a declaration form for the building society or bank undertaking to distribute the estate in accordance with the will or intestacy law but without having to obtain either probate of the will or letters of administration. Those organisations which have this power are not obliged to exercise it but they generally do.

- Building societies and National Savings are governed by the Administration of Estates (Small Payments) Act 1965. This allows them to refund individual accounts up to £5,000 each without production of a grant of probate or letters of administration.
- You cannot sell stocks, shares or land from the estate without probate (except in the case of land which is held as joint tenants as this passes automatically on death).
- If the administration is disputed or if a person intends to make a claim as a dependant or member of the family, his or her claim

is 'statute-barred' six months after the grant of probate. This does not matter much with small estates but would be very risky for the administrator of a more substantial estate to distribute without obtaining probate.

- A lay executor who managed to realise the assets of an estate without probate might miss the obligation to report matters to the Inland Revenue for inheritance tax (IHT) purposes, especially where a substantial gift had been made in the seven years prior to the death. This could result in serious consequences for the executor.

When and why letters of administration are needed

If someone dies intestate – that is, without making a will – the rules of intestacy laid down by Act of Parliament apply. As an administrator you have to apply for letters of administration for exactly the same reasons as an executor has to apply for probate. You may run into difficulties if someone else in the family is equally entitled to apply for letters of administration and you cannot agree who should apply. Generally speaking, the grant is made to the first applicant but, in the case of a dispute between equally entitled administrators, the Registrar of the Probate Registry should be consulted.

'Letters of administration with will annexed'

If a will deals with part but not all of the administration (for instance, where the will says who gets what but fails to appoint an executor), the person entitled to apply for letters of administration makes the application to the registrar, attaching the will at the same time. The applicant, called the administrator in this case, is granted 'letters of administration with will annexed'. The applicant can now distribute the estate in accordance with the will or, if the will fails to cover an essential point, in accordance with the rules of intestacy.

Who can apply for letters of administration?

Chapter 10 contains a list that sets out in detail the order of those entitled to apply for letters of administration and also deals with the distribution on intestacy.

Some preliminary matters

The executor's job

The people who deal with what you own when you die are called your personal representatives. If they are appointed by a valid will or codicil, they are known as executors; when they are not appointed in this way, as happens in an intestacy, they are known as administrators. In either case, they will usually have to obtain an official document from the Probate Registry to show that they are the people with legal authority to deal with the property of the deceased. In the case of executors, who are said to 'prove' the will, this document is called a grant of probate, also referred to as a probate of the will or, for short, the probate. Administrators, on the other hand, obtain a grant of letters of administration. The document which constitutes the probate or the letters of administration is sometimes referred to as the grant of representation. The task of executors as well as of administrators is referred to as the administration of the estate.

A valid will operates from the moment of its maker's death, so that executors have full authority to act as soon as a person dies. This authority is effective, even though the will will not yet have been formally proved in the way the law demands. When the will is proved by the issue of a grant of probate, it merely confirms and makes official the powers the executors have had since the testator's death. An important distinction between probate and letters of administration is that administrators have no legal authority to act until the grant of letters of administration is issued to them.

It can happen that there is a fully valid will which does not appoint executors or where the executors have died or are unwilling to act. In this case, the nearest relatives will usually apply for letters of administration. Deciding who can apply for letters of administration can cause difficulty if the family does not get on. It makes it hard to decide who will arrange the funeral and who will take charge of the house. The procedures for making the application are the same as for executors, but instead of a grant of probate the grant is called 'letters of administration' or 'letters of administration with will annexed'. In effect, the rules of intestacy fill in the gaps where there is an incomplete but otherwise valid will. Even though they are administrators and not executors, those involved have to deal with the distribution of the estate in accordance with the will. If the will appointed executors but the person entitled to the residue has died, the rules of intestacy would usually produce the substitute beneficiary.

Executors not willing to act

There may be a number of reasons why someone might wish to renounce his or her appointment as executor: for instance, a relative or friend who had had no contact with the testator for a long period, or someone who simply does not want to be troubled with the chore and responsibilities of the administration.

It is possible for any executor to renounce his or her right to take out a grant of probate.

A form of renunciation can be obtained from Oyez Straker★ (phone the head office for details of your nearest branch). Alternatively, the Probate Registry will send a form, called a 'power reserved letter', for the executor to sign. This means that the executor takes no active part in the administration although he or she can be called back if necessary.

If one of the executors renounces, the substitute (if one is named in the will) automatically comes in, unless he or she also renounces.

It is possible for a person named as executor in the will to appoint an attorney for the purpose of obtaining the grant; the attorney then acts as if he or she had actually been named as the executor in the will. (The appropriate form for this can be obtained from Oyez shops.)

A personal representative who has obtained a grant can appoint an attorney to act for him or her in the rest of the administration. Usually the power lasts for one year and relieves a personal representative of the form-signing part of the administration. It can be useful where the executor is abroad. (Since 1985 there have been rules enabling an attorney to act during the incapacity of another, and in some cases this can cover the incapacity of an executor.) The rules are complicated and, if any question of incapacity through old age or mental illness arises, you should check with the Probate Registry.

Nominations

There previously existed a system of nominating some kinds of property in favour of a particular person, to take effect on death – for example, the money in a National Savings Bank account, National Savings certificates and certain specified government stock. Since 1981, no new nominations of that sort can be made but such nominations as are in existence will be honoured.

A nomination applies whether or not a will mentions it and is not revoked or affected by a will made afterwards. The choice of a particular person to benefit under a discretionary trust is sometimes called a nomination or an appointment. You may come across either term in an insurance policy.

Joint property

No application for probate would have to be made if all the assets in the estate (houses, bank accounts, etc.) are held in joint names as joint tenants, one of whom survives. In such a case, the property automatically becomes wholly owned by the surviving joint owner and all that is required is to register the death certificate with the appropriate authority such as the Land Registry or bank (but inheritance tax may be payable on the value of the half-share passing by survivorship to the other joint owner).

Accounting to the Inland Revenue

Even where probate is not required, the Inland Revenue rules demand an account of all property in the estate, if the combined value of the estate – including the value of all jointly held property, and non-exempt lifetime gifts – is more than £240,000. The Inland Revenue account has to be completed by the executors, even if they could otherwise administer the estate without a grant of probate.

When to use a solicitor

Any number of complexities can arise in connection with the administration of an estate. Often the personal representatives are busy people, without the time to cope with the legal side of an administration and would not contemplate administering an estate without employing a solicitor. The solicitor carries insurance in case he or she makes a mistake. Another executor making a mistake might be personally liable.

In many cases, a good knowledge of the law is essential when the deceased owned his or her own business, for instance, or was a partner in a firm, or was involved in an insurance syndicate, or where there is agricultural property, or when family trusts are involved.

If the deceased was married but left no will and the estate comes to more than £125,000 (after deducting the value of the chattels including the car), the surviving spouse will get the first £125,000 and a life interest in half the remainder provided that there are children. In this case, the complications likely to arise from the life interest make a solicitor's advice and help worthwhile. The same applies where, on an intestacy or under the will, some of the property is to pass to children who are under the age of 18. Their rights are called minority interests and particular legal problems can arise regarding them. This is so whether the children are 17 months or 17 years old.

Another situation which usually requires legal advice is one in which, on an intestacy, some long-forgotten relative is entitled to a share in the estate. For example, a brother may have gone to Australia 40 years ago and not have been heard of since. In such a case, the Australian brother (or his children if he has died) is entitled to exactly the same share as the sister who lovingly nursed the deceased through his last years of illness. The problems involved in tracing relatives who have apparently disappeared generally require careful handling, as does the situation if they are not found.

Home-made wills, particularly on printed forms, sometimes contain ambiguities or irregularities which can create difficulties, and legal help about the interpretation may be needed to avoid errors. An executor who wrongly interprets a will and fails to distribute to a lawfully entitled beneficiary may well become financially liable for the consequences of his or her mistake.

A solicitor should also be consulted if there is a possibility of anyone seeking a share, or a larger share, of the deceased's estate under the Inheritance (Provision for Family and Dependants) Act 1975.

If the estate is insolvent – if the debts exceed the value of the assets – care is required. The same applies where, although the estate is solvent, there are not sufficient funds to pay all the legacies in full or there is no residue. If you arrange a funeral but there is no money in the estate to cover it you will have to foot the bill.

Solicitors' fees

A solicitor's fees for dealing with an estate are paid out of the deceased's property. They are a legitimate expense, like the funeral expenses and the IHT. Along with any other debts and taxes, legal costs are usually paid from the assets of the estate, after which the remaining monies are distributed to the beneficiaries.

There is no longer a recommended scale of fees for solicitors. The Law Society used to suggest, as a guide, the following as a basis for fees in normal probate cases: 3 per cent on a gross estate between £2,000 and £10,000; 2 per cent on the next £40,000 (that is, between £10,000 and £50,000); and lower rates for estates in excess of £50,000.

Solicitors nowadays should charge fees in accordance with the Solicitors' (Non-Contentious Business) Remuneration Order 1994. This sets out the various elements that can affect the final fee, including the time spent, the complexity of the estate and its value. The order also sets out the rights of clients to information and interest.

Clearly, the charges will be considerably less for a straightforward administration than for one in which complicated matters arise, although the solicitor may not know about them at the outset.

If the will states that a bank is to be the executor, it is worth talking to the bank at an early stage if you wish to challenge its fee scales, as banks still tend to calculate their charges according to a percentage of the gross estate. Typical charges for a simple case would be 4 per cent of the first £250,000, with 1 per cent levied on the excess over £250,000. Most banks charge a minimum fee of £1,500 or £2,000 but there can also be additional fees.

The Law Society tells solicitors that they should give their clients the 'best information possible' about the likely costs when they take instructions, so do remember to ask at an early stage for a 'terms of business letter' if you are not told.

Do-it-yourself

There are examples of people sorting out legal problems themselves and conducting quite complicated cases without legal help. Some 'litigants in person', as they are called, have taken cases to court alone, and many people have bought or sold a house without a solicitor. Whereas a litigant in person and a do-it-yourself house-buyer cannot expect special treatment from the other side, a personal representative will find that special arrangements are in place at the Probate Registry to help him or her to obtain probate without a solicitor.

What has to be done

In most cases, personal representatives will have to deal with the following matters:

- find out if there is a will or not, and confirm that he or she is the executor or administrator
- attend to the formalities such as organising the funeral, securing the property, notifying the registrar of deaths, collecting mail
- find out the nature and value of the assets in the estate at the date of death
- find out details of the debts (advertise for creditors, if relevant, see Chapter 8)
- prepare a detailed list of the assets of the estate and of the debts, for the purpose of IHT
- open an executor's bank account in order to be able to pay monies in or out during the administration. To do this the executors will have to provide evidence of identity and complete the forms required by the bank
- work out the amount of IHT payable and arrange any necessary overdraft or other credit. If there is sufficient money in a building society account, arrangements can be made to use this money
- prepare and send off the documents required by the Inland Revenue and the Probate Registry

Applying for probate: the procedure

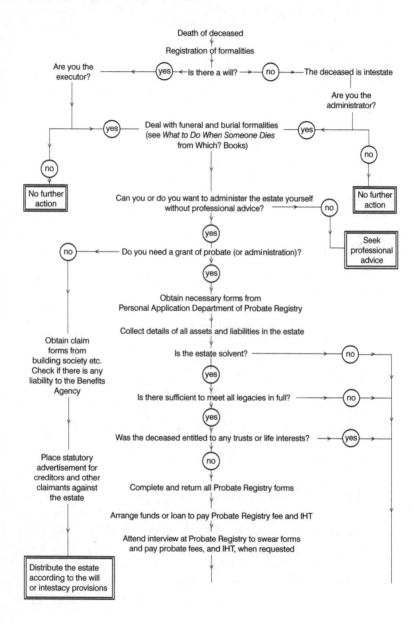

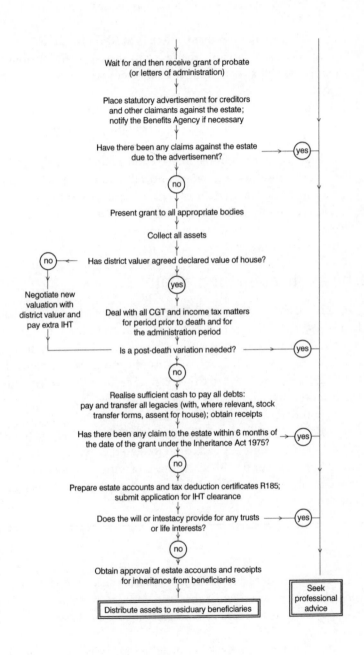

Wait for and then receive grant of probate
(or letters of administration)

Place statutory advertisement for creditors
and other claimants against the estate;
notify the Benefits Agency if necessary

Have there been any claims against the estate
due to the advertisement? → yes

no

Present grant to all appropriate bodies

Collect all assets

no ← Has district valuer agreed declared value of house?

yes

Negotiate new
valuation with
district valuer and
pay extra IHT

Deal with all CGT and income tax matters
for period prior to death and for
the administration period

Is a post-death variation needed? → yes

no

Realise sufficient cash to pay all debts:
pay and transfer all legacies (with, where relevant, stock
transfer forms, assent for house); obtain receipts

Has there been any claim to the estate within 6 months of
the date of the grant under the Inheritance Act 1975? → yes

no

Prepare estate accounts and tax deduction certificates R185;
submit application for IHT clearance

Does the will or intestacy provide for any trusts
or life interests? → yes

no

Obtain approval of estate accounts and receipts
for inheritance from beneficiaries

Distribute assets to residuary beneficiaries

Seek
professional
advice

- visit the Probate Registry in person to swear the papers
- pay the IHT
- receive the grant of probate or letters of administration
- send an official copy of the grant to the bank, the insurance company, and so on, and get from them what belongs to the estate
- sell any property unless there are good reasons to postpone the sale or transfer the property directly to the beneficiaries
- pay the debts
- deal with outstanding income tax and capital gains tax (CGT) for the period up to the date of death and for the subsequent administration period (no CGT is payable upon death) and obtain clearance from the Capital Taxes Office
- pay the legacies; hand over the bequests
- distribute or invest the residue.

The application for probate

There is a Personal Application Department in each of the Probate Registries, which has special staff, forms and procedures designed to smooth the path of the inexperienced layperson. However, the help and advice given by the Personal Application Department of a Probate Registry is confined to getting the grant of probate or letters of administration, and the personal representative is generally left to carry out the rest of the administration.

In cases where IHT is payable, the Capital Taxes Office (a branch of the Inland Revenue) is geared up to help the layperson but great care is needed to ensure that a mistake or omission does not have financial consequences that fall on the shoulders of the personal representative.

Example

Mary Josephine Blake has died. Robert, her son, and Matthew Seaton, her son-in-law, are her executors. Robert and Matthew have agreed that they will not instruct a solicitor in connection with the administration of the estate.

Matthew is the businesslike member of the family and can find the time, so it was agreed that he would run the administration. He had known of his appointment as one of the executors, but had never been shown the will itself. The will had been drawn up by a solicitor and put in Mrs Blake's deed box.

The date of Mary Blake's death was 8 April 2003.

Robert was reasonably sure that there was no other will because his mother had always used the same solicitors. Nevertheless, he made a thorough search of the house.

Mary Blake's will (example)

THIS WILL dated 16th August 2001 is made by me MARY JOSEPHINE BLAKE of The Firs, Willow Lane, Tadby, North Yorkshire

1 I revoke all earlier wills.

2 I appoint as my executors and trustees my son Robert Anthony Blake of Hall Farm, Woody Bay, North Devon and my son-in-law Matthew John Seaton of 14 Twintree Avenue, Minford, Surrey.

3a) I give the sum of £500 to each of my grandchildren providing they survive me and attain 18.

b) I give my jewellery to my daughter Emma Seaton.

c) I give £100 to Help the Aged and declare that a receipt from an officer of the charity shall be a discharge to my trustees.

4. I give to my son Mark Douglas Blake free from inheritance tax

(a) my house known as The Firs and I direct that any mortgage on the house shall be repaid from my residuary estate

(b) my car and my personal belongings and the contents of my house except for my jewellery.

5. My trustees shall hold the rest of my estate upon trust as follows:

a) to pay debts executorship expenses and any inheritance tax arising on my death

b) to divide the residue equally between my son Robert Anthony Blake and my daughter Emma Seaton

c) if either of them should die before me leaving children those children shall on reaching 18 take equally between them the share which the deceased parent would otherwise have inherited.

6. My trustees shall have the power to invest as though they were beneficially entitled.

7. I would like my body to be cremated.

Signed by the testator in our presence
and attested by us in the
presence of the testator and
of each other

}   Signed *M. J. Blake*

Signed – Witness 1
Full name
Address

Signed – Witness 2
Full name
Address

Releasing the will

If a will is lodged in the bank, the executor has to sign for it (if he or she collects it in person), or acknowledge its safe receipt in writing (if it is sent to him or her by post). Where several executors are named in the will, the bank may ask for all their signatures before releasing the will to one of them on the understanding that in due course all the executors will sign an acknowledgement.

Sometimes the will may be held in a solicitor's office safe. There should be no need for the solicitor to keep the will, and he or she should release it to the executors against their signatures if they all sign a receipt for it. If the solicitor is also one of the executors, he or she will expect to be involved in the administration but if his or her own firm is to deal with the administration of the estate make sure you are clear about the basis on which the firm will charge (see *Solicitors' fees*, above). If the solicitor who was appointed an executor has left the firm concerned, or has retired, he or she must be contacted but may be prepared to renounce as executor, leaving you free to administer the estate without having to use a particular firm of solicitors.

First formalities

Matthew read the will at once to see what it said about burial or cremation. He had no intention of arranging a formal reading of the will to the family after the funeral. This ritual now happens mostly (though not entirely) in the world of fiction. It is usual to inform the beneficiaries of the contents of the will at an early stage although you should remember that anyone can obtain a copy once probate has been obtained. There is a slight risk that the will might be found invalid for some reason, or that a later will might be found, or that there is not enough in the estate to pay out all the legacies, so that no legacy can be positively confirmed until after probate is granted and the estate administered. This might be a reason to wait but, the beneficiaries might become upset if the contents of the will are kept from them.

Matthew then telephoned an undertaker, who explained what he would have to do in order to register Mrs Blake's death and obtain a death certificate together with the disposal certificate which the undertaker would need to produce at the crematorium (see *What to Do When Someone Dies* from Which? Books).

A payment can be claimed from the state (contact your Benefits Office and ask about the Social Fund) to cover the reasonable cost of a funeral only if there is insufficient money in the estate to cover the will and the person responsible for it is in receipt of income support, or family credit or housing benefit. If a deceased person had been receiving income support, it would be wise for the executor to complete form RFE1 to be sure that no refund is due to the Benefits Agency. A late demand could prove embarrassing to an executor who had already distributed the residue of the estate.

Mary Blake had been a widow; her will gave the main part of her estate to her three children, Emma, Robert and Mark. The first £255,000 of her estate would be exempt from IHT but, with the exception of the charitable gift, the whole of the rest of the estate would be liable for tax.

She had given the house to Mark, who was unmarried and lived at home with her at the time of her death. The effect of the will was that any IHT due on the house, as well as the outstanding mortgage debt, were to be paid out of the residue of the estate, so that Mark would inherit the house without having to find any money to meet those liabilities. Had it not been for the specific direction in the will to this effect, he would have had to take the house subject to the mortgage although, in this case, the endowment policy was assigned to the building society so the mortgage was repaid automatically.

The general rule is that IHT is paid from the residue, but that any charge on an asset still binds the person who inherits that asset. For instance, if an overdraft had been secured by the deposit of shares with the bank, the person inheriting the shares, not the residuary legatee, has to settle the overdraft unless the will or codicil says otherwise. (The testator might have added a codicil specifically to deal with this.) However, it can be put into the will that this shall not apply in a particular case and that, for example, the proportion of tax attributable to the house should be borne by the person who inherits it. It is safest to state your wishes in regard to this quite clearly in your will.

In order to deal with post that continues to arrive after the death it is possible to arrange with the post office that all mail will be redirected to one of the executors. An application form for this can be obtained from any post office. A fee is payable depending on the number of months the service is needed. This forwarding service is useful where, after a death, a house will be standing empty. In Matthew's case, he had a word with Mark, who promised to send to him all his mother's mail.

Matthew also realised that he would have to check that the insurance on the house was adequate and valid. In cases where the house has to remain empty after the death of its owner it is important to safeguard the house and the contents.

Any valuables should be removed for safe keeping (don't forget to notify your own insurers if you are looking after the valuables). Advise the police and see if a neighbour is willing to keep an eye on the house for you.

You may wish to keep the services running but you might find that you have to turn off the water to maintain insurance cover through the winter. Discuss the situation with the insurer to make sure you are as fully covered as possible.

If there is a car it will cease to be covered by the deceased's policy although, as a short-term measure, the insurer may agree to fire and theft cover if the car remains in a garage.

Executor's actions

In the example, Matthew's next step was to register the death of Mrs Blake with the Registrar of Births, Marriages and Deaths. Once he had registered the death, he was able to obtain a number of copies of the death certificate that would be needed on several occasions over the next few weeks, as well as the disposal certificate for the under-taker. He also made arrangements to meet Robert, so they could look over the assets and decide who would do what in order to achieve an efficient administration.

In Mrs Blake's deed box Matthew and Robert found a number of other documents, including a life insurance policy, some National Savings Certificates, a building society account book, some Premium Bonds and some share certificates. They put them back into the box, together with the will, and Matthew took the box home.

From reading the will, Matthew satisfied himself that he had full authority to act as an executor with his brother-in-law Robert. Because he lived in Devon, Robert asked Matthew to deal with the correspondence and day-to-day matters of the administration, and left all the formalities to him. But after looking over the house together, Matthew made a point of specifically getting his brother-in-law to confirm the arrangement in writing. Apart from the courtesy of doing so, this was sensible. Robert was as much an executor as Matthew, but the letter made it clear what Matthew would do on Robert's behalf. On the other hand, they would still both have to sign the probate documents and claim forms. Robert knew that he was legally responsible for the proper administration of the estate along with Matthew.

Matthew and Robert were both aware that the duties of an executor involved much work and a lot of responsibility. Executors have to make sure that all the testator's wishes are carried out as far as is possible. They owe a duty of the utmost faith not only to the deceased but also to the creditors of the estate and the beneficiaries. They are under an obligation to realise the maximum benefit from the estate and can be challenged by the beneficiaries or the creditors if they fail to meet their obligations. They must therefore keep all matters of the administration of the estate entirely separate from their own personal affairs and be able to show, later on, by the prepa-ration of estate accounts, that all the assets of the estate could be accounted for.

Provided that they keep the necessary receipts and a separate note of the amounts involved, they are entitled to recover any expenses reasonably incurred in the administration of the estate. On the other hand they cannot claim payment for time spent.

Collecting the information

Matthew and Robert each knew quite a lot about Mrs Blake's affairs and both were interested in dealing with the administration, although Matthew would take the lead, so there was no doubt in their minds that they should proceed, as quickly as possible, to obtain the grant and deal with the administration themselves.

Within a few days, Matthew had assembled most of the available documents regarding the late Mrs Blake's property. He opened a large file with different sections for each organisation he would need to contact (bank, insurance company, etc.) so that he would have an immediately accessible record of all the correspondence – both letters to him and copies of his own – and avoid getting in a muddle.

He took a copy of the will for this file, keeping the original will itself in an envelope safely away from hole punches, staples and other office paraphernalia that might damage it and raise questions at the Probate Registry.

He then started to prepare a list of all the assets, with an estimate of the value of each. He was able, from the documents he had found in the house, together with information from Robert, to compile a provisional list of the assets that made up the estate.

Provisional details of Mrs Blake's estate

Assets	£
Rockley Building Society	80,000
Barminster Bank	1,900
National Savings Certificates	5,000
Premium Bonds	4,000
Stocks and shares (estimated)	100,000
The Firs, Willow Lane, Tadby	225,000
Bridstow – with-profits policy	5,000
Immortal Life – endowment policy	90,000
Jewellery	1,500
Car	4,000
Contents of The Firs	7,000
Private pension arrears	200
Old-age pension arrears	78
	523,678

carried forward

brought forward

Liabilities

The funeral	2,200	
Household bills	300	
Rockley Building Society mortgage	25,000	
Probate fees and expenses (approx)	1,000	
		28,500
Approximate net value of the estate		495,178

Estimated inheritance tax

Net value of estate	495,178
Less nil-rate band	255,000
Estimated IHT	240,178

@ 40%	= 96,071

Matthew left a column at the right-hand side blank so that he could fill in the actual figures alongside the estimates as they became known. He put this provisional a list of assets right at the front of the file for easy access.

Valuation of the assets

Matthew now had a good idea of what was likely to be involved in administering the estate. He would have to write to the bank manager, the building society and the insurance company etc. to find out the precise value of some of the assets, along the following lines:

Dear Sir,

Re: Mary Josephine Blake deceased

I am an executor of the will of the late Mary Josephine Blake, who died on 8 April 2003. My co-executor is her son, Robert Anthony Blake of Hall Farm, Woody Bay, Devon.

The estate includes the asset described below. Please let me know the value of this asset at the date of death, together with any accrued interest.

I enclose a copy death certificate. When the grant of probate has been obtained, I shall send an office copy of it to you for your inspection. Please let me have a claim form for signature by the executors.

Particulars of asset:
Name in which held:
Reference number:
Additional information required:
Yours faithfully,

National Savings

Matthew obtained a claim form DNS 904 (Death of a holder of National Savings) from a post office and entered full details of Mrs Blake together with her Savings Certificates and Premium Bonds.

He confirmed on the form that none of these savings was held jointly or in trust and that Mrs Blake had left a will for which he intended to obtain a grant of probate, and that he was an executor. He could indicate on the form whether he wished to keep assets in National Savings or have the money repaid. There were quite a number of National Savings certificate books among Mrs Blake's papers, some going back many years, containing printed certificates from several of the various issues of savings certificates that have been made over the years. Some of the new certificates had a computerised holder's number.

There were several addresses listed on the form to which the completed form could be sent, depending on the types of savings involved. Because there were National Savings Certificates among Mrs Blake's property, he sent the completed form to the National Savings and Investments* department in Durham. That office would also arrange for the Premium Bonds to be dealt with. With the form, he sent the securities themselves (Savings Certificates and the Premium Bonds).

A valuation of the Savings Certificates would be sent to Matthew from the office concerned, but the Department would check for unclaimed prizes. The Premium Bonds did not need to have an official valuation. They retain their face value, and no question of interest arises. They cannot be nominated and cannot be transferred to beneficiaries but may be left in the prize draws for 12 calendar months following the death, and then cashed. The money can be reinvested in new bonds in the name of the beneficiary but these will have to wait three months before becoming eligible for inclusion in the prize draw. National Savings should be notified of the bondholder's death as soon as possible. Any prizes received after the bondholder's death should be returned to the Bonds and Stock Office for it to determine and confirm that the deceased's estate is eligible and entitled to receive it. Where it happens that a prize warrant has been paid into the deceased's bank account after the date of death but before either the bank or the Bonds and Stock Office has been notified to freeze the account or stop payment, the Bonds and Stock Office will ask for the prize to be returned so that a new warrant can be sent to the executors after probate has been registered.

Where the value of all National Savings accounts or bonds (including interest and any Premium Bond prize won since the date of death) is £5,000 or less, it may normally be paid out without any grant having been obtained. National Savings will, however, ask if a grant is being obtained and, if so, may refuse to pay without sight of it unless the savings were held jointly or in trust.

Bank accounts

Mary Blake did not have a Girobank account. When a Girobank account holder dies, his or her account is administered according to the rules of ordinary banking practice.

Matthew knew that Mrs Blake had kept an account at the Tadby branch of the Barminster Bank. He found the cheque book, the paying-in book and the bank statements in a drawer in the house. When a bank is given notice of a customer's death, cheques drawn on that account are returned unpaid with a note 'drawer deceased', and all standing orders or direct debit mandates cease. Any cheques drawn by the deceased but not met on presentation because notice of death has been lodged at the bank should be regarded as a debt due from the deceased to the payee. (Plastic cards should be cut in half, so that they cannot be used fraudulently.) If any payments are to be made to the account, the amounts will be held by the bank in a suspense account for the time being.

Normally, a bank must not disclose to other people the details of how much is in a customer's account and what securities, deeds or other papers or articles are held, let alone hand them over. The exception is where the information is needed by the executors or administrators after a death so that the IHT accounts can be completed.

Matthew wrote his standard letter (see above) to the bank manager of the Tadby branch, concluding with these details:

Particulars of asset:
Name in which held: Mary Josephine Blake
Account number: 00860727
Additional information required: please let me know whether Mrs Blake kept a deposit account at your branch and, if so, the balance at the date of death and the interest accrued to the date of death but not yet added to the account, and whether she kept a deed box at your branch, or otherwise deposited any documents with you.
Yours faithfully,

Matthew also asked the bank to let him know the details of any standing orders and direct debits on Mrs Blake's account, so that he could decide whether any further steps were necessary. For instance, if she had had a direct-debit arrangement for her gas supply he would write to the gas company explaining that she had died and that therefore the standing order would cease, but informing it that he would settle any outstanding payment when the house was transferred to its new owner.

Joint bank accounts

When assets are held in joint names, it may be that the holders intended that, in the event of a death, the deceased's share would pass to the survivor. If not, it is necessary to fix a value on the share that belonged to the joint owner who died. In the case of a joint bank account, for instance, the executors might sometimes have to find out the source of the money paid to the credit of the account as this indicates the proportions in which the credit balance on the date of death was held. It may be necessary to identify payments into the account over a period of years and to calculate the respective total contributions to the account. The credit balance at the date of death would then be divided between the joint account holders in those proportions. If it is impossible to show who contributed what, or if the items in the account are too numerous or complicated to make it possible to distinguish the sources, the balance might be considered to be held equally by its joint holders.

However, where the joint account holders are husband and wife, it is presumed in the absence of evidence to the contrary that, even if all the money came only from the husband or only from the wife, it is held by them equally. Therefore, half the balance on the date of death would be taken as the value belonging to the spouse who has died. Circumstances may also show that a joint account held by an unmarried couple is owned equally between the joint account holders. It is best to settle any dispute in this area by agreement as the law can be vague on joint ownership disputes.

A joint account held by a couple has the advantage that the survivor can continue to draw on the account even though the other account holder has died. As it can take weeks or even months to get a grant of probate this allows the survivor to have continued access to ready cash. The balance in a personal joint account will usually pass automatically to the survivor and so bypasses the will (unless it is a trust account or some other specific agreement was made between the joint account holders). Nevertheless, the share of the deceased is included as an asset of the estate for IHT purposes – unless the survivor is the surviving spouse, in which case it is an IHT-exempt transfer.

With any assets held jointly – building society accounts, savings bank accounts and investments, for instance – similar principles apply.

Building society account

Matthew had found the Rockley Building Society passbook and in it was the address of the branch where the account was originally opened. He wrote to the manager of the branch, so that a note of the death could be made on the passbook and to ensure there was no possibility of some fraudulent person making withdrawals on the account. With the letter, he sent the passbook. He was aware that the amount shown in the book might not necessarily be the current balance of the account because there may have been further payments in or withdrawals. He therefore added the following paragraph to his letter:

I shall be grateful if you will let me know the capital balance standing to the credit of the account at the date of death, and a note of all interest due but not added to the account at that date.

Can you also let me know what interest was credited to the account in the tax year ending 5 April 2003?

This information is usually sent out automatically to account holders.

Insurance policies and the house

Matthew wrote his standard letter of enquiry to the Bridstow Insurance Company. He had found a life insurance policy with this company among the documents in the deed box. It provided for the payment of £5,000 on Mrs Blake's death. Matthew found that it was a with-profits policy, which meant that, in addition to the £5,000 to be paid to the executors by the insurance company, a further amount might be due. In the letter to the local branch manager of the insurance company, Matthew gave the following details:

Particulars of asset:
   Name in which held: Mary Josephine Blake
   Description of asset: life insurance policy, issued 14 June 1972
   Reference number: policy HPX 941/37
Additional information required: as this policy was with-profits, please let me know the amount payable on death in addition to the sum assured.

Matthew had now begun the procedure for valuing the property left by Mrs Blake. Even where he knew or had a fair idea of the value of an asset, he still asked the organisation concerned for a written valuation in case he should need evidence of the value of any item.

Valuation of the house

Matthew now turned his attention to the question of valuing the house. Most people have some idea of the current value of the houses in their locality. It is not essential in the first instance to obtain a professional valuation from a firm of surveyors and valuers.

Whether you have a professional valuation or not, your estimate will be checked sooner or later by an official called the District Valuer if the estate is large enough to incur IHT. The District Valuer is employed by the Inland Revenue but the job has little to do with taxes as such. He or she is concerned with the valuation of land, houses, factories, shops, offices and so on for many official purposes. He or she is an expert on valuation and knows the value of every sale in his or her district so there is no point in trying to understate the value of a house. However, for possible savings on

IHT, you may decide to put down your lowest reasonable estimate of value. The District Valuer may query your figure later on if it is too low, but perhaps not if it is on the high side. As there is IHT to pay on the estate Matthew would be wise to bring in a professional valuer to prepare a valuation as his valuer could then argue the case with the District Valuer if it were challenged.

However (particularly in an estate where there is no IHT payable), pushing for a higher estimated value could mean less tax in the long run if there is a possibility that any future sale might be subject to CGT. The value for IHT is the beneficiary's base cost for CGT purposes, so a low IHT value might mean a larger gain on any future sale. (Usually the private residence CGT exemption will apply, but this is not the case if the property does not become the beneficiary's main residence.)

Matthew estimated the value of The Firs at £225,000. Where a house is not going to be sold it is possible to agree a value for the house with the District Valuer before applying for probate, but this can delay matters.

If the house was joint property

As explained earlier, there are two different ways in which people may own a house or land jointly: as joint tenants or as tenants in common. Married couples usually hold property as joint tenants, and business partners as tenants in common, but you can choose which you want.

Where a house is owned by joint tenants, the share of the first to die passes to the survivor automatically on death. The survivor of joint tenants acquires the other half-share merely by surviving, irrespective of anything the will may say. The terms of the deceased's will do not apply to it at all. In the case of tenants in common, however, the share of the first to die forms part of that person's estate; that share may, of course, pass to the spouse (or whoever is the co-owner) under the will, but that is not the same thing as the share passing to him or her automatically as happens when it is a joint tenancy, and it may go to someone quite different. Whenever a house is held in the joint names of two people (whether married or not) the value of the deceased's person's share has to be declared for IHT purposes.

The value of a share in a jointly held house can vary depending on whether it was held as joint tenants or as tenants in common. That would be the first thing for the executor to find out (from the deeds and documents) in the process of valuing the share in a house on the death of one of the joint owners.

If it was held as tenants in common, the executor will have to know the proportions in which it was held in order to estimate the value of the share of the deceased at the date of death. For joint tenants it will automatically be half and half (or equal shares if there are more than two joint tenants).

The vacant possession value at the date of death is the starting point in calculating the value of the deceased's share of the house for IHT. Suppose it is the figure of £200,000. In the case of a joint tenancy or a tenancy in common held in equal shares, that figure must be divided by two to determine the share of the one who has died. This would give a figure of £100,000.

But this is not yet the true net value of the deceased's share. Because it was only a share in a house and because the other joint owner still has the right to live there, it can be argued that the deceased's share must be worth less than precisely half of the full value; the value is reduced by the very fact that someone can still live there. For IHT, 'value' means the price a buyer would pay in the open market on the day of death. It is hardly likely that a buyer (if one could be found) would pay as much as half of the vacant possession price for a half-share, when there is a stranger still living in the house.

It can therefore be argued that the proper value of the half-share (in the case of a tenancy in common held in equal shares) is half the vacant possession value less something for the mere fact of its being held jointly. The £100,000 for half the vacant possession value might well be depressed by about 15 per cent to £85,000 on this account. There is no rigid formula that applies to this aspect of the valuation and it is difficult to arrive at a figure because, in practice, shares in jointly owned houses are hardly ever sold. Nevertheless, the expert valuer should be able to decide on a figure. Some District Valuers may accept this basis of the value of the share in a house held by the deceased jointly with someone else, but it is arguable. Sometimes valuation officers do not accept any reduction for the 'forced sale' factor but a hypothetical valuation cannot, in any case, be absolutely accurate, and a tolerance of 10 or 15 per cent either way is usually regarded by valuers as acceptable. In cases like this the cost of engaging a professional valuer should be covered by the better result he or she should achieve in negotiations with the District Valuer.

When the property is owned jointly by husband and wife, valuation officers do not then allow any such reduction in the value because of what is called 'related property' provisions which apply under the Inheritance Tax Act. However, if before the death the property was jointly owned by, say, brothers and sisters, or two or more friends, or parent and child, or any two people not married to each other, it is worth arguing for a reduction in the valuation.

A situation can arise when a property is in the sole name of the deceased but the surviving occupier claims that he or she has a beneficial interest in the property in his or her own right. If that claim is accepted or substantiated in court proceedings the reduced value would be declared for IHT purposes. Legal advice should be taken in such a case.

Account must also be taken of any outstanding mortgage debt on jointly owned property. Suppose that it is £20,000; then the deceased's share of this debt would normally be half, that is £10,000. The result would be that the value of the deceased's share of the house less the mortgage debt would be £75,000.

Matthew was not involved in the problem of valuing a share in a jointly owned house, because he knew that the house was in Mrs Blake's name alone. If Matthew had been uncertain whether the house was in her name alone or in joint ownership and there was no declaration of trust or other evidence of joint ownership among Mrs Blake's documents, he would have to examine the title deeds.

The outstanding mortgage

There was a mortgage on the house, on which £25,000 was still owing according to a statement from the building society which Matthew had found in Mrs Blake's papers. The statement gave the position as it was on the previous 1 July, and it would therefore be necessary to obtain an exact figure showing the position at the date of Mrs Blake's death. He wrote this letter to the building society:

[Date]

Dear Sir,

Re: Mary Josephine Blake deceased

I am an executor of the will of the late Mary Josephine Blake, who died on 8 April 2003; my co-executor is her son, Robert Anthony Blake. I enclose the relevant death certificate.

Mrs Blake owned the house where she lived: The Firs, Willow Lane, Tadby, on which there is an outstanding mortgage with your society.

The reference number is AME716. Please let me know exactly how much capital was outstanding on the mortgage at the date of death, and also the amount of interest due up to that date.

Could you also please advise me of the amount to be paid under the Immortal Life Assurance Society endowment policy? Please let me know what formalities there are in this respect and send the claim form for completion. I do not appear to have any record of the date on which the mortgage was made. Please let me know this.

Yours faithfully,

There had been little discussion so far about whether Mrs Blake's son Mark would continue to live at The Firs or whether he would sell it. What was to happen would have to be Mark's decision once the administration was completed but the decision could not be made final until then in case there were some large debts to pay which were not yet known about. If such debts were to amount to more than the residue of the estate, the house might have to be sold to pay for these even though it had been specifically left to Mark in the will.

Shares and unit trusts

In this section of the book the company names have been taken merely to illustrate the workings of administering an estate and to give an air of reality. The prices and dividends and other figures are in no way intended to reflect the actual performance of the shares or the companies over the period covered.

Matthew next turned his attention to the question of finding out the value of another item which made up Mrs Blake's estate: the shares.

In the deed box, together with the will, Matthew had found a bundle of share certificates for various holdings, which he listed.

Matthew had made a rough estimate of what those shares were worth on the date of death by looking up the closing prices in the paper. Now it became necessary to work it out exactly in accordance with the accepted formula for valuing shares for IHT. This formula applies to shares which are bought and sold on the London Stock Exchange. The shares of all well-known large companies and a great number of others – as well as government securities and similar investments – are quoted on the London Stock Exchange.

On any particular day, there are sales of shares in nearly all the big companies (or plcs), and the prices often vary depending on the prevailing circumstances. At any one time two prices are quoted – the higher is that at which people buy and the lower at which people sell. The closing prices are the two prevailing prices of the share at the time in the afternoon when the stock exchange has closed dealing for the day.

The value of the holding

To work out the value which is officially recognised for probate purposes, it is necessary to know the closing prices on the day of the deceased's death. *The Stock Exchange Daily Official List* gives the closing prices, the required figures, in a concise way. If the death was at the weekend, prices from the official list for the Friday or for the Monday may be used and the executor may mix the Friday and Monday prices to his or her (that is, the estate's) advantage.

You can now access *The Stock Exchange Daily Official List* on the Internet. The local reference library may take it, as might a very large branch of a bank. If you telephone your bank manager, quoting the securities you wish to value, he will be able to find out and let you know the closing prices for each share for the date of the death in question (but you will be charged for the valuation). If there is a long list it is probably better to write to the bank. Alternatively, a stockbroker would be able to provide this information quite easily, either on the telephone in the case of a few quotations, or by letter if there are more. When a stockbroker makes a valuation, his or her charge is based on a percentage of the value of the shares.

Anyone can obtain back copies of *The Stock Exchange Daily Official List* for a relatively small sum – contact FT Interactive Data★ for details.

Matthew decided to buy a copy of the official list to make the valuation. It arrived within five days. He found that six of the companies in which he was interested were quoted in the official list. The government stock was classified under British Funds. The unit trust was quoted in the unit trust section.

In each case, Matthew found the price quoted. He was then able to adopt the official formula to work out the value of each for probate purposes. The formula is this: take as the figure a price which is one-quarter up from the lower to the higher figure. If the two figures in the quotation column of *The Stock Exchange Daily Official List* are, for instance, 100p and 104p, then you take 101p as the value; if the two prices are 245p and 255p, then you take 247.5p as the value. The prices quoted in the official list are often prices for every £1 share held; the nominal value of a share may be 20p, 25p, £1, or any one of many other amounts. It bears no relation to the actual value of the holding.

Matthew then prepared a complete table showing the share values. The shares turned out to be worth, on the date of death, £135,680 – considerably more than his first rough estimate of £100,000.

Number of shares	Description	Value per share pence	Value of holding £
2,500	Centrica plc	180	4,500
3,000	BT Group plc	190	5,700
5,000	National Grid Transco	360	18,000
1,000	Tesco plc	200	2,000
6,000	Marks & Spencer plc	300 (xd)	18,000
7,500	Prudential plc	450	33,750
1,500 units	HSBC investment fund	182	2,730
£50,000	5% Treasury Stock 2008	10	51,000
			135,680

Matthew wanted to check that he had got the correct holdings of the shares. For example, there might have been rights issues for which Mrs Blake had not yet received the certificates. So he wrote a letter to the registrar of each company concerned. The address of the registrar usually appears on the counterfoil of the dividend warrant. The counterfoil also acts as a certificate of income tax paid, so people should keep it in a safe place. An executor may not always find the counterfoils for all share holdings simply because the deceased may not have kept them, or they may be at the bank if the dividends were credited there directly from the company, or they may be with the deceased's accountant. There is a book called the *Register of Registrars*, kept in some reference libraries, which gives details of the registrar of each company quoted on the stock exchange. Alternatively, the executor could telephone the head office of the companies concerned to find the proper address for the registrar. Quite often the 'registrar' is another company such as 'Lloyds TSB Registrars Ltd' or 'National Westminster Registration Services Ltd'. (The registrar for government stocks would be the Accountant General at the Bank of England's head office; for other stocks it would be the appropriate registrar's department or finance department.) Matthew got the full address for the HSBC investment fund from the unit trust information columns of *The Times*.

The standard letter he wrote was as follows:

[Date]
Dear Sir,
Re: The estate of Mary Josephine Blake deceased
...............shares in................plc
Certificate no. 57713

I am one of the joint executors of the estate of Mrs Blake, who died on 8 April 2003. The only other executor is the deceased's son, Robert Anthony Blake.

I enclose a copy of the death certificate for noting in your records. I am in the course of preparing the papers for the grant of probate, and among the deceased's papers I have found the certificates for the above holding. I shall be grateful if you will confirm to me the holding as above registered in the deceased's name. Please also confirm to me that there are no unclaimed dividend or interest payments held at your offices.

I look forward to hearing from you as soon as possible so that I can finalise the probate papers.

Yours faithfully,

Matthew had now set about valuing all the securities he had been able to find belonging to Mrs Blake on the date of her death. (He knew that he might later have to account to the Inland Revenue for income tax on any income from the securities which he received while he was administering the estate.)

Unit trusts

If you own shares in one company, you do not know how well that company is going to perform and therefore what profits it will earn, which directly affects the value of the shares. Many people consider it sensible to spread the risk by owning shares in a number of larger companies.

Some investment managers have specialised in this, and it is possible to buy units in a pool of investments in which the investment managers specifically aim to spread the risk. With unit trusts, you do not buy and sell specific shares in companies but buy and sell a specific number of units. This 'unit trust' industry is itself very specialised; investment managers now specialise in different funds so that units can be bought in a portfolio consisting, for example, of property companies, of industrial companies or of electrical companies.

Matthew noted that Mrs Blake held units in an HSBC (Japan Growth) unit trust; HSBC, in this case, is the trust fund manager. The certificate was for units in its 'Japan Growth fund', which means that the money is invested in a wide spread of companies quoted on the Tokyo Stock Exchange.

In his letter to HSBC unit trusts Matthew asked the trust manager to confirm the closing prices on the date of Mrs Blake's death and the value of the holding. HSBC's reply in due course gave this as £2,730; Matthew filled in the list of assets accordingly.

Private companies

Although older 'Ltd' certificates are still quite valid, all companies whose shares are quoted on the stock exchange are now registered with the words 'Public Limited Company' or 'plc' at the end of the name. Private companies, whose shares are not quoted on the stock exchange (and which cannot always be freely sold), all have the word 'Limited' or 'Ltd' at the end of their name.

Valuing shares in a private company not quoted on the stock exchange requires expert help as a rule. Sometimes the secretary or accountant of the company concerned can state the price at which shares have recently changed hands, and this may be accepted for probate purposes. If not, detailed and possibly difficult negotiations may have to be undertaken and, unless the shares are of comparatively small value, it would be worthwhile to get an accountant to handle the matter. The basis of valuation is different depending upon whether the interest in the company is a minority or a majority shareholding.

Ex-dividend

Matthew noticed that the price for Marks & Spencer plc had the letters 'xd' beside it, which means that the price was quoted 'ex-dividend'. This means that if the shares are sold, the seller – not the buyer – will receive the next dividend on these shares. The price the buyer pays is therefore lower than he would otherwise pay, to the extent of the dividend he is forgoing. This is because the company prepares the actual dividend cheques in advance in favour of the owner at that time, so if the shares are sold before the company sends out the cheque on the day the dividend is due, it will still go to the seller. This usually happens about six weeks before the date for payment of dividends.

In this case, the share's price went ex-dividend on 23 March 2003, so Matthew made a note to expect a dividend cheque in May. Because the price does not therefore reflect the full value of the shares, the dividend must be included as another asset in Matthew's list. By phoning the registrar of the company, he found out that the dividend to be paid on the shares was .055p each, so he calculated that the dividend would be £330. This would have to be included as a separate asset in the Inland Revenue account of Mrs Blake's estate.

Pensions

Matthew found the papers relating to the pension scheme operated by his late father-in-law's former employers. It was a contributory pension scheme under which he had received a pension until his death and which then provided a pension, of half the amount, for Mrs Blake for the rest of her life. There was only one point arising which was strictly relevant to the administration of Mrs Blake's estate: the proportion of the month's pension due up to the date of her death. Matthew wrote to the secretary of the pension fund quoting the reference number he found on the papers:

Dear Sir,

Re: Mary Josephine Blake deceased

You will be sorry to hear that Mrs Blake of The Firs, Willow Lane, Tadby, died on 8 April 2003. I enclose a copy of the death certificate. As you know, she was receiving a widow's pension from the fund administered by you.

I am administering the estate. Can you please let me know if any pension is still due and, if so, how much.

Please also advise if any capital sum is due to the estate under your pension scheme.

Yours faithfully,

Employers' occupational pension schemes, which provide for the payment of a pension to a former member of the company's staff, vary in form and detail. Many are based on the employee's final salary; in some, the pension is calculated according to the contributions made to the pension fund by the company and by the member during the years in which he or she was employed by the company. This had been the basis of the pension which Herbert Blake had been receiving during his years of retirement. The scheme then went on to provide for the payment of a further pension to the widow of a pensioner, being a proportion (in this case half) of the earlier pension. In these circumstances, no other payment, such as a capital payment to the executors, was due under the scheme.

Quite often a pension scheme provides that a capital sum should become payable on the death of one of its members. For instance, if a member were to die while still an employee, that is, before retirement, the scheme might provide for the return of the contributions which had been made over the years by the member, and from which he has derived no benefit, because he did not survive to collect his pension. If the lump sum that represents this return of contributions were part of the deceased's estate, it would have to be declared for IHT. However, in most schemes nowadays it would be paid 'at the trustees' discretion' and not be subject to IHT. Such schemes provide that the trustees may select who is to receive the capital sum (but they are bound by the rules of the particular scheme, and some are quite restrictive). They may pay it all to the widow or they may share it between any number of dependants or pay it to the executors as part of the estate. If they pay it to the widow or to the dependants, the money forms no part of the deceased's estate. As a result, the discretionary payment to a widow or dependant is not subject to IHT.

Whatever the circumstances, it is probably best, where the deceased belonged to a pension scheme, to get a letter from the secretary of the pension fund to confirm the exact position regarding what the estate (as distinct from a dependant) is entitled to receive under the scheme. Even if it is only the proportion of the pension due for the last few days of life, a letter should be obtained to provide written confirmation for the purpose of IHT.

State benefits

Mrs Blake had also been receiving the state old age pension, or National Insurance retirement pension as it is properly called. Matthew found the pension book and noticed that she had not drawn her pension for the week in which she died.

Any arrears of pension, as well as the full pension for the week in which death took place, is paid to the executors after probate has been obtained. Pensions are paid on a specified day each week, for the week ahead. If a person collected the pension on Thursday and then dies on the following Monday, his or her estate would not be liable to refund any part of that week's pension. Where a person received the pension monthly or quarterly in arrears, or had it paid direct into a bank account, the death should be reported to the local office of the Department of Social Security, which will adjust the payment accordingly.

Matthew sent off Mrs Blake's pension book. The sum due for arrears of pension formed part of Mrs Blake's estate; it would have to be declared for IHT and included in the probate papers.

What to Do When Someone Dies from Which? Books includes a detailed account of National Insurance allowances and pensions that may be due after a death and how to obtain them after someone has died.

Contents of house and personal assets

The next item requiring valuation is the furniture and effects. This includes furniture in the house, household goods of all kinds, jewellery, clothes, the car and all personal possessions. It is not necessary to prepare a complete list, nor to state the respective values of different kinds of articles – they can all be lumped together.

Where the person who has died was sharing the house with a husband (or wife) or any other person, it is important to realise that it is only the deceased's household goods, effects, furniture and so on which need to be included in any valuation for tax purposes. A husband and wife may have regarded all of the property as being jointly owned by the two of them so that, on the death of either, it becomes wholly owned by the survivor. In such a case, one-half of the value of all the contents should be included. If the deceased owned any particular items outright, the full value of those items will have to be included. (There may be specific items bought by the husband or the wife particularly for him- or herself, or acquired by way of inheritance from their own respective families. Such items could quite possibly have been regarded by them as belonging to one or the other, not owned by the two of them jointly.) The executors should discuss the matter with the other person concerned to ascertain precisely what was owned by the deceased, what was owned by the other person and what was owned jointly.

It will usually be assumed that, in the case of a husband and wife, the items are owned jointly. If property is held by joint tenants, it will become owned by the surviving owner regardless of the provisions of the will or intestacy although part of the value will have to be declared for tax purposes. In the case of other people, for example an unmarried couple, it is usually assumed that the person who paid for an item owns it. Obviously, the provisions in a will (or indeed, intestacy) can operate only on the property which is found to be part of the deceased's estate, and no tax is payable on anything owned by someone else.

The make and age of the car are the principal factors which affect its value; its condition is another consideration. A study of the prices being asked for second-hand cars by local garages or dealers will give an indication of the value to within about £50. Do not forget to deduct any outstanding loan. If the car is on hire purchase, contact the hire purchase company to obtain its consent to sale. The remaining articles are not so easily valued. It is better to put a separate valuation on items of particular value, such as things worth more than about £100, when making a calculation of the total value of the effects. This might apply, for example, to a particular piece of jewellery, or a picture, especially if its value is reasonably well established, perhaps because it was recently purchased or had been valued recently by an expert for insurance (although the insurance value is unlikely to be the same as the probate value).

Matthew was not sure whether any of Mrs Blake's jewellery was worth a lot. He put into a box her wedding ring, a gold watch, several necklaces, one of which seemed to be made of gold with a ruby pendant, a pearl tie-pin (perhaps itself an heirloom) and the diamond brooch mentioned in the will. The local jeweller made a list of these items and asked Matthew whether he needed the valuation for probate or insurance purposes. For probate purposes, it is the value for which they could be sold which is needed; insurance value would be the cost of replacement, which is often considerably higher. The total value of Mrs Blake's jewellery came to £1,500. Matthew had to pay a valuation fee for which the jeweller gave him a receipt when he gave him the official valuation certificate.

Matthew would include the valuation fee in the expenses he would recover from the estate as executors' expenses in the administration account. If a valuable painting or piece of jewellery is disclosed, questions may arise about the origin of the item and when it was purchased. If earlier generations had not been completely honest, Matthew might receive an embarrassing questionnaire about such an item to find out when it had been acquired and at what cost.

The other items Matthew had to consider were the paintings. He had found, among the papers, the insurance policy for the home and contents and, with it, the latest endorsement for the renewal and review of the sum insured. In the contents section items above £300 had to be specifically mentioned. In that section, the paintings were specifically shown as £600, £500 and £400 respectively, which was considerably less than he had thought as Mrs Blake had always told everyone how valuable they were. Matthew decided to obtain a verbal estimate of their value by taking them to a local auction house.

General valuation

More difficult to fix is a value for the great bulk of the household furniture and effects. How do you decide what the tables, chairs, beds, linen, cups and saucers, carpets, TV set, clothes and all the rest of it are actually worth? You have to decide what price they would get if sold to best advantage on the day of death. This means in practice what they would fetch at an auction. Of course, the second-hand value of the great majority of items is considerably less than the cost when new. For IHT, you do not consider the cost of replacement, but the price they would fetch if sold second-hand. The Capital Taxes Office (as it is still called) of the Inland Revenue does not expect you to provide an expert's valuation, or one that is accurate to within a few pounds, but a valuation that is honest and sensible, and says what the executor really thinks the items are worth.

This was Matthew's approach to the problem. He spent a Saturday afternoon going around the house with his brother-in-law Mark, assessing what was in the house. Where necessary, they discussed when, where and by whom various items had been bought, in order to exclude items which belonged to Mark already. Matthew made a few notes as they went along. In due course, he totted it all up. It came to more than his first guess. The figure he finally arrived at for the furniture, pictures and effects (excluding the jewellery which had been separately valued) was £11,000, plus £4,000 for the car.

One other article needed special consideration: the dishwasher. Matthew found that Mrs Blake was buying it on hire purchase and there were four more payments of £20 each to be paid. How should this be dealt with in his valuation of Mrs Blake's property? Strictly speaking, the dishwasher itself was not something which belonged to Mrs Blake; it still belonged to the finance company. What she had owned – and which consequently had passed to the executors – was a right to become the owner of the dishwasher, when the remaining instalments had been paid, together with a right to use the dish-washer in the meantime. But it is not necessary to go through the solemn process of trying to value something so esoteric as a right of this kind. It is sufficient to take a common-sense attitude by valuing the article as if it had been part of what the deceased owned, along with everything else, and then to treat the instalments still to be paid as a debt due from her. This is what Matthew did about the dishwasher. His estimate of its current second-hand value, which he put at £220, was included as part of the £11,000, the value of the furniture and effects. The four outstanding hire-purchase instalments of £20 each he would include as a debt of £80. He ignored the fact that these instalments were not actually due at the date of death but only over the next four months. Matthew would have applied the same process of valuation if it had been the car, or any other articles, which Mrs Blake had been paying for on hire purchase. Where the figures are large, as for example on a car, it would be better to declare the net value as an asset after deducting the outstanding debt, rather than bringing this in as a separate debt.

Matthew now considered the simplest asset of them all: cash. In Mrs Blake's handbag, in the drawer of the desk, and in one or two other places, Matthew found odd sums of cash: £80 in all.

Income tax and capital gains tax

Income tax due before the date of death is calculated on a person's total income in the tax year which runs from 6 April to 5 April the following year. PAYE works so that tax is deducted week by week, or month by month on the assumption that the taxpayer will go on having income throughout the year. If he or she dies during the year, the PAYE assumptions are upset because the taxpayer did not live to receive the income throughout the tax year, and a tax repayment will be due because the full year's allowances can then be set against the income to the date of death. Also, if the taxpayer was not liable for tax because his or her income did not exhaust his or her allowances, he or she may be entitled to a tax repayment if bank interest is taxed before he or she gets it. (From 6 April 1999 it was no longer possible to reclaim the tax deducted from dividend payments.)

Personal representatives should explain the situation fully to the local inspector of taxes, and if necessary go to see him or her about any repayment that may be due because too much income tax was levied on the deceased during the tax year in which he or she died. Although tax is claimed only on the amount of income received up to the date of death, tax allowances (such as a single person's or a married person's personal allowance) are granted for the full year, even if, as here, the death takes place early in the tax year. If Mrs Blake had an accountant, Matthew might find it more convenient to ask him or her to complete her tax returns to the date of her death.

Now Matthew wrote to the local inspector of taxes.

[Date]

Dear Sir,

Re: Mary Josephine Blake deceased

The tax affairs of the above-named have, I believe, been dealt with in your district, under reference B 246537. Mrs Blake of The Firs, Willow Lane, Tadby, died on 8 April 2003. Her son Robert Anthony Blake, of Hall Farm, Woody Bay, Devon and I are the executors of her will, and we are in the process of applying for a grant of probate.

The only income which Mrs Blake was receiving up to the date of her death consisted of: pension from her late husband's former employers' pension fund (which was paid tax-deducted); her state retirement pension; interest from a building society account from which tax is regarded as having already been deducted; and dividends from various investments. Please let me know if you require me to complete a tax return.

If there is any other information you require from me, please let me know. I shall need to know the amount of any repayment for probate purposes, so I look forward to hearing from you.

Yours faithfully,

Depending on the circumstances, Matthew is likely to receive a tax return or a tax claim for completion.

Until 1999 dividends were taxed at 20 per cent but the tax could be recovered by a non-taxpayer or by a taxpayer with surplus tax allowances. A higher-rate taxpayer would pay a total of 40 per cent tax on the gross dividend but the 20 per cent tax credit could be treated as a part-payment of the tax.

Since 6 April 1999 non-taxpayers have been unable to recover dividend tax credits from the Inland Revenue. The tax credits are now one-ninth of the dividend.

Income received after the date of death

Where income is received after the date of death, the personal representatives will be taxed, either by prior tax deduction or by assessment in the normal way. They do not pay higher-rate tax but, on final distribution, they will provide a certificate (R185) showing what tax has been deducted from the income they are passing on to the beneficiary. The beneficiary must then disclose that income as his or her own, but the certificate is evidence of tax having been paid so the beneficiary will only have to pay more tax if he or she is liable as a higher-rate tax payer.

The personal representatives are given no personal allowances to set against the estate income but they can set off against the income any interest paid on a loan raised to pay the IHT. (See Chapter 8 for further details of the executor's tax return.)

Strictly speaking, the personal representatives should notify the Inland Revenue within six months of the relevant year-end and complete a tax return. However, the Inland Revenue has recently extended its informal procedure to cover straightforward estates whose income for the administration period does not exceed £10,000. In these cases the personal representatives can submit a simple computation of the tax liability. In other cases a self-assessment return will be required.

Debts and liabilities

If anyone had owed money to Mrs Blake, Matthew would have included it in the list of property declared for IHT. Any sums of money which are owed to the deceased count as assets. They are debts due to the estate. Items such as the dividend on the Marks & Spencer shares, the pensions due to the date of death and any income tax repayment fall within this category.

Debts due from the deceased have to be listed, too. Any money which she owed reduces what she owns for the purpose of calculating her total property: the liabilities are deducted from the assets. These debts can consist of almost anything: fuel bills, tax, telephone account, amounts due on credit cards or credit accounts, hire-purchase debts, an overdraft, for example. In addition, the funeral expenses are deducted (but not the expenses for administering the estate).

Mrs Blake had a few debts. Matthew found an unpaid bill for gas, a telephone account, and the hire-purchase debt for the dishwasher. In the course of the first few weeks after Mrs Blake's death Matthew received two more bills and these he added to the list: a bill for servicing the car and another for some wines and spirits. Matthew assembled the invoices for these items and wrote a short note to the companies and organisations which were owed money, explaining that they would be paid soon after probate was granted.

Not enough to meet the debts

Matthew had looked at all the assets and liabilities that he could find and had discovered very few debts and liabilities outstanding. In some cases, however, the debts can be a big problem in administering an estate. If you are involved in an estate where the deceased person had many debts and there is likely to be difficulty in being able to pay them, you should consult a solicitor if possible before you take the job.

However, if the estate is insolvent (that is, there are insufficient assets to pay all the debts), the question to ask is: which of the various creditors has priority if the deceased's assets will cover some but not all the debts in full? Acts of Parliament lay down a special order. There are priorities for creditors who have their loans secured by a mortgage; funeral, testamentary and administrative expenses come next in priority; then come VAT debts. It can thus happen that some creditors get paid in full and others get nothing. Or it can happen that all the creditors get at least something. In such a case, an executor will often not take upon him- or herself the administration of the estate but leave it for one or other of the creditors to take out a grant of letters of administration, as a creditor. There is little point in an executor getting involved where there will be no property actually to distribute to the beneficiaries.

If the estate is solvent (that is, there are sufficient assets to pay all the debts), the question is: out of whose share are the debts to be paid?

If there is any property which is mortgaged, then (unless the will specifies that the particular property should go to the recipient 'free from any mortgage debt outstanding against the property' or directs that all debts should be paid from the residue) the building society or other creditor in whose favour the property is charged can ask the person to whom the property has been left to pay the mortgage debt. If payment is not made, the building society can insist on the sale. If such a property is part of the residuary estate and is not mentioned specifically in the will, the loan is repaid from the residue and the residuary beneficiary gets what is left.

Apart from this, the debts are usually paid out of the residue. If there is not sufficient in the residue, pecuniary legacies will be reduced proportionately until enough money has been raised to pay all the outstanding debts. If all the pecuniary legacies do not cover the debts, then any other property specifically given by the will must be utilised. In such circumstances the various people entitled to these gifts must bear a due proportion of the debts. If necessary, the properties concerned will have to be sold. There is no distinction between land, buildings, leases and any other moveable personal property in this respect.

Advertising for creditors

There is a special formal procedure for advertising for creditors in the *London Gazette* and in a newspaper for the area in which the deceased held property.

Solicitors can put in this advertisement at any time after the death but the *London Gazette* will accept such a notice from ordinary personal representatives only after probate has been granted. A local newspaper will usually accept an advertisement at any time if it is satisfied that it is genuine.

Matthew had no reason to suppose that Mrs Blake had any debts apart from those about which he already knew, or for which bills or accounts would come in within the next few weeks. Nevertheless, he was aware that he would be responsible if he distributed the estate and a large unexpected claim was then made against it, so he decided to place the notices in any event.

Settling the value of the assets

It was not long before Matthew began to receive letters providing a precise valuation of the assets. He heard from National Savings and Investments about the savings certificates; he heard from the insurance company that the policy money and the profits to be paid amounted to a total of £9,100. The bank manager had handed a letter to Matthew and this letter stated the exact sum which stood to the credit of Mrs Blake's current account at the bank at the date of death: £1,900. The bank account was frozen as soon as the manager had been told of Mrs Blake's death. No further payment would be made out of the account either for cheques signed by Mrs Blake but not presented till after her death, or on banker's orders.

Matthew heard from the local Inspector of Taxes, who stated that a tax repayment would probably be due to Mrs Blake's estate, but required a tax form to be completed first. This did not worry Matthew because he knew that for the probate form he could put in an estimate of this figure, and notify the correct figure to the Capital Taxes Office at a later date.

Matthew also heard from the building society about the mortgage on the house: the amount outstanding on the mortgage on 8 April 2003 was £25,400. The building society told him that it had received a letter from the Immortal Life Assurance Society that the proceeds due on the endowment life policy was £85,300. Interest would accrue on this sum until it was actually paid. The building society sent a claim form to be signed by the executors so they could receive the balance after the mortgage had been repaid. Matthew would complete the claim form with Robert Blake as soon as probate had been granted. He would therefore expect to receive nearly £60,000 surplus from the life policy after repayment of the mortgage.

Then he heard from the secretary of the pension fund. There was £200 due for the proportion of Mrs Blake's pension for the part of the month of April during which she was alive. No other sum was due to the estate from the pension fund.

Matthew had also by now received all the letters from the company registrars, the Bank of England and the HSBC unit trust fund to which he had written, and most of these confirmed the matters which he had asked. However, there was one unexpected letter, from the registrar of Marks & Spencer plc. It read:

[Date]
Dear Sir,
Re: Mary Josephine Blake deceased

Thank you for your recent letter concerning the above-named deceased. I was sorry to hear of the death of our shareholder.

I confirm that there is a holding registered in the name of the deceased but the holding does not exactly match the holding of which you advised us. The deceased is registered as the holder of 7,200 Marks & Spencer plc Ordinary Shares. In 1988 there was a '1:5' bonus issue of shares and the certificate was sent out to the deceased on 31 July 1988 to her address at The Firs, Willow Lane, Tadby, North Yorkshire.

In case you are not able to locate the certificate, I enclose a declaration and a form of indemnity and guarantee for completion in due course against which we will be prepared to issue a duplicate certificate so that the shares may then be dealt with. Please let me know if I can be of any further assistance to you.

Yours faithfully,
Registrar, Marks & Spencer plc *

* This example is hypothetical.

This puzzled Matthew, because in the box with all the various deeds and documents belonging to Mrs Blake there were certificates totalling only 6,000 shares in Marks & Spencer.

When a company does not want to distribute its dividend but wishes to retain the cash within the company, it will sometimes 'capitalise' the dividend and instead issue additional shares (called a bonus, or scrip, issue).

It seemed to Matthew that what had happened was that the certificate had been sent out to Mrs Blake, but that she had not placed it with the existing certificates. He would now have to search through all his mother-in-law's possessions once more to see if it could be found anywhere. He also discussed the matter with Robert and Mark; they did not know anything about this certificate either.

They had another thorough search of all the possessions and papers in the house. The missing certificate was nowhere to be found.

The next day, Matthew went to the bank and showed the letter from the registrar to the bank manager and asked if the bank would have a search to see if there were any documents and papers held for Mrs Blake. There were none. This meant that the extra shares would have to be added to the value of the estate on the probate forms, and there would also be some additional IHT payable.

Matthew would have to add in a further 1,200 Marks & Spencer ordinary shares at a value of 300p, increasing the total value of the shares by £3,600. They would now therefore total £139,280. The dividend would also be larger.

The question of the issuing of the duplicate certificate for the lost shares could be dealt with when probate had been granted.

A rights issue is when a company offers its shareholders further shares at less than the market price. If at the date of death payment for a rights issue is due, the registrar should be contacted immediately to see if he or she will agree to postpone payment until probate is received. If not, the funds would have to be raised elsewhere (from the bank or by a loan from the executors or beneficiaries to the estate), because the payment may secure a valuable asset to the estate. If payment is not made as required, the rights will be lost.

The same point could arise if a deceased had just acquired shares in a newly privatised company. Usually the original subscription will be for only part of the price, and the balance will be payable by the owner of the shares some months later. If the date is missed, the share can be forfeited or lost so it is important to ensure that the money is available from some source. It is always wise to check the correct procedure with each company's registrar because practice can vary from company to company.

The Rockley Building Society had also replied telling him that the exact amount of capital held by Mrs Blake in the account was £80,400 and that there was a further £750 of interest accrued due at the date of death but not added to the account. The letter explained that interest was added on 20 June and 20 December each year, and that the December instalment had not yet been added to the book, which was why the capital balance was more than Matthew had expected.

Within a month of Mrs Blake's death, Matthew had collected all the necessary information about the estate of his mother-in-law. The funeral account, amounting to £2,200, was among the papers he collected together. Matthew was now able to complete the forms which would enable him to apply for a grant of probate.

Raising the inheritance tax

Fortunately for Matthew, The Firs made up a significant part of the value of the estate. This was important for IHT because land and houses are eligible for the instalment option. This means that the IHT due on the value of the house can be paid by ten equal instalments over a period of ten years. Interest is payable but the first payment does not have to be made for six months. As a result, Matthew will not have to raise a loan from the bank although he will have to pay IHT on the value of the rest of the estate before the grant of probate gives him access to the assets of the estate. He could see that the value of the estate on which the instalment option was available was £225,000 less the mortgage, on which the proportion of the IHT would be about £42,132 but he would have to find £71,834 to cover the balance of IHT due now.

	£	£
Total value of assets (except house)	342,834	
Less debts and funeral accounts	2,520	340,314
Value of house (before increase by DV)	225,000	
Less mortgage	25,400	199,600
Total value of estate		539,914
Total value of estate	539,914	
Less nil-rate band	255,000	
Tax due	284,914	

$$x\ 40\% \qquad = 113,965.60$$

Apportionment of IHT:

Value of assets
excluding the house $\dfrac{340,314}{539,914} \times 113,965.60 = 71,833.84$
Total value of estate   (payable immediately on application)

Value of house $\dfrac{199,600}{539,914} \times 113,965.60 = 42,131.76$
Total value of estate   (payable in instalments)

(At this stage Matthew was not aware of the adjustments he would have to make to his IHT calculations – see *IHT rectification* in Chapter 8).

In theory, the executors are faced with an odd dilemma. On the one hand, no bank or insurance company which holds money belonging to the estate is willing to hand any of it over to the executors until a grant of probate is obtained and produced to them; the probate is the only authority which can allow them to part with the money. On the other hand, the executors cannot obtain a grant of probate until they have actually paid the IHT, or at least most of it. How can they pay the tax without being able to get their hands on the wherewithal to pay it?

From National Savings

If there are funds in the National Savings Bank (and funds cannot be made available from anywhere else), these can be used to pay the IHT; so can National Savings certificates, yearly-plan and Premium Bonds, also British savings bonds, and government stocks on the section of the National Savings Stock Register kept by National Savings, and money from save-as-you-earn contracts. A special system operates between the Personal Application Department of the Probate Registry and National Savings which enables this to be done. (For obtaining payment from a building society, see below.)

Arrangements for paying IHT money

Generally, assets cannot be dealt with before there is a grant of probate. But if the person who died had a bank or building society account, it is possible that the bank or society will release money from the account for the purpose of providing finance for IHT (and probate fees). A cheque will be issued not to the executors but made payable to the Inland Revenue for the IHT and to the Paymaster General for the probate fees.

If the person who died had a Girobank account, the executors may, subject to satisfactory identification, borrow for the purpose of paying IHT, so that a grant of probate may be obtained. The borrowing is limited to solvent estates and to the amount of the credit balance in the deceased's account.

The Capital Taxes Office provides Form D20 on which to apply to a bank for the IHT to be paid out of the deceased's account. The notes which accompany the D20 form explain how to fill it in and what to do with it.

If this arrangement is not available, the executors will have to persuade a bank to give them a loan to cover the tax, which can then be repaid once probate has been granted. This can prove difficult if you do not have a friendly bank.

Probate application forms

The first step is to obtain the necessary forms from the personal application department of the Principal Probate Registry in London or your local district Probate Registry. They can also be downloaded from *www.courtservice.gov.uk*.

The Inland Revenue forms can be downloaded from the Inland Revenue (Capital Taxes) website (*www.inlandrevenue.gov.uk/cto*).

If the value of the estate is more than £240,000 (including the deceased's share of any jointly owned assets, the value of assets held in trust and any gifts made within the last seven years) then form IHT 200 must be completed.

Matthew knew that Mrs Blake's estate would exceed £240,000 so he telephoned the Capital Taxes Office to request the IHT forms. A few days later he received the following forms from the Capital Taxes Office:

- IHT 200 – The Inland Revenue Account
- IHT 210 – Notes to help fill in IHT 200
- SP1 – Supplementary pages
- IHT (WS) – A worksheet to work out the tax
- IHT 213 – The notes to help fill in IHT (WS)
- D20 and D21.

He also received IHT 14, a booklet which sets out the responsibilities of personal representations.

Matthew read through form IHT 210 (supp) which explained that IHT must be paid before he could apply for probate. Although the form explained what Matthew should do if he intended to work out the tax for himself he decided to let the Inland Revenue work it out.

He noted that, under the inheritance tax direct payment scheme he could draw on Mrs Blake's accounts to pay the IHT due if the bank or building society was part of the scheme. To do so he had first to apply to the Capital Taxes Office for an IR reference number on form D21 provided. He would then complete form D20, which would be sent to the bank at the same time as he sent the IHT 200 to the Capital Taxes Office.

Matthew then laid out form IHT 200 (see sample on pages 140–7) and the explanatory booklet IHT 210. The booklet gave a useful step-by-step guide to filling in the form, so Matthew referred to that guide as he completed each section of the IHT 200.

Once Matthew had filled in the first page of the IHT 200 with general information, he turned to page 2, which sets out a number of yes/no questions to establish what sort of assets were held by Mrs Blake.

Matthew answered 'yes' to questions like:

- Did the deceased leave a will?
- Did the deceased own any stocks or shares and did the deceased own any land or buildings?

He was referred to various supplementary pages which would need completing.

He then turned to page 3, which asked for details of the various assets held by Mrs Blake at the date of her death (some of which had to be entered on another supplementary sheet).

He worked through the form, putting the cost of the funeral on page 4 and the value of the house on page 5 together with details of the outstanding mortgage.

The explanatory booklet IHT 210 gave helpful advice on how to complete each section. In addition it set out a flowchart to help Matthew sort out which forms had to go to the Capital Taxes Office and which forms would have to go to the Probate Registry.

Matthew telephoned the Probate Registry and requested the relevant forms for making an application for probate. A few days later he received the following forms from the Probate Registry:

- Form PA1 – The probate application form
- Form PA1a – Guidance notes
- Booklet PA2 – A guide to help a person applying for probate without a solicitor
- Form PA3 – A list of probate fees
- Form PA4 – A list of probate registries and interview venues.

Matthew first read booklet PA2 and the guidance notes. He also read booklet IHT 14. He then gathered his notes together and read through the application form PA1 (see sample form on pages 148–51).

Matthew put himself as the first applicant in section C so that the grant of probate would be sent to him. He put Robert's name in section C8.

There were some other questions on form PA1 which could have been difficult to answer with certainty. For instance, Matthew did not know if Mrs Blake held any assets in another name but, after discussing the matter with Robert, he was satisfied that she did not. Matthew then arranged to meet with Robert, his brother-in-law and co-executor, in order to go through all the completed forms and to be sure that Robert was satisfied that they were correct. Robert and Matthew then signed the form.

Sending off the forms and paying inheritance tax

The back page of the Probate Application form PA1 sets out a checklist of forms to be sent to the Probate Registry but, where IHT is payable, it makes clear that form IHT 200 must be sent to the Capital Taxes Office rather than the Probate Registry. (If there is no IHT to pay, form IHT 205 should be sent to the Probate Registry.) The following flow-chart from IHT 210 shows the sequence of events.

Matthew read the guide PA2 again. Having decided that he wanted the Capital Taxes Office to work out the IHT he noted the order in which the forms had to be submitted and the offices to which the forms must be sent. He realised that matters would be further complicated because he was intending to obtain the IHT by submitting Form D20 to the Rockley Building Society.

The following list shows the additional steps which have to be taken to obtain advance payment of IHT from a building society:

1. Form PA1 and Form D18 were to be sent to the Probate Registry together with the original will and an official copy of the death certificate and a cheque for £140 (to cover the fee of £130 and for ten official copies of the probate).
2. The interview at the Probate Registry would then follow, after which Matthew would expect to receive Form D18 completed by the Probate Registry.

Steps involved in the granting of probate

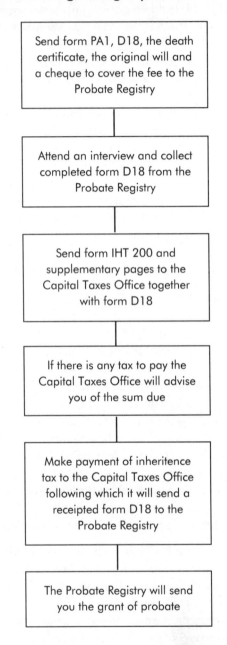

Send form PA1, D18, the death certificate, the original will and a cheque to cover the fee to the Probate Registry

Attend an interview and collect completed form D18 from the Probate Registry

Send form IHT 200 and supplementary pages to the Capital Taxes Office together with form D18

If there is any tax to pay the Capital Taxes Office will advise you of the sum due

Make payment of inheritence tax to the Capital Taxes Office following which it will send a receipted form D18 to the Probate Registry

The Probate Registry will send you the grant of probate

3. Completed Form D18 would then be sent to the Capital Taxes Office together with Form IHT 200 and the supplementary pages, following which Matthew would be advised how much IHT was required to be paid. (It would not include the IHT arising on the house as he had elected to pay that by instalments.)
4. Matthew would then be able to send Form D20 to the Rockley Building Society. Once payment has been made, the Capital Taxes Office will receive the form and then receipt it (to show IHT has been paid) and send it back to the Probate Registry. Probate will then be granted.

Fees

The probate fees are charges made by the Probate Registry for dealing with the papers and issuing the grant of probate. Form PA4 gives a list of the fees, as a guide: it would be wise to confirm the actual amount payable before you attend the interview at the Probate Registry.

The probate fee must be paid when the personal representatives go to the Registry to swear the papers. Payment can be made by cheque, banker's draft, postal order or in cash. In Mrs Blake's case, the total fees would come to £140.

Matthew would draw a cheque for £140, made payable to HM Paymaster General, on the executorship account which he and Robert had recently opened at the bank. The extra £10, on top of the £130 probate fees, was for ten official copies of the probate, at £1 each. Matthew had already arranged with the bank manager for the temporary overdraft.

Inland Revenue Account for Inheritance Tax

Inland Revenue Capital Taxes

Fill in this account for the estate of a person who died on or after 18 March 1986. You should read the related guidance note(s) before filling in any particular box(es). The notes follow the same numbering as this form, so section headings are shown by capital letters and the items in each section are on a dark background.

A Probate Registry, Commissary Court or Sheriff Court District

Name **A1** PRINCIPAL PROBATE REGISTRY   Date of Grant

B About the person who has died

Title **B1** MRS   Surname **B2** BLAKE

First name(s) **B3** MARY JOSEPHINE

Date of birth **B4** 24/ 6 /1925   Date of death **B5** 8 / 4 / 2003

Marital status **B6** WIDOW   Last known usual address

Surviving relatives

Husband/Wife **B8**

Brother(s)/Sister(s) **B9**

Parent(s) **B10**

B7 THE FIRS
WILLOW LANE
TADBY
NORTH YORKSHIRE

Postcode

Number of

Children **B11** 3

Grandchildren **B12** 3

Nursing / Residential home **B13**

Domicile **B14** ENGLAND & WALES

Occupation **B15** NONE

National Insurance number **B16**

Income tax district **B17**

Income tax reference or self assessment reference **B18**

C Solicitor or other person to contact

Name and address of firm or person dealing with the estate

C1 MR MATTHEW JOHN SEATON
14 TWINTREE AVENUE
MINFORD
SURREY

Postcode

DX number and town

C2 DX

Contact name and reference

C3

Telephone number

C4

Fax number

C5

For IR CT use

IHT 200

R2I4153 IRCT 02/02

Ⓓ Supplementary pages

You must answer all of the questions in this section. You should read the notes starting at page 10 of form IHT 210 before answering the questions.

If you answer "Yes" to a question you will need to fill in the supplementary page shown. If you do not have all the supplementary pages you need you should telephone our Orderline on 0845 2341000

		No	Yes	Page
● **The Will**	Did the deceased leave a Will?		✓	D1
● **Domicile outside the United Kingdom**	Was the deceased domiciled outside the UK at the date of death?	✓		D2
● **Gifts and other transfers of value**	Did the deceased make any gift or any other transfer of value on or after 18 March 1986?	✓		D3
● **Joint assets**	Did the deceased hold any asset(s) in joint names with another person?	✓		D4
● **Nominated assets**	Did the deceased, at any time during their lifetime, give written instructions (usually called a "nomination") that any asset was to pass to a particular person on their death?	✓		D4
● **Assets held in trust**	Did the deceased have any right to any benefit from any assets held in trust or in a settlement at the date of death?	✓		D5
● **Pensions**	Did the deceased have provision for a pension from employers, a personal pension policy or other provisions made for retirement other than the State Pension?	✓		D6
● **Stocks and shares**	Did the deceased own any stocks or shares?		✓	D7
● **Debts due to the estate**	Did the deceased lend any money, either on mortgage or by personal loan, that had not been repaid by the date of death?	✓		D8
● **Life insurance and annuities**	Did the deceased pay any premiums on any life insurance policies or annuities which are payable to either the estate or to someone else or which continue after death?		✓	D9
● **Household and personal goods**	Did the deceased own any household goods or other personal possessions?		✓	D10
● **Interest in another estate**	Did the deceased have a right to a legacy or a share of an estate of someone who died before them, but which they had not received before they died?	✓		D11
● **Land, buildings and interests in land**	Did the deceased own any land or buildings in the UK?		✓	D12
● **Agricultural relief**	Are you deducting agricultural relief?	✓		D13
● **Business interests**	Did the deceased own all or part of a business or were they a partner in a business?	✓		D14
● **Business relief**	Are you deducting business relief?	✓		D14
● **Foreign assets**	Did the deceased own any assets outside the UK?	✓		D15
● **Debts owed by the estate**	Are you claiming a deduction against the estate for any money that the deceased had borrowed from relatives, close friends, or trustees, or other loans, overdrafts or guarantee debts?	✓		D16

2

E Domicile in Scotland

- Has any claim for legal rights been made or discharged? No Yes
- How many children are under 18 ☐ or 18 and over ☐

F Estate in the UK where tax may not be paid by instalments

Quoted stocks, shares and investments *(box SS1, form D7)*	F1	£139,280
UK Government and municipal securities *(box SS2, form D7)*	F2	£
Unquoted stocks, shares and investments	F3	£
Traded unquoted stocks and shares	F4	£
Dividends or interest	F5	£ 396
Premium Bonds	F6	£ 4,000
National Savings investments *(show details on form D17)*	F7	£ 5,000
Bank and building society accounts *(show details on form D17)*	F8	£ 82,900
Cash	F9	£ 80
Debts due to the deceased and secured by mortgage *(box DD1, form D8)*	F10	£
Other debts due to the deceased *(box DD1, form D8)*	F11	£
Rents due to the deceased	F12	£
Accrued income	F13	£ 278
Apportioned income	F14	£
Other income due to the deceased *(box IP4, form D9, box PA1 form D6)*	F15	£
Life insurance policies *(box IP3, form D9)*	F16	£ 94,400
Private health schemes	F17	£
Income tax or capital gains tax repayment	F18	£
Household and personal goods *(sold, box HG1, form D10)*	F19	£
Household and personal goods *(unsold, box HG2, form D10)*	F20	£ 16,500
Interest in another estate *(box UE1, form D11)*	F21	£
Interest in expectancy *(reversionary interest)*	F22	£
Other personal assets in the UK *(show details on form D17)*	F23	£
Total assets *(sum of boxes F1 to F23)*	F24	£342,834

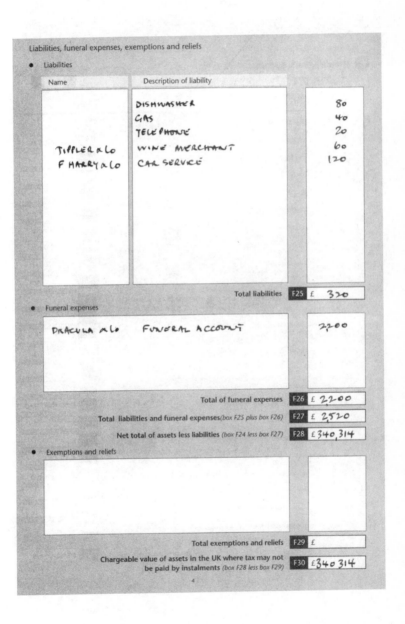

Liabilities, funeral expenses, exemptions and reliefs

- Liabilities

Name	Description of liability	
	DISHWASHER	80
	GAS	40
	TELEPHONE	20
TIPPLER & CO	WINE MERCHANT	60
F HARRY & CO	CAR SERVICE	120

Total liabilities **F25** £ 320

- Funeral expenses

DRACULA & CO	FUNERAL ACCOUNT	2,200

Total of funeral expenses **F26** £ 2,200

Total liabilities and funeral expenses *(box F25 plus box F26)* **F27** £ 2,520

Net total of assets less liabilities *(box F24 less box F27)* **F28** £ 340,314

- Exemptions and reliefs

Total exemptions and reliefs **F29** £

Chargeable value of assets in the UK where tax may not be paid by instalments *(box F28 less box F29)* **F30** £ 340 314

4

143

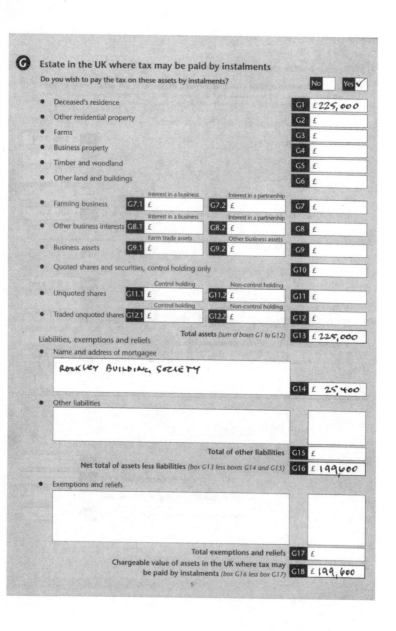

G Estate in the UK where tax may be paid by instalments

Do you wish to pay the tax on these assets by instalments?   No [ ]   Yes [✓]

- Deceased's residence   **G1** £ 225,000
- Other residential property   **G2** £
- Farms   **G3** £
- Business property   **G4** £
- Timber and woodland   **G5** £
- Other land and buildings   **G6** £

- Farming business   **G7.1** £ (Interest in a business)   **G7.2** £ (Interest in a partnership)   **G7** £
- Other business interests   **G8.1** £ (Interest in a business)   **G8.2** £ (Interest in a partnership)   **G8** £
- Business assets   **G9.1** £ (Farm trade assets)   **G9.2** £ (Other business assets)   **G9** £
- Quoted shares and securities, control holding only   **G10** £
- Unquoted shares   **G11.1** £ (Control holding)   **G11.2** £ (Non-control holding)   **G11** £
- Traded unquoted shares   **G12.1** £ (Control holding)   **G12.2** £ (Non-control holding)   **G12** £

Total assets *(sum of boxes G1 to G12)*   **G13** £ 225,000

Liabilities, exemptions and reliefs

- Name and address of mortgagee

  ROCKLEY BUILDING SOCIETY

  G14 £ 25,400

- Other liabilities

  Total of other liabilities   **G15** £

  Net total of assets less liabilities *(box G13 less boxes G14 and G15)*   **G16** £ 199,600

- Exemptions and reliefs

  Total exemptions and reliefs   **G17** £

  Chargeable value of assets in the UK where tax may
  be paid by instalments *(box G16 less box G17)*   **G18** £ 199,600

5

H Summary of the chargeable estate

You should fill in form IHT(WS) so that you can copy the figures to this section and to section J. If you are applying for a grant without the help of a solicitor or other agent and you do not wish to work out the tax yourself, leave this section and section J blank. Go on to section K.

Assets where tax may not be paid by instalments

- Estate in the UK (box WS1) — **H1** £ 340 314
- Joint property (box WS2) — **H2** £
- Foreign property (box WS3) — H3 £
- Settled property on which the trustees would like to pay tax now (box WS4) H4 £

Total of assets where tax may not be paid by instalments (box WS5) **H5** £ 340 314

Assets where tax may be paid by instalments

- Estate in the UK (box WS6) — **H6** £ 199,600
- Joint property (box WS7) — **H7** £
- Foreign property (box WS8) — H8 £
- Settled property on which the trustees would like to pay tax now (box WS9) H9 £

Total of assets where tax may be paid by instalments (box WS10) **H10** £199,600

Other property taken into account to calculate the total tax

- Settled property (box WS11) — H11 £
- Gift with reservation (box WS12) — H12 £

Chargeable estate (box WS13) **H13** £

Cumulative total of lifetime transfers (box WS14) **H14** £

Aggregate chargeable transfer (box WS15) **H15** £

J Calculating the tax liability

Calculating the total tax that is payable

- Aggregate chargeable transfer *(box WS16)* — J1 £ 539,914
- Tax threshold *(box WS17)* — J2 £ 255,000
- Value chargeable to tax *(box WS18)* — J3 £ 284,914

Tax payable *(box WS19)* — J4 £ 113965 60

- Tax (if any) payable on lifetime transfers *(box WS20)* — J5 £
- Relief for successive charges *(box WS21)* — J6 £

Tax payable on total of assets liable to tax *(box WS22)* — J7 £

Calculating the tax payable on delivery of this account

- Tax which may not be paid by instalments *(box TX4)* — J8 £ 71833 82
- Double taxation relief *(box TX5)* — J9 £ /
- Interest to be added *(box TX7)* — J10 £ /

Tax and interest being paid now which may not be paid by instalments *(box TX8)* — J11 £ 71,833 82

- Tax which may be paid by instalments *(box TX12)* — J12 £ 42131 78
- Double taxation relief *(box TX13)* — J13 £
- Number of instalments being paid now J14 / 10 *(box TX15)*
- Tax now payable *(box TX16)* — J15 £
- Interest on instalments to be added *(box TX17)* — J16 £
- Additional interest to be added *(box TX18)* — J17 £

Tax and interest being paid now which may be paid by instalments *(box TX19)* — J18 £

Total tax and interest being paid now on this account *(box TX20)* — J19 £

K Authority for repayment of inheritance tax

In the event of any inheritance tax being overpaid the payable order for overpaid tax and interest in connection with this estate should be made out to

Declaration

I/We wish to apply for a **L1** GRANT OF PROBATE OF THE WILL

To the best of my/our knowledge and belief, the information I/we have given and the statements I/we have made in this account and in supplementary pages **L2** D1, D7, D9, D10, D12 AD17 attached (together called "this account") are correct and complete.

I/We have made the fullest enquiries that are reasonably practicable in the circumstances to find out the open market value of all the items shown in this account. The value of items in box(es)

L3 are provisional

estimates which are based an all the information available to me/us at this time. I/We will tell IR Capital Taxes the exact value(s) as soon as I/we know it and I/we will pay any additional tax and interest that may be due.

I/We understand that I/we may be liable to prosecution if I/we deliberately conceal any information that affects the liability to inheritance tax arising on the deceased's death, OR if I/we deliberately include information in this account which I/we know to be false.

I/We understand that I/we may have to pay financial penalties if this account is incorrect by reason of my/our fraud or negligence, OR if I/we fail to remedy anything in this account which is incorrect in any material respect within a reasonable time of it coming to my/our notice.

I/We understand that the issue of the grant does not mean that

➔ I/we have paid all the inheritance tax and interest that may be due on the estate, or

● the statements made and the values included in this account are accepted by IR Capital Taxes.

I/We understand that IR Capital Taxes

● will only look at this account in detail after the grant has been issued

● may need to ask further questions and discuss the value of items shown in this account

● may make further calculations of tax and interest payable to help the persons liable for the tax make provision to meet the tax liability.

I/We understand that where we have elected to pay tax by instalments that I/we may have to pay interest on any unpaid tax according to the law.

Each person delivering this account, whether as executor, intending administrator or otherwise must sign below to indicate that they have read and agreed the statements above.

Full name and address	Full name and address
MR MATTHEW JOHN SEATON 14 TWINTREE AVENUE MINFORD SURREY	MR ROBERT ATHORN BLAKE HALL FARM WOODY BAY NORTH DEVON
Signature Date	Signature Date
Full name and address	Full name and address
Signature Date	Signature Date

Printed in the UK by St Ives Direct, St Ives plc. 92H 4155 02/02

Probate Application Form - PA1

Please use BLOCK CAPITALS

Name of deceased

Forenames MARY JOSEPHINE

Surname BLAKE

Please state where you wish to be interviewed (see enclosed PA4). You can be interviewed at the Controlling Probate Registry of your choice or at one of its interview venues. Please also specify dates when you will **not** be available for interview.

PRINCIPAL PROBATE REGISTRY
SOMERSET HOUSE

Please read the following questions and PA2 booklet 'How to obtain probate' carefully before filling in this form.
Please also refer to the Guidance Notes enclosed where an item is marked *.*

		Section A: The Will / Codicil	This column is for official use
*A1	Did the deceased leave a will/codicil? *(Note: These may not necessarily be formal documents. If the answer to question 1 is Yes, you must enclose the **original** document(s) with your application.)*	**Will** Yes ✓ No ☐ **Codicil** Yes ☐ No ✓ If **No** to both questions, please go to Section B	Date of will/codicil
A2	Is there anyone under 18 years old who receives anything in the will/codicil?	Yes ☐ No ✓	
A3	Are there any executors named in the will/codicil?	Yes ✓ No ☐	
*A4	Give the names of those executors who are **not** applying and the reasons why. Please see attached Guidance Notes. All executors **must** be accounted for.	Full names / Reason A,B,C,D,E	A = Pre-deceased B = Died after the deceased C = Power Reserved D = Renunciation E = Power of Attorney

		Section B: Relatives of the deceased	
*B1 - B6 Please refer to the Guidance Notes		Number (if none, write nil)	Under 18 / Over 18
	Please state the **number** of relatives in **each** category and complete each category fully (i.e. B1, B2 etc.). If there are no relatives in a particular category, write 'nil' in each box and move onto the next category.	B1 Surviving **lawful** husband or wife	nil
		B2a Sons or daughters who survived the deceased	3
		b Sons or daughters who did **not** survive the deceased	nil
		c Children of person(s) indicated at '2b' **only** who survived the deceased *	n/a
		B3 Parents who survived the deceased	nil
		B4a Brothers or sisters who survived the deceased	nil
		b Brothers or sisters who did **not** survive the deceased	nil
		c Children of person(s) indicated at '4b' **only** who survived the deceased *	
		B5 Grandparents who survived the deceased	nil
		B6a Uncles or aunts who survived the deceased	nil
		b Uncles or aunts who did **not** survive the deceased	nil
		c Children of person(s) indicated at '6b' **only** who survived the deceased *	

Section C: Details of applicant(s)

This column is for official use

Please note that the grant will normally be sent to the first applicant. Any applicant named will be required to attend an interview. It is, however, usually only necessary for one person to apply (please see PA2 booklet, page 3).

C1   Title   Mr ☑ Mrs ☐ Miss ☐ Ms ☐ Other ☐   I.T.W.C

C2   Forename(s)   MATTHEW JOHN

C3   Surname   SEXTON

C4   Address   14 TWIN TREE AVENUE
     MINFORD
     SURREY

Postcode: _____

C5   Telephone number   Home _____
     Work _____

C6   Occupation

C7   Are you related to the deceased?   Yes ☑   No ☐

If Yes, what is your relationship?   Relationship: Son-in-law,

C8   If there are any other applicants, up to a maximum of three, give their details. (Note: All applicants named in Sections C1 and C8 must attend an interview.)

Details of other applicants who wish to be named in the grant of representation. (Please give details as C1 to C7.)

MR ROBERT ANTHONY BLAKE
HALL FARM
WOODY BAY
NORTH DEVON

SON OF THE DECEASED

C9   Name and address of any surviving lawful husband or wife of the deceased, unless stated above.

Postcode:

*C10   If you are applying as an attorney on behalf of the person entitled to the grant, please state their name, address and capacity in which they are entitled (e.g. relationship to the deceased).

Postcode:

Relationship:

C10a   Has the person named in section C10 signed an Enduring Power of Attorney?   Yes ☐   No ☐

C10b   If Yes, has it been registered with the Public Guardianship Office?   Yes ☐   No ☐

		Section D: Details of the deceased	This column is for official use
*D1	Forename(s)	MARY JOSEPHINE	
*D2	Surname	BLAKE	True name
*D3	Did the deceased hold any assets (excluding joint assets) in another name?	Yes ☐ No ✓	Alias
*D4	If Yes, what are the assets?		
	And in what name(s) are they held?		
D5	Last permanent address of the deceased.	THE FIRS, WILLOW LANE TADRY NORTH YORKSHIRE Postcode:	Address
D6	Date of birth		
D7	Date of death	9ᵗ APRIL 2003 Age:	D/C district and No.
D8	Was England and Wales the permanent home of the deceased? If No, please specify the deceased's permanent home.	Yes ✓ No ☐	L.S.A. D.B.F.

*D9 Tick the last **legal** marital status of the deceased, and give dates where appropriate.

Bachelor/Spinster ☐
Widowed ✓
Married ☐ Date:
Divorced ☐ Date:

Note: These documents (✦) may usually be obtained from the Court which processed the divorce/separation.

(If the deceased did **not** leave a will, please enclose official copy* of the Decree Absolute.)

Judicially separated ☐ Date:

(If the deceased did **not** leave a will, please enclose official copy* of the Decree of Judicial Separation.)

*D10 Was the deceased legally adopted?   Yes ☐   No ✓

*D11 Has any relative of the deceased been legally adopted?   Yes ☐   No ✓
(If Yes, give name and relationship to deceased.)   Name:
Relationship:

D12 Answer this section **only** if the deceased died **before 4th April 1988 or** left a will or codicil dated before that date.

D12a Was the deceased illegitimate?   Yes ☐   No ✓

D12b Did the deceased leave any illegitimate sons or daughters?   Yes ☐   No ✓

D12c Did the deceased have any illegitimate sons or daughters who died leaving children of their own?   Yes ☐   No ✓

Important - please complete the checklist overleaf before submitting your application

Important

Checklist

Please return your forms to the probate registry which controls the interview venue at which you wish to be interviewed (see PA4) otherwise your application may be delayed.

Before sending your application, please complete this checklist to confirm that you have enclosed the following items:

1	PA1 (Probate Application Form)	✓
2	Either IHT205 (signed by all applicants) or D18 (signed) Note: Do not enclose IHT Form 200 – **this must be sent to C.T.O.** (see PA2)	✓
3	Original will and codicil(s), **not a photocopy** Note: Do **not** attach anything to the will/codicil	✓
4	Official copy of death certificate or coroner's letter, **not a photocopy**	✓
5	Other documents as requested on PA1 – please specify	
6	Please state number of official copy grants required for use in England and Wales (see PA3)	10
7	Please state number of official copy grants required for use **outside** England and Wales (see PA3)	✓ **For official use only** (sealed and certified)
8	Please state total amount of cheque enclosed for fee (made payable to HMPG) including cost for the number of official copy grants stated in 6 and 7 above.	£ 140

Note: If you do not enclose all the relevant items, your application may be delayed.

Official Use Only

Type of grant:

Power reserved to _____ [Name of executor/s]

Will message: with a codicil / and _____ codicils (delete as appropriate)

Limitation _____

Min interest   Yes / No

Life interest   Yes / No

Figures:- DNE / amounts to Gross: £

Net: £   Fee paid: £

Clearing:-

Title:-

Footnote:-

At the Probate Registry

On the day appointed for their interview at the Probate Registry, Robert Blake and Matthew went to Somerset House in the Strand in London. (You can go to the Probate Registry that is most convenient for you.) Matthew took with him to the Probate Registry the file with all the papers he had accumulated in connection with Mrs Blake's estate so that he could check the accuracy of the forms they would be asked to swear as being correct. They made their way to the Personal Application Department as directed and handed in the form they had been sent.

A few minutes later they were asked to the room of the commissioner who would deal with their case.

The information which Matthew had supplied had been translated on to a formal printed legal document, the executor's oath. The commissioner explained that before signing they ought to be completely satisfied that the details in the forms were true in every respect. As personal representatives, they were responsible for ensuring that everything was completely and accurately stated. Robert and Matthew carefully went through each part of the oath and account, which seemed to tally exactly with the information which Matthew had supplied.

Satisfied that everything was in order, both Matthew and Robert signed the oath in the space provided at the end. They also signed the original will, as indicated to them by the commissioner; the oath contained a clause identifying the will as Mrs Blake's. Then, at the request of the commissioner, each of them stood up in turn, held up a copy of the New Testament in the right hand and repeated aloud these words after the commissioner: 'I swear by almighty God that this is my name and handwriting, and that the contents of this my oath are true and that this is the will referred to.' As each said the words 'name and handwriting' the commissioner pointed to their signatures on the oath, and likewise with the will.

Instead of swearing on the Bible (New Testament or Old Testament), a personal representative who has grounds for objecting to taking an oath can affirm by holding up his right hand and saying: 'I solemnly and sincerely affirm that this ...'. People who follow other religions can take the oath on a book holy to them. It is a serious offence if you swear or affirm that the contents of the documents are true when you know they are not.

The commissioner signed beneath each of their signatures and signed the will below where they had signed it.

Matthew was then given Form D18 which he would need to send with Form IHT 200 to the Capital Taxes Office.

The grant – probate or letters of administration

While there may be an interval of six weeks or more between lodging the probate papers and being asked to come to the Probate Registry to sign and swear them, after that things tend to move quickly. If there is no IHT to be paid – for instance where the net estate is less than £255,000 or where all the deceased's property goes to the spouse – the grant of probate (or letters of administration) will be issued within a few days.

In Matthew's case, matters took a little longer because arrangements had to be made to pay the IHT, but after a few weeks the grant of probate arrived – see page 155.

Any property which passes by survivorship does not 'devolve to' the personal representatives but goes automatically to the survivor. (This is why it is excluded from the value of the personal estate even though it is not excluded from calculations for IHT, where applicable.)

At the end of the document, it stated the value of the gross and net estate (that is, before and after deduction of debts), but the amount of tax was not disclosed. The press often publish in the newspapers the value of the estates of famous people who have died. It is seldom a true indication of their wealth because it takes no account of any jointly owned property nor any trusts to which they are entitled, nor, for that matter, of the IHT to be paid out which will reduce the estate.

Attached to the grant of probate was a photocopy of the will, the original will being kept at Somerset House in London; Matthew noticed that each page of the copy will bore the impress of the court's official seal. It was accompanied by a note which very briefly explained the procedure for collecting in the estate and advised representatives to obtain legal advice in the event of any dispute or difficulty.

The grant was what they had been striving for. It confirmed that they were now entitled to deal with Mrs Blake's property, pay her debts, and then distribute the property in accordance with her will. It is a public document in the sense that anybody, including any beneficiary, and even the press, can obtain a copy of it or of the will from Somerset House for a small fee. Copies of the will or the grant can also be obtained at the Probate Registry where they were issued.

IN THE HIGH COURT OF JUSTICE
The Principal Probate Registry

BE IT KNOWN that **MARY JOSEPHINE BLAKE**

of **The Firs, Willow Lane, Tadby, North Yorkshire**

died on the **8th** day of **April 2003**
domiciled in **England and Wales**

AND BE IT FURTHER KNOWN that the last Will and Testament of the said deceased (a copy of which is annexed) was proved and registered in the High Court of Justice and that Administration of all the estate which by law devolves to and vests in the personal representative of the said deceased was granted by the said Court on this date to the Executors

MATTHEW JOHN SEATON of **14 Twintree Avenue, Minford, Surrey**

and **ROBERT ANTHONY BLAKE** of **Hall Farm, Woody Bay, North Devon**

It is hereby certified that it appears from information supplied on the application for this grant that the gross value of the said estate in the United Kingdom does not exceed £567,834 and the net value of such estate does not exceed £539,914.

DATED the **10th** day of **July 2003**

REGISTRAR/PROBATE OFFICER
Extracted by the Executors in person

Chapter 8

The administration

This chapter describes what happens after the grant of probate, and follows the example used in previous chapters.

Gathering the assets

As soon as he had the grant of probate, Matthew lost no time in proceeding with the administration. Enclosed with the probate were the ten sealed copies of it that he had asked for. This enabled him to proceed with the administration more quickly because instead of having to send the probate in turn to each organisation requiring to see it, he could send a copy to the bank, the insurance company and National Savings at the same time.

Matthew wrote a similar letter to all those who had to see the probate: the insurance company, the secretary of the firm's pension scheme, the Department of Social Security (about the arrears of retirement pension) and the Inspector of Taxes (about a tax refund). He was careful to quote their reference in all cases.

[Date]
[Reference]:
Dear Sir,
Re: Mary Josephine Blake deceased
I enclose a sealed copy of the probate of the will of the above for registration with you together with a completed claim form. Please return the probate to me when this has been registered, and send me what is due to the estate as described in your letter to me of ...

Yours faithfully,

He had previously obtained payment application forms for the National Savings assets. He now completed and, together with Robert, signed this form as executor, and returned them to National Savings with a sealed copy of the grant of probate.

To the bank manager, Matthew wrote the following letter:

[Date]
[Reference]
Dear Sir,
Re: Mary Josephine Blake deceased
I now enclose a sealed copy of the probate of the will. Please return it to me when you have recorded details of it. Will you also close the deceased's current account at your branch and transfer the money in it to the executorship account which my co-executor (Robert A. Blake) and I recently opened at your branch.

Yours faithfully,

There was £1,900 in Mary Blake's current account when she died. Banks as a rule do not allow the credit on the deceased's bank account to be treated as available for the executors' use until probate is obtained. As a result a person may be faced with paying overdraft interest to a bank even though there is money available in the same bank which will eventually be available when probate has been granted.

Within a few days, the £9,100 from the Bridstow Insurance Company arrived and, not long after, the money from National Savings, including £4,000 from the Premium Bonds. No Premium Bond prizes had been declared in the interim. Premium Bonds are not transferable and must be repaid, though the other National Savings products do not have to be encashed but can be simply transferred to beneficiaries after probate. On some types of National Savings there is a limit to the total amount any one person is allowed to hold, but this limit can be exceeded if the excess is the result of transferring to the inheritor the savings held by the deceased. National Savings Certificates are exempt from income tax.

When a copy of the probate was returned by one of the organisations that owed money to the estate, Matthew sent it off to one of the others who had not yet seen it. All who had to pay money to the executors required to see it and enter details of it in their records; this is often referred to as 'registering the probate'.

Soon all the money which was to be paid to the estate had been received by Matthew and paid into the executorship account at the bank. Matthew kept a note of all of these:

	£
Life insurance	9,100.00
Premium Bonds	4,000.00
Building society account (less IHT)	9,166.18
Savings certificates	5,000.00
Pension from employers	200.00
Pension from state	78.00
Dividend payable on Marks & Spencer plc shares	396.00
Total amount received	27,940.18

The building society figure was for less than the amount declared at the date of death because the first instalment of IHT had been paid from it. The Marks & Spencer dividend was greater than originally calculated because Mrs Blake's holding consisted of 7,200 shares, not 6,000 as thought.

Finding unknown creditors

A personal representative is obliged to make full enquiries to discover what debts the deceased had. In addition there is a procedure which involves advertising for creditors. After obtaining probate, the personal representative should put an advertisement in the *London Gazette* and a local newspaper announcing that all claims against the estate should be made by a certain date, which should be at least two months after the appearance of the advertisement. There is a standard way of setting out the notice. When this is done in the official way, the personal representative will be quite safe to distribute the assets of the estate on the basis of the debts known to him or her on the date by which claims have to be made.

If a personal representative does not advertise for creditors in this way, there is always a danger, however slight, that after he or she has parted with the assets to the beneficiaries, some unknown creditor appears on the scene and justifiably claims that the deceased owed him or her money. If that were to happen, the personal representative would have to pay the debt out of his or her own pocket if he could not recover the money from the beneficiaries. He or she should also contact the Benefits Agency if the deceased was receiving income support, as a refund may be due to the Agency if the deceased had not disclosed all his or her capital to it.

Lost share certificates

Now that probate had been granted, Matthew could deal with the question of the lost share certificate for 1,200 shares in Marks & Spencer plc. Each company registrar may have a different procedure to replace a lost certificate. Matthew looked over the forms which the registrar of Marks & Spencer had sent to him. There was a statutory declaration which he and Robert had to sign to the effect that they had made all due searches and had not found the certificate, that they believed it to be lost, and that, so far as they were aware, Mrs Blake had not sold or signed any form of transfer of those shares.

There was another form which they were required to sign; an indemnity to the company against any loss which might be suffered if the certificate should later turn up in the hands of some rightful owner. The registrar would be prepared to issue the duplicate certificate only if Matthew and Robert signed this form of indemnity. On the same form, there was a section for a bank to guarantee the indemnity so that the loss would not fall on Matthew and Robert at some time in the future. Matthew discussed this matter with the bank manager at the Barminster Bank, and the bank agreed to countersign the form of guarantee for a fee of £35 which would be deducted from the executors' account. To complete the statutory declaration, Matthew and Robert had to swear it before a solicitor. Any solicitor will be prepared to do this but will charge £5 per person for this service.

There was no need for Robert to come to London to attend to this one item; it was not necessary for them both to sign in the same place or at the same time, so Matthew sent the form to Robert. Within a few days he received the declaration back from Robert and went to find a solicitor. Most high street solicitors will swear you to a document at short notice even if you have had no previous dealings with the firm (although you may not be seen immediately if you have not made an appointment). Matthew and Robert each made a note of the £5 cash which they had paid out to the solicitors because this was a proper expense of the administration of the estate to be reclaimed.

Matthew then wrote to the registrar of Marks & Spencer plc, enclosing the sealed copy probate, the statutory declaration, the indemnity, the guarantee and the share certificates for the 6,000 shares. By 1 August he had received back the new share certificate showing the names of himself and Robert, the executors of Mary Josephine Blake, as the registered owners of 7,200 Marks & Spencer shares.

He would leave the rest of the shares to be dealt with later when he knew which were going to be sold and which were going to be retained and distributed to the beneficiaries.

IHT rectification

When there has been no provisional agreement with the District Valuer about the value of a house, the first contact with him or her is likely to be after probate has been obtained. Where this happens, the value of the house as finally agreed with the District Valuer may be higher than the value included in the Inland Revenue account. This results in a further payment of IHT having to be made at this stage.

Matthew heard from the District Valuer for Tadby, who considered that his figure of £225,000 for The Firs was too low. After some bargaining, they agreed that the figure should be £227,500, so that a further £1,000 of tax (for the extra £2,500 at 40 per cent) would be due. In fact, Matthew had elected to pay IHT on the house by instalments so that he did not have to arrange a bank loan to cover it. His intention now was to pay the tax as soon as he had received sufficient funds to do so. Additional tax might also become due if the executors discovered some asset of which they had had no knowledge when the papers were signed. They might, for instance, find that the deceased had had a deposit account at a bank which was different from the one where he had kept his current account. When this happens, details have to be given to the Capital Taxes Office and it may be necessary to sign a further, corrective, document.

Occasionally, if an asset was mistakenly overestimated in value, or if a new debt appears, there may be some IHT to be returned to the personal representatives. Having sent a tax return and a copy of probate of the will to the inspector of taxes, Matthew told the inspector that he expected the administration of the estate to be completed very shortly and asked the inspector if he would require an income tax return to be completed for the period from the date of death until 5 April 2004.

Matthew then realised that the legacy of £100 payable to Help the Aged was exempt from IHT because it was a gift to a charity. This would reduce IHT by £40 (40 per cent of £100). He could now write to the Inland Revenue to apply for clearance on Form IHT 30 (see page 167).

Selling shares

Matthew knew that he had to set aside £1,600 to pay the legacies (£500 to each of the three grandchildren and £100 to Help the Aged). There was also the mortgage and other debts to pay off. IHT on the house had been paid. Matthew knew that the mortgage would be paid off from the life policy proceeds, but having discussed it with Robert and Emma they decided to sell some shares because they both wanted some spare cash.

Matthew then arranged to sell the Treasury Stock and Unit Trust through the bank, sending sealed copies of the probate and the certificates for the registrars. The bank let him have a stock transfer form for each holding, which Matthew and Robert signed.

It is not advisable for the inexperienced to sell shares direct without a broker. When it is done through the bank, it is the bank's broker who does the actual selling. If Matthew or Robert had been in the habit of buying and selling shares, they would probably have gone to one of their own brokers. If a broker is used, find out his or her commission rates before giving dealing instructions. Selling through a bank's broker attracts a commission just as selling through any other broker does, often with a minimum fee of, say, £15 per holding. The bank may also charge a dealing fee.

The formalities for selling and transferring government stock (so-called gilt-edged) are very similar to ordinary shares, but the registrar is the Bank of England.

The sales of Mrs Blake's Treasury Stock and Unit trust raised a total of £53,780 after deduction of commission and fees. This amount bears no direct relation to the value of the stock or units at the date of death but is the result of the price of investments on the day of sale. Matthew paid the money, which was sent to him ten days later, into the executors' account. He made a note of the prices at which the shares were sold and the net proceeds of sale, to compare with the value at the date of Mrs Blake's death in case there should be liability for CGT. The tax does not apply to government stocks.

Paying off creditors

There were no further assets to collect in. Matthew had now received all monies due to the estate. After the proceeds of sale from the stock and unit trusts were received, on 3 September, and after paying the bank charge (£25) for dealing with the indemnity for the replacement of the Marks & Spencer share certificate, the balance on the executors' bank account was rather large to have in a bank current account so Matthew wrote the following letter to the bank:

[Date]
Dear Sirs,
Re: Executors of Mary Blake
Please take this letter as my authority and instruction to you to open a deposit account in the names of the executors of Mary Blake and to transfer at the end of each banking day either to or from the deposit account sufficient to leave £1,000 to the credit of the executors' account.

Yours faithfully,

In this way he knew that there would be money available for cheques to meet the debts but also that the money would be earning interest. He sent the letter to Robert for his signature before posting it to the bank.

He then wrote to the Rockley Building Society:

[Date]

Dear Sirs,

Re: Mary Blake (deceased)

Probate has now been granted so I enclose a sealed copy of the probate with the signed claim form for the Immortal Life Policy. Could you please arrange to discharge the mortgage from the proceeds and send me the balance due, together with a statement accounting for the interest on the life policy proceeds and the mortgage to the date of discharge?

Yours faithfully,

On 17 September he received a letter and statement back from the Rockley Building Society enclosing a cheque for the balance due of £59,900, which included net interest of £400 for which a tax-deduction certificate was enclosed.

Dear Sir,

Mary Blake deceased

The balance on the mortgage account at the date of death was £25,400. The net proceeds of the policy with Immortal Life were £85,300. We therefore enclose a cheque for the balance of £59,900 together with a final statement and tax certificate in respect of interest.

Yours faithfully,

Matthew then wrote a letter back to the building society.

[Date]

Dear Sir,

Re: Mary Josephine Blake deceased

Further to your letter, please send all the deeds and documents to me, together with the official certificate of discharge.

On the question of insurance for the building, we wish to continue the existing policy, but to have it transferred to the name of Mr Mark Douglas Blake (to whom the property has been left), and to take the opportunity of increasing the cover to £197,500. Will you please arrange this (and let me know the increase in premium), or put me in touch with the insurance company so that I can do so?

Yours faithfully,

Matthew paid the cheque into the bank account and kept the tax certificate for later.

He then arranged to pay the other debts, including the gas bill, telephone account, garage bill, and wines and spirits bill, and he also paid the undertaker's bill. These were as listed on Form IHT 200.

Another task was to deal with the hire purchase on the dishwasher. He had written to the finance company soon after Mrs Blake's death to explain that no instalments could be paid until after the grant of probate was obtained. He now decided that the easiest thing to do was to pay all the outstanding instalments in one. Rather than go through the trouble of continuing the hire-purchase agreement in Mark's name, he sent to the finance company a cheque for what was outstanding – £80 plus a nominal £1 for the actual purchase of the machine. He got a receipt, and there was no further difficulty.

He could, if he had preferred, have arranged for the agreement to be continued in Mark Blake's name, or put it into the names of the executors, in which case he would still have paid the instalments out of the estate.

Income tax return

The executors have two questions to answer: first, is a tax return necessary to settle the tax affairs of the deceased up to the date of his or her death and, second, is a tax return necessary to deal with the income received by the executors during the administration of the estate.

The tax affairs of the deceased
Generally speaking, any income of the deceased received before his or her death should be included in a tax return. If the deceased has kept up to date with his or her tax returns the final return prepared by the executors will have to cover only the period from 6 April before his or her death to the date of death although the full amount of personal reliefs will be available to set against the income and capital gains received or realised in that period. As a result a refund of tax may be due.

Income received by the executors

Executors have to pay basic- or lower-rate (20 per cent) tax on any income they receive. The remaining net income is then paid to the beneficiary with an R185 certificate giving details of the tax which has already been paid on that income.

Although the executors do not receive any personal reliefs for income tax they do not pay higher-rate tax. (Different rules apply to certain trusts).

However, there is one permitted deduction: if Matthew had taken out a loan to pay IHT, the loan interest could have been deducted. Technically, the Inland Revenue could object to a deduction of interest for probate fees, as opposed to IHT, but some inspectors do not take this view.

The executors are also liable for CGT on chargeable gains realised on the sale of assets (including houses) in the estate. In this case, they are allowed the same exemption as an individual for the year in which the deceased died, and the following two years, although the rate of tax is now 34 per cent.

The tax inspector sent Matthew an income tax return form to be completed for the year from 6 April 2002 to 5 April 2003 because Mrs Blake had not received the tax return at the date of her death. Technically, he should complete a return for the two days from 6 April to 8 April 2003 (the day Mrs Blake died), but the inspector would probably accept a letter setting out the position. Matthew decided that the administration of the estate was fully completed by 12 October 2003, so he asked the tax inspector for a tax form to complete for that period. The administration of an estate is completed as soon as all the assets and liabilities are known and paid; it is irrelevant whether or not the estate has been distributed to the beneficiaries of the will.

If the administration had continued beyond 5 April 2004, Matthew would have had to complete another income tax return form for the next tax year (6 April 2004 to 5 April 2005) for all the income and capital gains up to the date when the administration was finally completed.

The tax return would be quite straightforward.

There was also £600 of interest added to the account at the Rockley Building Society since the date of death, but again this had already had income tax at 20 per cent deducted from it. There would also be the Marks & Spencer dividend and interest from the executor's bank account.

Capital gains tax

The other matter to be considered on the income tax return was CGT. This presented no problem because the only items which had been sold were the Treasury Stock (on which no CGT is assessed) and the HSBC unit trust (whose sale value would have to have exceeded the annual exempt allowance for any tax to be levied). The house was treated as having been transferred to Mark for £227,500 so there was no gain on that transfer.

The last tax matters

For all the other questions on the income tax return Matthew could write in 'none', but there were one or two other sections to complete, simply to explain that this was a case of an administration of an estate. The form required only one signature, so Matthew completed this and sent it to the Inspector of Taxes with a letter:

[Date]
Dear Sir,
Re: The estate of Mary Josephine Blake deceased
I enclose the income tax return for the period to 12 October 2003, the date on which the administration of the estate was formally completed.

Please confirm that all income and capital gains tax matters have been finalised so that I may distribute the estate.

Please send me Forms R185 for the two residuary beneficiaries of the estate.

Yours faithfully,

Two weeks later Matthew heard from the Inland Revenue. It returned the dividend payment counterfoils which were the estate's evidence of tax credit. These would be necessary when preparing the final distribution of cash to the beneficiaries and sending to them the tax-deduction certificates for income tax paid from the estate on income received. The Inland Revenue confirmed, as requested, that it had now closed its file.

IHT clearance (Form IHT 30)

If it had not been for the fact that he had decided to exercise the instalment option to avoid paying IHT straight away on the house, Matthew would have been able to make his final adjustments of the IHT sooner, following which he could then complete and submit form IHT30, which confirms the IHT liability of the estate.

As it was, he wrote to the Capital Taxes Office confirming the final value of The Firs at £227,500 and notifying it that he now wished to pay all the IHT due on the house. He also requested the Office to note the charitable gift in its assessment.

A little later, Matthew received the final assessment for £960 (extra IHT on the house less £40 refund for the charitable gift), which he paid. He could now complete two copies of form IHT 30.

Form IHT 30 has the effect of fixing the value of assets conclusively as at the date of death. If a sale of a house, for example, is expected to raise a much larger figure than that disclosed or agreed with the District Valuer, it may be taken as an indication that a higher valuation should have been put on the particular asset concerned. So it may be prudent, in such a case, to wait until Form IHT 30 is obtained before going ahead with the sale, because until the form is obtained the question of value can be re-opened.

The distribution

Matthew and Robert had now collected in all the monies due to the estate and paid all the debts. They now had to distribute the assets in accordance with the will.

Some of the assets are handed over directly to the beneficiaries. Other assets, such as the shares and the house, have to be transferred by deed or other document. The residue may include a particular asset but it will also include the cash remaining after everything else has been paid.

All the expenses involved in the administration of the estate had been paid out of the executorship account at the bank. These expenses included the cost of copies of the probate, the bank's charge on the transfer of shares and the Land Registry fees relating to the transfer of the house. His own out-of-pocket expenses, on postage and such matters as fares to London to visit the Probate Registry, and to Tadby to visit the house, were refunded out of the executorship account, and so were Robert Blake's expenses as the other executor. Personal representatives are not entitled to be paid for the time they devote to the administration of the estate, unless the will specifically says so, but, on the other hand, they are not expected to dip into their own pockets. Matthew discussed matters with Robert, and they worked out that their total expenses were £340, including the £140 paid to the Probate Registry.

The personal effects

The will left 'furniture and effects' in the house to Mark. He took them over with the house itself including the three paintings, and they became his property without any formalities. Matthew asked Mark to write a letter addressed to the executors, confirming that the furniture and effects, and car were now in his possession as owner, and were no longer part of the estate. A car may or may not be covered by the expression 'personal effects'. It is included in the term 'chattels', but it is much better, in a will, to make clear that the testator's intention had been carried out by dealing with a car specifically, as Mrs Blake had done.

Legacies

The executors were now in a position to pay the legacies and distribute among the beneficiaries the specific bequests. Robert and Matthew signed a cheque on the executorship account for the pecuniary legacy which Mrs Blake had given and sent it to Help the Aged with a request that the charity provide a receipt. Matthew received the receipt a week or so later.

Matthew had also received a letter from Mark confirming safe receipt of the household contents and the car, although he asked Mark to sign the transfer section of the log book so he could register the change of ownership without problems.

Finally, Matthew spoke to Emma and asked her to let him have a written acknowledgement that she had received the jewellery.

Children under 18

The £500 legacies due to each of the grandchildren were a different matter. There is no problem for children over 18 years old but, for those under 18, there arises the legal difficulty that money or property cannot safely be handed over to a minor – even a 17-year-old. A person under 18 does not have the legal capacity to give the executors a valid receipt so there is always the risk that any minor who received his or her money from the executors before being of age might spend it on some frivolous purchase and then demand the money again after his or her eighteenth birthday on the grounds that the executors should not have given it to him or her when he or she was so young.

The £500 could not be paid to the grandchildren directly as they were all under 18. The executors, therefore, had to invest the money until each child, on becoming 18, could receive his or her share (plus the interest it had earned meanwhile).

Matthew and Robert decided to open deposit accounts for the three grandchildren in their own names. Because the grandchildren will not earn enough income to pay tax, they can have the interest on the account paid without any tax deducted. To do this they must complete a 'self-certification' form available from banks and building societies. It would be possible for the executors to pay out the interest for the children's benefit, but Matthew and Robert thought that it would be better for it to accrue in the account until they each became 18.

Matthew also realised that he should consult an independent investment adviser on how best to invest the legacies for the grandchildren in order to comply with the proviso of the Trustee Act 2000. An alternative solution may be provided by the Children Act 1989, which gives those with parental responsibilities the right to receive money or property on behalf of the child. Under this provision Matthew could have paid the legacy to the parents, who would then have been responsible for its safe investment.

When an administration is long and complicated, it is possible that the legacies will not be paid for several years. When the legacy is then paid, the legatee receiving the legacy is entitled not only to the actual amount of the legacy but also to interest (currently at 6 per cent per annum) from the date one year after the date of death until payment of the legacy. This is taxable as income in the hands of the recipient, but it is deductible against any income earned in the administration for income tax purposes.

Transferring /dividing shares

It is often necessary to sell some or all of the shares held by a person who has died in order to pay the debts, IHT or the legacies or to meet the expenses of administering the estate. When this happens, it is then the remaining shares which get divided according to the will.

When shares or unit trust holdings are sold within a year of a death for less than the value on the date of death, the total of the gross selling price of all such investments can be substituted as the value for IHT. The sale has to be made by the executors; once the shares have been transferred into the names of the beneficiaries, it is too late to claim a reduction of IHT. Adjustment is made by a corrective document. Where the market for shares has fallen generally, this can be a valuable relief if some shares have to be sold.

Whether the shares are sold or not, it is necessary for each company in which shares are held to see a copy of the probate. A letter addressed to the registrar of the company at the head office will always ultimately reach the right destination, but Matthew had already found out the names and addresses of the registrars when he wrote to them to confirm the holdings.

In a case where a sole executor is also the person entitled to the shares under the will, the company will usually provide its own form in order to complete the transfer.

Where the shares are to be sold, or where (as in Mrs Blake's case) the shares are to be transferred direct to the beneficiaries entitled to have them under the will, it is usually possible to send the probate to the registrar of the company at the same time as sending the transfers of the shares to be dealt with by him or her.

Dividing up shares

The unsold shares – not having been left to anyone else – comprised part of the residue of the estate. This meant that, under the will, Mrs Blake's two children, Emma and Robert, were entitled to the shares equally. It might have been necessary to value the shares again if they were not dividing every shareholding equally because their relative worth would have changed since the date of death and because Emma and Robert were entitled to equal value.

Mrs Blake had owned investments of a kind which Matthew might well have chosen. He suggested that Emma and Robert, who were entitled to the residue of the estate, should divide between them the unsold investments which their mother had held, and they agreed.

It is possible to divide up each existing holding of shares equally between the beneficiaries. Then each one gets exactly the same. This is what Robert and Emma, on Matthew's advice, decided to do.

Alternatively, the beneficiaries can agree in writing who is to take over what shares on what day, using the stock exchange closing prices as shown in the financial columns of the national press. A cash payment to achieve exact divisions can be made out of any balance in hand. If no agreement is possible, all the shares should be sold and the beneficiaries should get their entitlement in cash. Then there can be no argument about who gets what, but from an investment point of view this may not be the most advantageous thing to do.

It can happen with unit trusts that the amount held is such that the manager of the fund will not split it, because the split holding would be below the minimum holding allowed or would not be of the correct denomination (for example, some funds specify that holdings must be in multiples of 50 units). In such a case it may be easiest either to sell the whole holding, or to transfer the whole holding to one or other of the beneficiaries, and make a cash adjustment to compensate the other beneficiary, so that they all end up receiving an equal share of the estate.

Formalities of transferring shares

Matthew took the share certificates, together with the copies of the probate, to the Tadby branch of Barminster Bank, and asked the manager to deal with them. Where executors employ the bank to lodge the transfers for registration, they may as well let the bank do the whole thing, and merely send the certificates to the bank manager with appropriate detailed instructions (about who is to get what) for the necessary action.

The bank would debit any fees from the executorship account. Some banks do not charge, treating it as a courtesy service to their customers; others charge between £2 and £6 per shareholding, but this fee includes the service of providing and completing the transfer forms and submitting them to the registrars.

It is also possible to obtain transfer forms (called Con 40) from an Oyez Straker* shop and to complete them for each of the shareholdings held and send them to the companies concerned so that the beneficiaries can be registered as the new owners. This form has to be completed by entering the name of the company concerned or the unit trust or gilt-edged stock, as appropriate, and specifying the number of the holding and the particular type of the security ('Ordinary shares of 25p each'). In any event it is sensible to check with the registrar to see what procedure is used by each company and whether it has its own particular form for transferring shares to beneficiaries.

A separate form must be used for each different transferee, so in Matthew's case there were two separate transfer forms for each holding because half of the holding was going to Robert and half to Emma. There is a space where names of the present owners (the transferors) have to be inserted. In this case, it was the executors. Although on the company's register the shares may still be in the name of Mrs Blake, the registrars will accept the transfer in the executors' names provided a sealed copy of the probate has been registered or is sent at the same time. As far as the registrar is concerned, the sealed copy of the probate operates as the transfer from Mary Blake to the executors, but a charge may be made if probate has to be registered at the same time as the sale.

The full name and address of the transferee (Robert or Emma, as appropriate) has to be entered on each of the stock transfer forms, so that there will be one set of transfer forms for each of them.

Stamp duty is no longer payable on shares transferred from executors to beneficiaries, provided that a certificate is endorsed on the transfer form in the following terms: 'I hereby certify that this instrument falls within category ... of the Schedule to the Stamp Duty (Exempt Instruments) Regulations 1987'. Where the shares are a specific legacy, it is category 'B'; where they are part of the residuary estate, it is category 'E'; where they are transferred by way of entitlement under the intestacy rules, it is category 'C'.

Eventually, Matthew received back the sealed copies of the probate and, some time later he heard that the new share certificates showing Emma and Robert as the owners of their new holdings of shares had been issued to them. This was proof of ownership of the shares.

Capital gains tax

Matthew had to consider the CGT position. Capital gains can arise when assets are sold or transferred for more than they cost when they were bought or more than their probate value (that is, their value at the time of the owner's death). However, for tax purposes, a proportion of the increase in value, between the date of purchase or inheritance and the date of sale or disposal, is disregarded. For disposals prior to 6 April 1998 the proportion is calculated by indexation – that is, by reference to the retail price index. For disposals from 6 April 1998 onwards, indexation has been replaced by taper relief. The taper relief will reduce the amount of chargeable gain according to how long the asset has been held after 5 April 1998, up to a maximum of ten years. The rates of taper relief are more generous for business assets than for non-business assets.

When shares are to be transferred to the beneficiaries and are showing a gain since the date of death, it might be better to sell the shares within the estate and give cash to the beneficiaries, and for the beneficiaries then to buy back the shares with the cash: they then obtain a higher base value for any future sale. If a beneficiary is paying 40 per cent on his or her top slice of income, his or her CGT rate will be the same, whereas the executor's rate will be, as mentioned earlier, 34 per cent.

Every person is allowed a certain amount of gains in each tax year (from 6 April to the following 5 April) without paying any tax, and any losses can be offset against any gains. In April 2003 this exempt amount was raised to £7,900. The executors of an estate also have the annual exemption of £7,900 per year, independently of the beneficiaries who are entitled to the assets. This offers considerable scope for avoiding or lessening gains, and utilising losses to be offset against gains. The £7,900 exemption for executors is available for the tax year in which the deceased died, and for each of the two following tax years. If, therefore, the beneficiaries are likely to have their own gains in any of these years, it might be better for the executor to continue to hold the shares in the administration of the estate, and if they need to be sold at a gain, which would be taxable if the beneficiaries owned the shares, the executors can use part of the £7,900 exemption. Taper relief is also available, unless its use creates or increases a capital loss.

Treasury or Exchequer stock and similar so-called 'gilts' are exempt from CGT.

In Matthew's case, the unit trust which had been sold had shown a slight gain but was well within the £7,900 exemption.

Where the gains are likely to be more than £7,900, it may be thought prudent to take professional advice as to how to minimise CGT. The sale could, in such a case, perhaps be split between the executors and the beneficiaries in such a way that there would be more than one £7,900 exemption available for any one tax year. Matthew had to make a record of what had been sold within the administration period for the purposes of any income tax return.

In Mrs Blake's estate, the house will be transferred to Mark. Where, as often happens, the house has to be sold, CGT will be assessed on the rise in value since the date of death, based on the probate value. Where a property is sold for less than the probate value within four years of the death, the sale price may be substituted for the probate value. All costs, such as estate agents' and legal costs, can be deducted, and there is also a taper relief. Any gain will be liable to CGT, subject to the executors' £7,900 exemption, which relates to all sales in the tax year concerned. The disposal showing the costs and net gain would have to be included in the executors' tax return.

Recent developments

Note that the Land Registration Act 2002 came into force on 13 October 2003. The changes set out below should be borne in mind when reading the sections on transfer of property.

- Land Certificates and Charge Certificates have been abolished. The Land Registry* will issue a new owner with only a copy of the register entries called a Title Information Document, which is an official copy of the entries on the master register together with the title plan.
- The Land Registry has also issued a new range of forms.
- From 13 October 2003 all new leases in excess of seven years and transfers of existing leases with at least seven years to run must be registered.

Transfer of a house (registered/unregistered)

Where a mortgage is outstanding at the time of death and there is nothing in the will about having it paid off out of the residue, the house may have to be sold so that the mortgage can be repaid from the proceeds of the sale and the beneficiary would get the balance of the money. (But, as with Mary Blake, many people nowadays have a mortgage protection policy or a mortgage backed by an endowment policy, so that the mortgage can be repaid automatically on the death of the borrower.) Where the house is going to be transferred outright into the name of a beneficiary, the building society may be prepared to let the beneficiary continue with the existing mortgage. He or she can, of course, apply to any source – another building society or bank, for example – for a new mortgage if that gives a better deal.

Registered property

The title to Mrs Blake's house was registered. It was not strictly accurate, therefore, for Matthew to have spoken of the deeds of the house when he wrote to the Rockley Building Society although it is common practice even in the legal profession to do so. He really meant the charge certificate, which the building society held as security for the money it had lent. When a house has a registered title and a mortgage on it is completely paid off, the building society hands back the charge certificate to the owner, together with an official acknowledgement that the money due under the mortgage has been paid. This acknowledgement is on a special Land Registry form, known as Form DS1.

There is another system in operation called 'END' (electronic notification of discharge). Some building societies and banks use this system to confirm to the Land Registry that a mortgage has been discharged. Nevertheless, it is still necessary for the owner to send the charge certificates to the Land Registry and to apply for the charge to be removed from the register.

As mentioned above (see box), since October 2003 the procedure at the Land Registry has changed fundamentally in that the Land Registry issues a Title Information Document (TID) rather than land certificates. So, now when the owner sends the charge certificate, together with Form DS1 and Form DS2 (the application to register the discharge, which is on the back of Form DS1) to the Land Registry, he or she will receive from the Registry the TID, which will show that the mortgage has been deleted from the title. In this way, the owner obtains formal proof of his or her ownership, free from any mention of a mortgage.

It can happen that the property is left in the will to people who have only a life interest – for example, where a wife grants her husband the right to live in the house for the rest of his life. In this case there will be two trustees (usually the trustees of the will) who will become the owners of the legal title to the property and hold it on trust for the husband. Alternatively, other forms of trust may have been created. In either case there are certain entries which must be made at the Land Registry.

Mrs Blake was currently registered at the Land Registry as being the owner – or registered proprietor, to use the official expression – of The Firs, Willow Lane, Tadby. To prove that the executors had now replaced her, the probate would have to be registered with the Land Registry. And there was a further step involved: to transfer the house into Mark Blake's name.

All three steps – removing the details of the mortgage, substituting the names of the executors for Mrs Blake's, and substituting Mark Blake for the executors – could be dealt with in a single application to the Land Registry.

Matthew received the following 'deeds' from the Building Society by registered post: the charge certificate, Form DS1 (for the discharge of the mortgage) bearing the seal of the building society, and a number of old papers relating to the property. (There may well be a charge to pay to the building society.)

Matthew then prepared the form to transfer the ownership of the house into Mark Blake's name. He obtained from the Oyez shop a copy of Land Registry Form AS1 (Assent or Appropriation of the whole land).

The document by which personal representatives transfer a house to the person entitled to it under a will or intestacy is called an 'assent' (accent on the first syllable), and they are said to *assent* (accent on the second syllable) to the property vesting in the person entitled to it. Form AS1 was not difficult to complete. It asked for the title number and the address of the property. Then the name of the deceased had to be filled in and then the names of the executors. Finally, Matthew put in the name of the recipient, Mark Blake and his address. Each of the two executors had to sign the form in the presence of a witness, whose address and occupation also had to be given.

Form AS1 can also be used for a leasehold house or flat, in which case the landlord usually has to be notified. Depending on the terms of the lease, the landlord may be entitled to receive a copy of the completed form and to demand a fee. Great care should be taken when transferring leasehold property to ensure that there are no outstanding liabilities or, if there are, that they are taken over by the new owner along with the obligation to comply with the covenants contained in the lease.

When Form AS1 had been completed, signed by Robert Blake and Matthew, and witnessed, Matthew completed the application form AP1 and sent all three forms to the appropriate district office of the Land Registry, with a covering letter.

[Date]
[Ref. Title number]
Dear Sirs,
Re: The Firs, Willow Lane, Tadby, North Yorkshire
I enclose a sealed copy of the probate of Mary Josephine Blake's will, charge certificate for The Firs, Willow Lane, Forms DS1 and AS1 together with form AP1 and cheque payable to HM Land Registry for £70. Please cancel the mortgage and register Mark Douglas Blake as the new owner.

Please then return the copy of the probate and a copy of the new entries on the title to him.

Yours faithfully,

The £70 fee was for registering the assent to Mark Blake, based on the value of the house (there was no fee to pay for cancelling the mortgage). Land Registry fees are based on the value of the house being dealt with, that is, bought or transferred. Where the dealings are not 'for value' (that is, not a sale), an abatement is applied:

Scale 2	value	fee
	£	£
0–100,000	40	
100,001–200,000	50	
200,001–500,000	70	
500,001–1,000,000	100	
1,000,001 and over	200	

There is a box in the application form AP1 which must be completed to show the value.

Some weeks later, Mark received a copy of the revised entries on the title (Form TID) in which he appeared as the registered proprietor. The reference to the mortgage to the Rockley Building Society had been deleted but there was a note on the title that the property might be liable for more IHT. This was a routine formality and not appropriate for a case in which the IHT had been paid in full and a clearance certificate issued. At the same time, the Land Registry returned the copy of the probate. Thus Mark Blake became registered as the owner of the house in substitution for his late mother, and the mortgage was cleared.

This is the procedure which must be followed irrespective of whether the ultimate owner of the property, under the will, is a beneficiary or the executor (or administrator). Even if the property is left wholly to a single executor, Form AS1 still needs to be completed, to transfer ownership of the property from the executor (in that capacity), to him- or herself as absolute owner.

Unregistered property

If the title to a house is not registered at the Land Registry, the procedure for transferring the house to the person entitled to it is likely to be less straightforward. To find out whether the title is registered or not, it is necessary to inspect the deeds. If there is no evidence of a title number with the deeds, it may mean that the title is not registered. Registration of title has now become compulsory everywhere, which means that the title of an unregistered property must be registered on a change of ownership whether or not it has been purchased or acquired by a gift or inheritance. It is now necessary to register a title even when a house changes hands on a death. If a bundle of deeds has been found, they should be checked to make sure they are not the pre-registration deeds (if they are, they will have a Land Registry stamp on the outside cover). If in doubt you can make an index map search at the Land Registry (on form SIM) which will tell you if the land in question is registered or not.

In the case of unregistered deeds, the executor, after paying off the mortgage if there is one, should find among the deeds and documents one deed which is the conveyance of the property to the deceased when he or she bought it. (If the house is leasehold, it is called an assignment.) This is the deed prepared at the time the house was bought and which transferred ownership of it to the deceased. If the deceased acquired the property by inheritance the executor will be looking for an assent, which is the deed used by executors to transfer a property into the name of a beneficiary who has inherited the property through a will or intestacy.

Imagine that Mrs Blake's house had an unregistered title and that the executors had wished to put the house into Mark Blake's name now that he was entitled to it. When he paid off the building society mortgage Matthew would have received from the building society the title deeds to the house. These would have included the mortgage deed, on the back of which would now be a receipt, bearing the official seal of the building society acknowledging that all the money due had been paid off. The building society sometimes leaves the date blank, so complete it with the same date as the assent. The title deeds would also have included the deed of conveyance or assignment prepared when the house was acquired by Mrs Blake and her late husband. Matthew would also have needed the original grant of probate. He would then have to prepare an assent. This should be completed on Land Registry Form AS1, which can be used for assents of both registered and unregistered land.

Where there are any complications such as restrictive covenants on the property, the executor should take legal advice to make sure he or she is not left with any personal liability for them. In the case of a joint ownership by joint tenants, as a rule, no assent is needed; a death certificate is sufficient to prove the survivor's title and should be placed with the deeds, although it should be shown to the Land Registry, which will note the change on the title register if the land is registered. The AS1 form of assent must still be used, however, even where the beneficiary is the only personal representative (or one of several), writing what, in effect, is an assent to him- or herself.

If the property is a leasehold house, the assent should contain a covenant by the beneficiary to observe the terms of the lease. Details of the lease should appear in the assent and the landlord should be notified; the landlord may be entitled to a copy of the assent itself and may demand a fee, depending on the terms of the lease, in the same way as for a title that is already registered. The assent must be signed by the executor and the beneficiary in the presence of a witness who must then add his or her signature, address and occupation.

An assent is not liable for stamp duty but, even in the case of unregistered freehold land, it now has to be registered within two months. Unregistered leasehold land must be registered if the lease has more than seven years to run.

As registration is now compulsory, the executor will have to make the application him- or herself or seek legal assistance.

To summarise, these are the main steps to be taken.

- It is necessary to register the probate at the Land Registry to establish that the executor is the person entitled to deal with property.
- Any mortgage will have to be paid off or arrangements made for the beneficiary to take it over.
- An assent must be completed by the executor transferring legal ownership to the beneficiary. If the deeds contain covenants, a clause should be included in the assent passing responsibility for observing those covenants to the beneficiary. (A lease will always have covenants, including the obligation to pay the rent.)

An application for first registration on Form FR1 must be sent with Form AS1 to the Land Registry. As well as completing the forms the executor or person dealing with the registration will have to pay the fee and make out a schedule of all the pre-registration deeds (including the repaid mortgage) which are being sent to the Land Registry. This application should be made within two months of the assent.

If the deceased was in financial difficulties or halfway through a divorce, you should not dispose of any assets unless you are sure you have kept back enough to meet the liabilities or until the claims have been settled.

If you attempt to register an unregistered property without legal assistance you may well receive some technical enquiries from the Land Registry about the deeds which you have sent to it. It is much more straightforward to transfer property which is already registered than to make a transfer of unregistered property and then have to deal with a first registration.

Final steps

Matthew was about to take the last step in the administration, the final distribution of the residue. The debts had been paid, no further claims had come in. All the other property had been distributed and all that was left was the money in the bank account. Personal representatives should consider carefully everything they have done before parting with the remaining cash.

Matthew went through everything that he had done in connection with the executorship from the moment Mrs Blake had died some six months before. He looked again at every asset in the estate, at each debt and at each expense, to see that everything had been done properly. This is important if several people are sharing the residue, and it would have been more important still if there had been any dissent within the family. He also asked his fellow executor Robert Blake to look over the papers. Reviewing all his actions over the previous months, Matthew found everything to be in order. So he now set about preparing the estate accounts.

Accounts

It is not necessary that these accounts should take any particular form as long as they are clear and accurate. It is useful to have a separate note of the income received, so that the calculation of the tax credit due to each beneficiary is more straightforward.

Matthew knew that the accounts were correct because the final balance to be distributed according to his accounts matched exactly the closing balance at the bottom of his last bank statement. This showed him that he still had the correct amount of money left. If these figures are not the same, something is wrong, and Matthew would have to look at everything – starting with the adding-up.

It is, of course, unlikely that the values of all the assets shown in the IHT 200 at the date of death will match exactly the money received when the accounts are closed or transferred. Interest will have accrued and shares may have risen or fallen in value.

Some estate accounts show the value of the assets at the date of death and then the transactions taking place during the administration. Matthew felt that a straightforward account would be sufficient as he had already discussed the increase in value of The Firs with Mark, Robert and Emma. They were also quite aware of the changes in the values of the shares that they would receive.

MARY JOSEPHINE BLAKE (deceased)
CAPITAL ACCOUNT

Assets	£
The Firs, Willow Lane, Tadby	227,500.00
Immortal Life – endowment policy	85,300.00
Bridstow Assurance – life policy	9,100.00
Rockley Building Society	81,000.00
Barminster Bank	1,900.00
National Savings Certificates	5,000.00
Premium Bonds	4,000.00
1,500 units HSBC Investment Fund (sold)	2,730.00
£50,000 5% Treasury Stock 2008 (sold)	51,000.00
Retained shares	85,550.00
Jewellery (valued)	1,500.00
Car (estimated)	4,000.00
Contents (estimated)	11,000.00
Private pension arrears	200.00
OAP arrears	78.00
Cash	80.00
	569,938.00

Liabilities	
Funeral account	2,200.00
Household bills	320.00
Mortgage on The Firs	25,400.00
Probate fees	140.00
Executors expenses	200.00
Land Registry fees	70.00
Guarantee for missing shares	35.00
Carried forward	28365.00

brought forward		28365.00
Inheritance tax – 1st payment	71,833.82	
payment on The Firs	42,131.78	
final adjustment	960.00	114,925.60
Balance transferred to distribution account		426,647.40
		569,938.00

INCOME ACCOUNT

Received

	Tax	Net
Rockley Building society – after 8/4/03	25.00	100.00
Marks & Spencer dividend – after 8/4/03	44.00	396.00
Interest – executor's bank account	7.50	30.00
Transfer to distribution account	76.50	526.00

THE DISTRIBUTION ACCOUNT

Received

Balance from Capital Account made up as follows:		
The Firs	227,500.00	
Retained shares	85,550.00	
Jewellery	1,500.00	
Car	4,000.00	
Contents	11,000.00	
Cash balance	97,097.40	
		426,647.40
Balance from income account		526.00
		427,173.40

Distribution

Legacies –	the grandchildren	(£500 each)	1,500.00
	Help the Aged		100.00
	Mark Douglas Blake	the car	4,000.00
		the contents	11,000.00
		The Firs	227,500.00
The residue –	Robert Anthony Blake	1/2 shares (value)	42,775.00
		1/2 balance	48,761.70
	Emma Seaton	1/2 shares (value)	42,775.00
		jewellery	1,500.00
		1/2 balance less	
		jewellery	47,261.70
			427,173.40

In the capital account, he included the capital balance in the building society account at the date of death and interest accrued to that date. The income account includes the interest accrued after the date of death. The other interest payment represents the further interest due to the date of closing of the executor's deposit account.

In the income account, Matthew included the receipts of all the income received after the date of death, so they were excluded from the capital account to avoid recording the same item twice.

He hoped that the way he had drawn up the accounts could readily be understood as showing what had happened to all the assets of the estate since the date of death. He then sent them to Robert, Emma and Mark for their approval. They signed them and returned them to him. If he had been worried that a beneficiary might challenge his accounts he could have arranged for them to be professionally audited as a precaution.

Income tax again

The only other matter to deal with was the income tax deduction certificates in Form R185. This form (which can be obtained from the Inland Revenue) should be completed by the executors when income, which has already had tax deducted from it, is being paid to beneficiaries. The beneficiary discloses the income on his tax return but he will be given credit for the tax already paid when the Inland Revenue makes an assessment on the beneficiaries' income for the year. Part of the cash which Robert and Emma (who were entitled to the residuary estate) would receive was income earned or received during the administration.

Matthew completed the certificates in Form R185 as indicated on the forms. The 'trust' referred to was 'the estate of Mary Blake deceased'; the income was the 'total interest from Rockley Building Society and the executor's bank account from which tax has been deducted at source'. In the second column he entered the tax deducted, and in the last column the net income. The Marks & Spencer dividend was entered in a separate box as the tax deducted was 10 per cent and not 20 per cent as for bank interest.

Matthew then signed the forms, ready to send them to Robert and Emma.

Inheritance (Provision for Family and Dependants) Act claims

Certain people can claim a share in the estate if they feel they have not been given 'reasonable provision' by the deceased's will or even by the rules operating on intestacy (see Chapter 9).

The rules of the Inheritance (Provision for Family and Dependants) Act 1975 state that a claim must be made within six months of the date of probate being granted (unless there are some very special circumstances, in which case the time limit may be extended by the court). If there is any question at all that someone may make a claim, the safest thing to do is not to distribute the estate until at least six months have passed since the date of probate.

In this particular case the whole family felt that the provision was reasonable because Mark had always lived in The Firs and was younger than Robert and Emma and had yet to establish himself properly in life. By contrast, Robert and Emma were already settled and had secure incomes and their own homes, and it was therefore very unlikely that any such claim, if it were made, would be successful.

The residue

With the final accounts Matthew sent to Emma and Robert the R185 form and the cheques, which had been signed by Matthew and Robert, for which he asked them to sign a formal acknowledgement. When the cheques were cleared, there would be nothing left in the executors' account. He would tell the bank to close the account when all the cheques had been cleared.

In this way, the administration by the executors was brought to an end. Matthew bundled all the papers together, including the original probate and the signed copy of the accounts, and put them in a large envelope to be kept in a safe place, theoretically for 12 years (where there are any life interests under any trusts in the will, the papers should then be kept for 12 years after final distribution following the death of anyone with a life interest). The probate could be kept as a family document.

The administration of the estate was now over except for the payments of legacies to the grandchildren in a few years' time.

Chapter 9

Problems and disputes

It is a sad fact that the death of a family member can trigger a dispute within the family. The first sign of trouble is often preceded by the remark 'It's not the money that I'm bothered about. It's the principle of the matter.'

Another sad fact is that the cost of a dispute can reach astronomical levels and consume the value of the estate which is in dispute.

However, disputes do arise and have to be dealt with. They fall into two main categories. First, there are disputes over the will. Was it valid? Was it fair? Was it forged? Second, disputes can arise over the administration of the estate of the deceased person. Are the executors or administrators acting improperly or failing to do what they should be doing? Have they paid out to the wrong person or are they refusing to tell the beneficiaries what they have done. This chapter first deals with both kinds of problems, and then discusses other common issues.

If you are involved in a dispute over a will or administration the best advice you will get is to try and settle it as quickly as possible, and perhaps to have a word with the Probate Registry. If that cannot be done you will almost certainly need to instruct a solicitor who knows his or her way round court procedures.

Problems with the will

Executors responsible for administering an estate and getting probate of the will are strictly regulated by law. They also commonly face problems which can slow progress and can mean, at the worst, that the rules of intestacy apply.

No will can be found

The deceased person may never have made a will but what if one of the family believes that he or she did make one and it cannot be found? If a thorough search of papers and possessions fails to discover the will, one step is to write to local firms of solicitors and banks who might have been employed to make or keep a will on the deceased's behalf. If all enquiries fail, the rules of intestacy apply.

Was it signed properly?

The will should be carefully checked to ensure that it has been signed by the testator and that the testator's signature has been witnessed by two witnesses (who must not be beneficiaries to the will). Both witnesses must have been present when the will was signed. As executor, if you have any doubts about the signing of the will, check with the witnesses. If the will has not been properly signed and witnessed, the Probate Registrar may declare it invalid or at the very least require a sworn affidavit to explain the irregularity.

Was the will dated?

If it is not dated, you have a problem. Do the witnesses remember when it was signed? If so, the Probate Registry will require an affidavit to explain the lack of a date. Sometimes, it is apparent that a will has been changed or that some other document has been attached. Take all the documentation you have to the Probate Registrar, who can advise whether any of it should be counted as part of the will.

Is it the last will?

Even if you find a will which is properly dated and witnessed, it may not necessarily be the last will the deceased made. The older the will, the greater the chance that a later will or a codicil exists changing its terms. Always make further enquiries to be sure. Remember, too, that even an apparently valid will may have been wholly or partly invalidated by a subsequent marriage or divorce.

Problems with the testator

Did the testator have 'testamentary capacity'?

In order to make a valid will, a testator must understand what he or she owns, understand the effect of the will and recognise individuals to whom he or she might have responsibilities – for instance, a wife with young children. As executor, if you believe the testator lacked testamentary capacity, you need medical evidence to support your case and should take legal advice.

Was the testator threatened or improperly influenced?

Anyone wishing to challenge the will on these grounds must show that the testator was induced to make it by force, fear or fraud or that in some other way the will was not made voluntarily. Legal advice should be taken before attempting to challenge a will on these grounds.

If someone decides to challenge the will, he or she may apply to the Probate Registry for a 'caveat'. This prevents an application for probate being made. It covers all registries and lasts for six months. If not renewed, it lapses. While it is in force, probate cannot be issued. If a caveat has been registered, as executor, you first have to resolve the problem with the applicant. If you cannot, you have to issue a warning to the Probate Registry which has the effect of beginning a court action to settle the dispute. This is an area requiring specialist knowledge, so seek legal advice at an early stage.

Is the will or distribution on intestacy unfair?

If it is generally agreed by the beneficiaries that the will (or intestacy) has not made reasonable provision for all the interested parties, they can enter into a 'post-death variation'. This has the effect of rewriting the will or intestacy rules. (It can be used to reduce IHT in some cases; see Chapter 3.) This step must be taken within two years of the death. If the variation reduces the share of a beneficiary who is under 18, the court's approval must be obtained. If you wish to make such an agreement, take legal advice. If there is no agreement and the matter remains in dispute, the only recourse is to take the dispute to court. Probate actions can be very expensive, in effect transferring a substantial proportion of the estate from the beneficiaries to their solicitors and barristers. If there is no alternative, the claimant has to take proceedings under the Inheritance (Provision for Family and Dependants) Act 1975 (see *Claims by ex-spouses, dependants and family members*, below).

Other problems with wills

Bankrupt beneficiaries
If you suspect that a beneficiary is bankrupt, you should make further enquiries, including a search on form K16 at the Land Charges Registry. Any payments due to a bankrupt must be made to his or her trustee in bankruptcy who must produce a S.307 notice under the Insolvency Act 1986.

Missing beneficiaries
If you have to find beneficiaries, use what detective qualities you have. In addition to family networks and newspaper advertisements, you could use the Internet to track down missing people. Genealogists can be engaged for intractable problems on a 'no-find no-fee' basis – check that their finding fee is a reasonable proportion of the sum involved. Another solution, if the circumstances are appropriate, is to obtain a court order permitting distribution or to pay the money into court under the provisions of s.63 of the Trustee Act 1925.

Problem executors or administrators
If it appears that a personal representative is unsuitable or is failing to carry out his or her duties, an application for removal can be made to the High Court. Before doing so, it is wise to ask the Probate Registrar or a solicitor with specific experience for advice.

Negligence by executors and administrators
If the administration is being conducted by an executor who is also a solicitor, or if you have instructed a solicitor to deal with the administration for you, he or she is liable at law if he or she is negligent. For example, if the solicitor misinterprets the will and pays out to someone who should not have benefited, or if he or she acts in another negligent way, he or she can be ordered to pay compensation for the loss. As a solicitor, he or she must hold insurance to cover this possibility. If you are a lay executor, always

take advice when a problem crops up which you do not understand. Otherwise you may be personally liable if things go wrong. If you act on advice from a solicitor (preferably in writing) and the advice is wrong, the solicitor is liable.

A common oversight is to fail to advertise for debts in the *London Gazette*. If you distribute the estate before realising that the deceased owed money, you may be faced with meeting the debt yourself.

Problems can also arise because an executor fails to read the will carefully or misinterprets what effect some technical point of law may have on the way in which the estate is to be divided.

If in doubt, do not be too proud to take advice. It could save you, and the beneficiaries, a lot of money.

Claims by ex-spouses, dependants and family members

If there is an ex-spouse to whom maintenance is still being paid following a divorce or separation, he or she is entitled to make a claim against the estate, so remember to take this possibility into account. The extent of the claim will depend upon the size of the estate and the other claimants. Similarly, a cohabitee or child of the deceased who considers the will to be unfair can make a claim against the estate under the provisions of the Inheritance (Provision for Family and Dependants) Act 1975. Under the Act, the claimant has to file a claim no later than six months after the grant of probate or letters of administration. If there is any risk of a claim being made, executors should limit any distribution made during that six-month period. Those entitled to claim under the relevant legislation are:

- the husband or wife of the deceased
- the former husband or wife of the deceased if they have not remarried or relinquished their claim in matrimonial proceedings
- a cohabiting partner of the deceased who has lived with the deceased for at least two years immediately prior to the death
- a child of the deceased
- a person treated as a child of the family by the deceased (this would normally include any stepchildren).
- any other person who was being wholly or partly maintained by the deceased at the date of his or her death.

Having the right to claim does not mean that a person automatically wins the case if a claim is made, especially where the applicant has not been dependent on the deceased. Legal costs of the action are a matter for the court to decide. A claimant is not paid automatically by the estate nor are the claimant's costs paid automatically from the estate.

Joint property

If two people own a house as joint tenants and one dies, the deceased's share passes automatically to the survivor. But, if they own the house as tenants in common and one dies, the share becomes part of the estate. If the survivor does not wish to sell the house and agreement cannot be reached for the survivor to buy out the estate of the deceased person, the executors have to apply to the court for an order for sale. This can be tricky if children of the deceased are living in the house. Seek legal advice if this becomes a problem. See also Chapter 4.

Court of Protection

If the affairs of the person who has died have been administered by the Court of Protection (in cases of mental illness, for example), there are formalities to go through with the court before the assets of the deceased can come under the control of the personal representatives. This usually requires the 'receiver' to file final accounts at the Court of Protection but, if all parties agree, that requirement can be waived. The receiver is the person appointed by the court to look after the financial affairs of people who cannot look after themselves, known as 'patients'.

Foreign property

Generally speaking, if a deceased person owned property or land in another country, the laws there determine what happens to the property at death and overrule what is said in the English or Welsh will. Seek advice from a solicitor with specific knowledge of the relevant law of the country involved. The Law Society★ can provide names of suitable solicitors.

Foreign domicile

If the deceased person had a foreign domicile (that is, the country which was recognised as his or her permanent home), the law of the country of domicile applies to the administration of the estate although probate (or letters of administration) will be required to deal with English and Welsh property owned by such a person.

Caveats and citations

If you wish to prevent the issue of a grant of probate because you believe the will is invalid or that the applicant has no right to apply, you may file a caveat at the Probate Registry. This prevents probate being issued while the problem is resolved. If you simply want to know when probate is issued, you should make a standing search.

If the caveat is challenged by a warning, that has the effect of commencing a probate action.

A citation is a document issued by the Probate Registry (upon application) calling on a person to explain why he or she has not taken a certain step, for example, why has there been no application for probate if that person is shown in the will to be an executor.

Other probate disputes can end up in the High Court or in the Chancery Division. In either case the proceedings will be costly and you will need advice. Neither court is DIY territory.

Chapter 10

Intestacy

This chapter looks at intestacy and how a person's estate is distributed when there is no will.

Letters of administration

When a person has died leaving no will, the people who administer the estate are called administrators (as opposed to executors, who are named in a will). The procedure adopted by executors applying for a grant of probate is broadly the same as that adopted by administrators applying for a grant of letters of administration but there is little point in a relative applying for letters of administration if the estate is insolvent.

The nearest relatives, in a fixed order, are entitled to apply for the grant. If the nearest relative does not wish to apply, he or she can renounce his or her right to do so in which case the next-nearest becomes entitled to be the administrator, and so on, down the line of kinship as set out in the list below.

The order of entitlement to apply for letters of administration where the deceased has died totally intestate (that is, leaving no partially effective will) is:

- the deceased's spouse
- the children of the deceased or their issue★ if a child of the deceased has died before the deceased
- the parents of the deceased
- the brothers and sisters of the whole blood or their issue, if any of the brothers and sisters have died before the deceased

★ 'Issue' means your children and all subsequent generations arising from them, that is, your grandchildren, your great-grandchildren and so on.

- the brothers or sisters of the half-blood or their issue (as above)
- the grandparents
- the uncles and aunts of the whole blood or their issue (as above)
- the uncles or aunts of the half-blood or their issue (as above).

If none of these comes forward, the application can be made by the Treasury Solicitor on behalf of the Crown or by a creditor of the deceased.

Until 1970, the only blood relationships which the rules governing intestacy recognised were legitimate ones; an illegitimate person could not claim any interest. Now, no distinction is made between legitimate, adopted or illegitimate relationships. They are all treated equally. Normally, an affiliation order or guardianship order from the court would be required to prove an illegitimate child's claim to his or her father's estate, but genetic blood testing can now be used if the deceased father's parents are still alive, and DNA testing can also be used.

An adopted child is deemed to be the legal child of his or her adoptive parents and has exactly the same inheritance right as the adoptive parents' other (natural) children, but adoption removes any rights he or she may have had in law to his or her natural parents' estate. Similarly, the natural parents of an adopted child lose their right to claim against the estate of that child under intestacy laws. (However, a natural parent can, of course, still benefit such a child in his or her will and *vice versa*.)

Distribution on intestacy

When it comes to distributing the estate, the executors follow the directions of the deceased according to the will; administrators must apply the intestacy rules laid down in the Administration of Estates Act 1925.

The division of the net estate where a person has died without leaving a will depends on the value of what is left and what family survives. The net estate is what remains of the estate after paying the debts, the funeral expenses, the expenses of getting letters of administration and administering the estate.

Inheritance tax (IHT) will be payable on the basis of the distribution of the property according to the intestacy rules, that is, no tax is payable on anything that goes to the surviving spouse. IHT is payable on the balance, once the nil-rate band has been used up. The following list sets out where your money goes if you fail to make a will.

The distribution of your estate if you die intestate

If there is a surviving spouse:

(i)   if there are no children and no relatives, the spouse gets everything

(ii)   if there are children, the surviving spouse gets the chattels, £125,000 and a life interest in half the remainder. The children get the other half of the remainder immediately but have to wait until the death of the surviving spouse before getting the outstanding half (in which the surviving spouse had a life interest). If any of the children are under 18 or have died before their parents, the statutory trusts apply★

(iii)   if there are no children or grandchildren but the deceased's own parents are alive the surviving spouse gets the chattels, £200,000 and half the remainder. The parents of the deceased get the other half of the remainder. If the parents have not survived but the deceased left brothers and sisters, those brothers and sisters will share the other half of the remainder (statutory trusts apply if any of the brothers and sisters are under 18 or have died before the intestate).

If there are children but no surviving spouse	the children share everything (statutory trusts apply)
If there is no spouse and no children or other issue of the deceased	the estate is taken by the relatives of the deceased in the following order:

★ The statutory trusts mean:

a) any property due to the children of a person who has died intestate is to be held on trust for them providing they are living at the date of death of the intestate and that they attain 18 (or marry under that age)

b) if a child of the intestate has died before the intestate but has left issue then such issue will inherit the share of the deceased parent. The share will be divided if there is more than one of them.

(i)   parents of the deceased

(ii) brothers and sisters of the whole blood or their issue

(iii) brothers and sisters of the half-blood or their issue

(iv) grandparents

(v)   uncles and aunts of the whole blood or their issue

(vi) uncles and aunts of the half-blood or their issue

(vii) the Crown.

How the rules work

If the deceased left a wife or husband

Example A

Deceased's family
Wife and three children.

Net estate
Personal effects (that is, strictly, 'personal chattels', including a car – because it wasn't used for business purposes – furniture, clothing, jewellery and all goods and chattels) and £9,500 (in savings bank, savings certificates). They lived in rented accommodation.

Division of estate under intestacy rules
All to wife, providing she survives her husband by 28 days.

Explanation
The surviving spouse takes the personal effects, no matter how great their value, and the first £125,000 of the rest. In the present example the net estate is less than £125,000, so everything goes to the surviving spouse, and the children get nothing. No other relatives (for example, parents) are entitled to any part of the estate. It would be the same in the case of a wife dying intestate, leaving a husband surviving her.

Example B

Deceased's family
Wife and three adult children.

Net estate
Personal effects and £185,000 including investments and value of house, which was owned solely by the deceased.

Division of estate under intestacy rules
(1) Wife gets:
(a) personal effects
(b) £125,000 plus interest on it at 6 per cent per annum from date of death (not, as for a pecuniary legacy under a will, one year from the date of death) until payment
(c) a life interest in £30,000 (that is, the income from £30,000 for the rest of her life).
(2) Each of the three children gets:
(a) £10,000 immediately
(b) £10,000 (or the fund representing the £10,000) on their mother's death.

Explanation
The intestacy rules give the widow all the personal effects, £125,000 (plus interest at 6 per cent from the date of death to the date of payment) and a life interest in half the remainder. The children share half the remainder immediately, and the other half on their mother's death. If one of the children had died before the father, leaving any children, then those grandchildren of the deceased would have shared their parent's proportion of their grandfather's estate. It makes no difference if the widow is not the mother of some or all of the children; where, for instance, their father has married a second time, the estate is shared as described between the widow and the deceased's children, both her children by him and her stepchildren (his children by his first marriage). Any children or grandchildren under age do not inherit immediately until they reach 18 or get married. Other relatives (parents or stepchildren of the deceased, for instance) get nothing.

This intestacy can create a very difficult situation for the wife if the value of the house is more than £125,000. In such a case a solicitor should be consulted.

Example C

Deceased's family
Wife and four children; two of them (A and B) are over 18 years old at the deceased's death, and two of them (C and D) are younger than 18.

Net estate
Personal effects and £219,000 made up of £129,000 of investments, and half the value of the house worth £180,000, which was owned as tenants in common in equal shares by husband and wife.

Division of estate under intestacy rules
(1) Wife gets:
(a) personal effects
(b) £125,000 plus interest on it at 6 per cent per annum from date of death until payment
(c) a life interest in half the remainder – £47,000 (that is, the income from £47,000 for the rest of her life).
(2) Each of the four children gets:
(a) £11,750; A and B will receive their sums immediately; the remaining £23,500 will have to be held by the administrators on trust until C and D respectively reach 18
(b) on their mother's death, a further £11,750 (that is, one-quarter of the £47,000 which had been the mother's life interest). The administrators should have invested the amount, so each of the children receives his or her share of the funds representing the £47,000. It may be worth considerably more by that time, because the capital may have increased in value, although all the income will have been paid to the mother until her death.

Explanation
As for example B, but the wife already owns half of the house, so only half the value of the house will be included in the estate because that is all the deceased owned. The wife may take the other half-share in the house as

part of her legacy of £125,000, in which case she could request that the house is transferred into her name and thus become the sole and absolute owner of it. If the house (or the deceased's share of the house) exceeds the amount to which the survivor is entitled under the intestacy rules, she may be able to acquire it by paying the balance to the estate, or by a post-death variation between herself and her children (providing they are at least 18 years old and agree).

Example D

The situation is as for example C, but the house was owned by husband and wife as joint tenants. Therefore, regardless of the intestacy rules, the wife acquires the rest of the house automatically and becomes the sole owner. The intestacy rules operate on the rest of the estate only, so the wife gets:

(a) personal effects

(b) £125,000 plus interest on it at 6 per cent per annum from date of death until payment

(c) a life interest in half the remainder – £2,000 (that is, the income from £2,000 for the rest of her life). The children get £500 each immediately (or on reaching the age of 18), and on their mother's death £500 each (or their equal share of the fund representing their mother's £2,000 life interest).

Example E

Deceased's family
Husband, mother, no children.

Net estate
Personal effects, £32,000 in investments.

Division of estate under intestacy rules
All to husband.

Explanation
Where there are no children, the surviving spouse takes all the personal effects, plus everything else up to £200,000. Mother gets nothing.

Example F

Deceased's family
Wife, mother and father, two brothers, no children.

Net estate
Personal effects, £225,000 in investments. House held as joint tenants passes into the sole name of the wife.

Division of estate under intestacy rules
(1) Wife gets:
(a) personal effects
(b) £200,000, plus interest on it at 6 per cent per annum from date of death until payment
(c) £12,500
(2) mother gets £6,250
(3) father gets £6,250.

Explanation
The surviving wife or husband takes the personal effects and £200,000 plus interest until payment. The rest is divided in two; the surviving spouse takes one half, and the other half is divided equally between the deceased's parents (the brothers get nothing). If only one parent had been alive, he or she would have received the whole of the parents' £12,500. If the deceased had no parents living, his brothers would share equally that £12,500; the share of any brother or sister who died before the deceased would be divided equally between the children of that deceased sibling.

Example G

Deceased's family
Husband, no children, no parents, no brothers or sisters, no nephews or nieces, no grandparents; one aunt, four cousins.

Net estate
Personal effects, £240,000 in investments.

Division of estate under intestacy rules
All to husband.

Explanation
If, apart from the surviving spouse, there are no parents or any issue of parents, and the nearest relations are aunts, uncles, cousins, or grandparents, the surviving spouse takes everything, no matter how much it is.

If the deceased left no wife or husband

Example H

Deceased's family
No wife, three surviving children, seven grandchildren, two of whom are children of a son who died some years before.

Net estate
£3,500, personal effects to the value of £500; total £4,000.

Division of estate under intestacy rules
(1) Each of the three surviving children gets £1,000 (a total of £3,000)
(2) Each of the two grandchildren whose father died before the deceased gets £500 (£1,000)
(3) The other grandchildren get nothing.

Explanation
Where there is no wife or husband, the whole estate is shared between the children equally. It makes no difference how big or small the estate is. The share of any child who has already died is shared equally between his or her children; this process of taking a deceased parent's share can go on to the third and fourth generations if necessary. Any children or grandchildren who are under age do not get a share until they come of age, or marry, and until that time the administrators hold the money for them as trustees.

Example I

Deceased's family
Two brothers.

Net estate
£3,000 including personal effects.

Division of estate under intestacy rules
£1,500 to each brother.

Explanation
If the parents of a bachelor or a spinster (or widow or widower without descendants) are both dead, the whole estate is shared between brothers and sisters equally. The share of a deceased brother or sister goes to his or her children. If a parent had been alive, he or she would have taken everything, and brothers and sisters would have received nothing. If both parents are alive, they share the estate equally.

Relatives of the whole blood take priority over relatives of the half-blood. If, for example, a bachelor whose parents are dead has one brother and one half-brother, the brother takes everything and the half-brother takes nothing. But if there is no brother of the whole blood, then a half-brother would take everything in priority to grandparents, or aunts, uncles or cousins. The same applies to other relatives of the half-blood: they take only if there are no corresponding relatives of the whole blood (or their descendants) to inherit a share. An adopted child counts as being a child of the full blood for the purpose of inheritance, and so does any illegitimate relative of the deceased.

Relatives by marriage do not count, nor do stepchildren.

Example J

Deceased's family
One aunt, two uncles, three cousins who are children of one deceased uncle, four cousins who are children of one deceased aunt, five other cousins who are children of the two living uncles; no children, no parents, no brothers or sisters, no grandparents.

Net estate
£60,000.

Division of estate under intestacy rules
(1) £12,000 each to the aunt and two uncles who are living (a total of £36,000)
(2) £4,000 each to the three cousins who are children of the deceased uncle (£12,000)
(3) £3,000 each to the four cousins who are children of the deceased aunt (£12,000).

Explanation
The aunt and uncles, being the nearest relatives, share the estate equally. But the children of any dead aunt or dead uncle share what the aunt or uncle would have received if he or she had survived long enough. So the estate is divided into five (£60,000 ÷ 5 = £12,000); the one-fifth share of the dead uncle is divided into three equal shares for his children (the three cousins on that side of the family), and the one-fifth share of the dead aunt is divided into four equal shares for the children (the four cousins on that side of the family). The cousins whose relevant parent is still alive get nothing.

It would be essential for the administrators to make sure that they were aware of all possible claimants before distributing the estate. They should therefore place the statutory advertisement in the *London Gazette* (and perhaps local newspapers) – see Chapter 8. It is up to anyone who claims to be a relative to prove that he or she is entitled; this is usually done by showing necessary birth, marriage and death certificates. If the administrators have any doubts at all whether the family tree is complete, they should seek legal advice. The only safe course for them, to guard against the possibility of some remote relative later coming forward, may be to pay the money into court or obtain insurance cover. The court can then discharge them from their duties as administrators, and any applicant must therefore apply to the court and show his or her claim.

Example K

Deceased's family
Five second cousins (relatives who have the same great-grandparents as the deceased).

Net estate
£10,000.

Division of estate under intestacy rules
Everything to the Crown (or the Duchy of Cornwall or the Duchy of Lancaster in those areas).

Explanation
Only relatives who can show that they are descendants of (or are) the deceased's grandparents can take a share in the estate of someone who died intestate. To be a descendant of the deceased's great-grandparent is not sufficient, and if there are no nearer relatives, the estate goes to the Crown. It is then called *bona vacantia*, property to which no one can claim a title. Often the Treasury Solicitor, who administers *bona vacantia*, makes a distribution of some or even all of the net estate, after paying the expenses, among those who can show a strong moral claim: where a distant relative has looked after the deceased for many years, for example, or where a void will has been made which would have left everything to a close friend. This may also happen where the deceased had been living with a woman to whom he was not married. But she is likely to do better by claiming under the Inheritance (Provision for Family and Dependants) Act 1975, because she would count as being someone who 'immediately before the death of the deceased was being maintained either wholly or partly by the deceased'. Alternatively, if they had been cohabiting for at least two years her claim would be much stronger. This would give her a right to claim reasonable provision – probably an income, but perhaps a capital sum as well out of the estate. Such a claim must be made within six months of probate being granted.

Anyone considering making a claim under the Inheritance Act (on an intestacy or also where there was a will) should certainly take advice.

Chapter 11

Wills and confirmation in Scotland

Advice on drafting wills in England (see Chapter 2) applies equally to wills in Scotland. Use clear and precise language, and avoid technical terms and anything not strictly essential. If there is ambiguity or a dispute about the meaning of a provision in a will which cannot be resolved by agreement, the matter may have to go to court, causing expense and delay. For this reason it is true to say that lawyers make more money from badly drawn-up home-made wills than they do from drafting them properly. Inheritance tax (IHT) and its exemptions, including the 'seven-year rule' regarding lifetime gifts and gifts with reservation, apply in Scotland. In other ways, there are considerable differences in law, practice and procedure between the Scots law of wills and succession and the law as it applies in England and Wales.

Making your will

Eligibility rules for wills in Scotland are the same as in England and Wales, with the exception that children aged 12 or over with their permanent home in Scotland can make valid wills there.

I, Mrs JEANNIE SCOTT or DEANS, residing at 999 Waverley Street, Glasgow G43 9ZZ for the settlement of my affairs after my death REVOKE all former testamentary writings made by me and declare this to be my last Will: That is to say I nominate my sister Griselda Scott and Robert Burns, residing at The Cottage, Alloway, Ayrshire and the survivor to be my Executors: And I convey to my Executors the whole estate, heritable and moveable, real and personal which shall belong to me at the time of my death: BUT THAT IN TRUST for the following purposes:-

FIRST	To pay my debts and funeral expenses and the expenses of winding up my estate:
SECOND	To give effect to any directions contained in any writings signed by me however informal and that free of tax and without interest unless otherwise stated:
THIRD	To pay as soon as convenient free of tax but without interest the following cash legacies namely (one) to John Lennon, residing at Central Park, New York the sum of One hundred Pounds and (two) to The Society for the Preservation of Ancient Solicitors the sum of Fifty Pounds (declaring that the receipt of their Treasurer will be a sufficient discharge to my Executors):
FOURTH	To deliver to my friend Victor Meldrew, residing care of the BBC free of tax as his own absolute property my oil painting entitled 'The Wreck of the Hesperus':
FIFTH	To allow my sister Griselda Scott the free use and enjoyment of my dwellinghouse at 999 Waverley Street aforesaid together with the whole household furniture, furnishings and contents thereof for as long as she may require it subject to a maximum period of two years from my date of death subject to her paying all ordinary maintenance costs, the rates and taxes falling on an owner or occupier in respect thereof and the cost of insurance for reinstatement value against normal risks: AND
SIXTH	To pay, convey and make over the residue of my said estate to my cousins equally among them and the survivors of them all as their respective own absolute property, declaring that the children of any of them who shall prede-cease me shall take, equally among them if more than one, the share which their parent would have taken had he or she survived me:

IN WITNESS WHEREOF I have subscribed these presents at Glasgow on 1 April 1999 before this witness:-

DJMcClean   *Deans*

Signature of Witness
Full Name of Witness   Douglas J McLean
Address of Witness   18 Dechmond Street, Parkhead, Glasgow
    G43 9LK
Occupation of Witness   Mechanic

Notes

In Scotland married women traditionally retained their maiden name and this is often reflected in legal documents, but it is not necessary to show both names. Hence 'Scott' is the deceased's maiden name and 'Deans' not an alias but her married name. 'Jeannie' is probably not the deceased's correct birth certificate name, but is in order in Scotland if this was how she was known.

Various persons are named but their addresses are not given. This is in order only where the person is clearly identified. It is better to give addresses.

The informal writings clause is very convenient to deal with small items. It is acceptable in Scotland.

The cash legacies are unrealistically small. Persons making wills should carefully assess the value of their estate and make a reasonable provision for legatees, who are often close friends.

The provision regarding the house illustrates that clear instructions can be given in a will, even though they may not be bequests of a traditional type.

Every will should contain a bequest of residue to avoid partial intestacy. The signing docquet is in accordance with current law and practice.

Legal rights

In Scotland you cannot disinherit your husband or wife or descendants completely. Whatever the will says, your husband or wife has a right to a third of your 'moveable estate' – that is, all your possessions except land and buildings. This fraction is increased to one-half if you do not leave any descendants. Similarly, the children between them have a right to one-third or, if you are a widow/widower when you die, one-half of your moveable estate.

The executors appointed under the will have a duty to make sure that a person entitled to claim either does so or renounces his or her claim, and in theory a person claiming these rights, known as 'legal rights', simply has to inform the executors. In practice there must be cases where estates are wound up in ignorance of the position.

The surviving spouse or children must choose between their legal rights and what they have been left in the will. They cannot have both.

Note: Not all items commonly regarded as property form part of a person's estate to be disposed of by a will. Further, such property outside the estate cannot be subject to a claim for legal rights. The most important examples are rights in a pension fund administered by trustees, whether established in connection with employment or personally, and certain types of insurance company bond. If you own either, check the precise legal status of your entitlement and leave appropriate instructions with the trustees as a separate exercise from making your will.

Children's legal capacity

In accordance with the Age of Legal Capacity (Scotland) Act 1991, an individual of 16 or over no longer has a guardian and is legally empowered to give a receipt for and obtain a transfer of money and property. The age of 'majority' remains 18 but this is of much less significance than in the past. There are two main consequences.

First, a will should refer to an age expressly – 'when she is 18' rather than 'when she comes of age' or 'when she attains the age of majority'. Second, many people feel that 16 is too young for a person to be placed in charge of large sums of money. If you prefer the legatee not to acquire control of the legacy until he or she is, say 21 or 25, you must set up a trust with special provisions to achieve this result. It is not enough just to provide that payment should be delayed.

A will which refers to children is interpreted to include natural and adopted children but not, unless specifically mentioned, stepchildren. Scots law presumes that, if a child is born to you after you have made a will, you would wish to make a new will including the addition to your family. Your existing will may do this by a provision in favour of 'all my children' but, if it does not or where the children to benefit are named, the child born later can apply to the court for the will to be set aside. In these circumstances, the court will do so unless it is satisfied that your real intention was to exclude the child.

Death of beneficiary

A person has to survive the deceased by only an instant in order to inherit. Where it cannot be known who died first, the younger is deemed to have survived the older, except in the case of a husband and wife, where simultaneous deaths are assumed. These rules can have unintended consequences so, as in England, it is normal to state a specific period of survivorship of, say, 14 or 30 days. This also has tax benefits, because if, say, a husband survives his wife by only a couple of days, their estates would be combined, which can increase the overall tax bill.

If the person to whom you leave the legacy dies before you, the legacy lapses, so that it falls into the residue of your estate. If the bequest was of a share of residue, the result can be complicated. Sometimes the share set free goes to the other named beneficiaries, sometimes there is a partial intestacy. The best solution is for the will to spell out what should happen if a beneficiary predeceases.

Who should be the executors?

All executors nominated in the will who survive the deceased are entitled to act, and unless they decline they are 'confirmed' – that is, officially approved by the sheriff court to administer the will. In all but the simplest estates, it is probably better to have two executors to guard against a sole executor acting incorrectly or becoming incapacitated or dying before completing the administration. There is no rule preventing a beneficiary from being an executor and in many cases, for example wills between husband and wife, this is the best course.

Signing the will

New rules introduced in Scotland relate to the validity of wills dated on or after 1 August 1995. Under these new rules, a will which complies with certain simple requirements (listed below) is now regarded as 'self-proving'. Unless it is challenged – for example, because the deceased did not sign it – the will is presumed to be valid. A will which does not comply has to be proved by a petition to the court, which involves expense and may not succeed. Accordingly, all wills should now meet the following formal requirements for self-proving status.

- The document must be signed by the testator at the end.
- If the document consists of more than one sheet, it must be signed on each sheet.
- The signature must be attested by one 'competent' witness,

who must sign immediately after the testator signs to acknowledge his or her signature. The witness's name and address should appear in the text of the document or in a 'testing' clause added at the end. This information need not be written by the witness and can be added after the event. Certain people are not competent to act as witnesses, mainly children below the age of 16, blind people (as they cannot see the testator signing) and those suffering from mental incapacity. It is not good practice for a person with an interest (such as a beneficiary) to sign, as this may become material if the will is later challenged. Similarly, a person may, but should not, act as a witness to his or her spouse's signature.

- Blind people may sign their own wills. Alternatively they (and other people who cannot write) may use another method. This involves a solicitor, advocate, sheriff clerk or justice of the peace reading the will to the testator and signing it after receiving the testator's authority to do so. The signature is then witnessed as above.

Storing the will

There is no official depository in Scotland where your will can be kept while you are alive. Because of this it sometimes happens that estates are dealt with wrongly on the basis that there is no will, or on the basis of an out-of-date will which has been revoked by a later one. It is not really safe to keep the will at home, nor is it sensible to leave it in a bank, because an annual charge will be made and when the time comes for it to be referred to it will be difficult for the family to get access to it quickly. Wherever it is, leave a note in your personal papers telling your executors where it is. Most solicitors provide safe storage for a will, free of charge.

After a person has died, his or her will is normally produced to the sheriff clerk in connection with an application for confirmation. The clerk keeps a copy in the court books, where it can be inspected by members of the public. The executor can also lodge the will in the Registers of Scotland★ in Edinburgh.

Revocation of a will

As in England, a will should contain a clause revoking all former wills. This ensures that the distribution of the estate is regulated by the most recent document. A will is also revoked if it is destroyed on your instructions, even if you are not present to see it done.

In Scotland, unlike England, a person's will is not automatically revoked by his or her subsequent marriage. Unless you make a new will, your husband or wife can only inherit if they claim legal rights (see above). Similarly, bequests to a husband or wife are not automatically invalidated by subsequent divorce or separation so, if a marriage breaks down, it is better to put the matter beyond doubt by making a new will without delay.

Co-ownership of money and property

Where money is contained in a joint bank or building society account, it is not necessarily owned in equal shares. There are two main types of joint account. The first requires both the account holders to sign cheques. The second, which is more common, is called an 'either or survivor account'. In this case, either holder can sign cheques while both are alive. On the death of the first holder, the survivor can continue to sign cheques. This type of account, however, regulates only the entitlement of the holder to withdraw and the bank to pay money; it does not determine who owns it. Ownership depends on who put money into the account and their intentions in doing so. Where only one holder put money in and made the account joint so that the other could also sign cheques, the money remains the property of the contributing holder. On the other hand, if the intention was to pool resources, each holder has a half-share of the balance. The law assumes pooling resources was not intended, so this has to be proved.

Where both holders contributed, the balance is divided according to the contributions made. If this is difficult to prove, the balance is divided equally.

These rules also apply to joint accounts held by married couples. It is perhaps more likely in the case of a husband and wife that their intention was to pool resources, but the presumption against pooling still applies, except in the case of 'housekeeping' accounts, which are shared equally unless the couple specifies otherwise.

Where a house is held in common ownership without a survivorship provision (called a 'destination'), each owner's share forms part of his or her estate on death and is dealt with either by the will or the rules of intestacy. The share each owner possesses – usually equal – is stated in the title deed to the property. A survivorship destination usually transfers the share of the first to die to the survivor. In some circumstances, depending on the wording of the title deed, you cannot change the destination. If you are free to revoke it, you must do so expressly in your will. When a marriage breaks down and either the husband or wife is taking over complete ownership, both must sign the transfer documents. This branch of law is complicated and you should get expert help.

Intestate succession

A person who dies without leaving a will is said to die intestate. Where there is a will dealing with only part of the estate, the result is described as partial intestacy. For example, a person may leave a will dealing with his or her house, furniture and savings, but overlook, say, his or her life policies. On his or her death the house, furniture and savings are distributed in accordance with the will, and the remainder of the estate by application of the intestacy rules. In general, total or partial intestacy is to be avoided, but there may be rare occasions when a person wishes to defeat legal rights claims and uses intestacy deliberately.

In certain circumstances, you can disinherit your children by dying without a will. Provided your estate is not too valuable, your surviving spouse's rights to the house, furniture and cash can swallow up the whole estate, leaving nothing for the children. If you had made a will which left everything to your husband or wife, your children could claim their legal rights to one-third of your moveable estate.

The rules of intestacy are set out in the Succession (Scotland) Act 1964 and represent what Parliament then considered to be a reasonable distribution for the average family. Now, some 40 years later, society has changed greatly and the rules are unsuitable for many lifestyles. For example, people who live together will never inherit under the 1964 Act, which gives rights only to legally married spouses. There is virtually no such thing in Scots law as a 'common-law spouse', because the old-fashioned law which regarded people as married by 'habit and repute' will almost never apply in modern circumstances. The rules allowing a cohabitee in England to apply to the court for a suitable provision do not apply in Scotland. At the present time this area of law is of interest to certain members of the Westminster and Scottish Parliaments, particularly in the context of gay relationships, and radical changes may be enacted in future.

Under the 1964 Act, the law does not discriminate between children born in or out of marriage or between natural or adopted children. A divorced person cannot inherit from his or her ex-spouse and, where a divorced person with a child remarries, the child cannot inherit from his or her step-parent.

In general terms, the division on intestacy depends on the size of the estate, the nature of the assets and which relatives survive. The more straightforward case of a single or widowed person's estate is dealt with first.

Deceased leaves no surviving spouse

When a person dies without leaving a surviving spouse, the estate passes to the surviving relatives in the following order: descendants (children, grandchildren and so on); brothers, sisters (and their descendants) and parents; uncles and aunts (and their descendants); grandparents; great-uncles and aunts (and their descendants); great-grandparents and so on until a relative is found to inherit. Different rules apply to different categories of surviving relatives.

Children
The children share the estate equally between them, with descendants of a child who died before the deceased generally taking that child's share. However, if all the children are dead, the grandchildren share the estate equally between them, the descendants of a dead grandchild taking the share that grandchild would have taken had he or she survived.

Brothers, sisters and parents

Where the deceased leaves no surviving children and no surviving parents, his or her brothers and sisters share the estate equally between them, with the descendants of a brother or sister who died before the deceased generally taking his or her share. However, if all the brothers and sisters are dead, their children (the deceased's nephews or nieces) share the estate equally between them, the descendants of a dead nephew or niece taking the share he or she would have taken. A child jointly adopted by a couple is treated as a full brother or sister of any other child they adopt or of any child of their marriage. Half-brothers and half-sisters get a share only if there are no full brothers or sisters or their descendants.

Where the deceased leaves no surviving no brothers or sisters (or their descendants) but leaves both parents they inherit the estate equally. If only one parent survives, he or she inherits the entire estate.

Where there are both brothers and sisters (or their descendants) and a parent or parents left, the estate is divided into two. One half goes to each group.

Uncles and aunts

Next in line are brothers and sisters of the deceased's parents – his or her uncles and aunts. The uncles and aunts share the estate equally between them, with the descendants of an uncle or aunt who died before the deceased generally taking his or her share. However, if all the uncles and aunts are dead, their children (the deceased's cousins) share the estate equally between them, the descendants of a dead cousin taking the share that cousin would have taken.

Grandparents

Next in line are the deceased's grandparents. They share the estate between them or, if there is only one alive, he or she inherits the entire estate.

Remoter relatives

After grandparents come great-uncles and great-aunts or their descendants (namely second cousins and second cousins once removed). The further the search extends for someone to inherit, the more complex the inheritance becomes.

The Crown

If, when a person dies and the debts and funeral expenses have been paid but no surviving relatives have been traced, the estate goes to the Crown's formal representative, the Queen's and Lord Treasurer's Remembrancer. This official advertises for claimants in local newspapers. If no relative claims the estate, the Crown may be prepared to make gifts from the estate to people with a moral but no legal claim to the estate, such as a cohabiting partner or a neighbour who gave substantial help to the deceased without payment. Further, if a relative turns up after an estate has been paid over to the Crown, he or she should be able to claim the inheritance.

Deceased leaves a surviving spouse

Briefly, the law provides first for the surviving spouse to receive 'prior rights'. Next come the 'legal rights' of the surviving spouse and any children. The remainder of the estate (if any) is taken by the nearest relatives.

Prior rights

These comprise rights to the house, its furnishings and a cash sum. Except in the case of larger estates, where intestacy is rare, prior rights often mean that the surviving spouse inherits the entire estate. The financial figures given here are reviewed from time to time and as at 2003 have not been changed since 1999.

The house

The surviving spouse is entitled to the house owned by the deceased, provided:

- it is situated in Scotland
- he or she was ordinarily resident in the house at the date of the deceased's death
- it is not worth more than £130,000.

Where the deceased owned a share of the house, the surviving spouse gets that share, provided it is worth less than £130,000 and the other conditions are satisfied.

The surviving spouse gets £130,000 instead of the house or share of the house if either is worth more than £130,000. If the house is

215

part of a larger property run as a business and it would be disadvantageous to separate the house, the surviving spouse gets the value (up to £130,000) instead of the house. This situation could particularly arise with a farm and farmhouse.

Where the house has a loan secured on it, the surviving spouse receives only the net value – the value of the house less the outstanding balance of the loan. This is so even if the deceased had a life policy to pay off the loan on death.

The furnishings

The surviving spouse is entitled to up to £22,000 of furnishings owned by the deceased. These need not be in a home owned by the deceased. For example, the couple's house may have been rented or belong to the surviving spouse already. Where the deceased's furnishings are worth more than £22,000, the surviving spouse selects items to this value.

Cash sum

If the deceased left no children or other descendants, the surviving spouse gets up to £58,000, but only up to £35,000 otherwise.

Legal rights

These come into play after prior rights have been taken. If there are surviving children, the surviving spouse is entitled to a third of the remaining net moveable estate (estate other than land and buildings). The children share another third between them. If there are no surviving children or other descendants, the surviving spouse's fraction is increased to one-half.

Calculating the size of the remaining net moveable estate in order to work out legal rights is complicated. Debts and liabilities of the estate must be set against either land and buildings (the heritable estate) or the moveable estate. While a loan secured over the house is a debt against the heritable estate and the funeral account and ordinary bills are debts against the moveable estate, IHT and administration expenses are apportioned between the heritable and moveable estates depending on their respective values. Finally, where the deceased owned heritable estate apart from the house, the prior rights cash sum of £58,000 (or, where there are children,

£35,000) is treated as having been taken partly from the other heritable estate and partly from the moveable estate.

Children normally share the money representing their legal rights equally. Where one of the children dies before the deceased, leaving children, these children – the deceased's grandchildren – share the dead child's share. Where all the children have died, all the grandchildren share equally. A child who renounces his or her legal rights while the deceased is alive does not share, nor can his or her descendants. A child's share can also be affected if the deceased gives him or her a substantial lifetime gift on marriage, for example, or to provide long-term income.

The remainder of the estate
After prior and legal rights have been met, any remainder of the estate goes to the deceased's nearest relatives. The order is children, grandchildren and remoter descendants, then brothers, sisters (or their descendants) and parents. The rules for division between these relatives are the same as where the deceased left no surviving spouse. If the deceased leaves no surviving relatives in the above categories, the surviving spouse inherits the entire estate.

Administering the estate

In Scotland, the persons legally responsible for dealing with an estate are the executors. Unless a will provides otherwise, they are not entitled to be paid for their services but, if they seek help, professional fees are chargeable to the estate. It is inadvisable to attempt the work yourself unless you are confident you have the necessary administrative and financial ability. Even then it is often wiser to leave the work to a competent professional person to minimise the emotional and family problems which can arise at the stressful time following a bereavement.

Appointment and confirmation of executors
'Confirmation' is the Scottish term used to describe both the English terms 'probate' (proof of a will) and 'letters of administration' (power to wind up where there is no will). Executors appointed by your will are called executors-nominate. If an

executor-nominate does not wish to act, he or she can decline to be confirmed. A simple signed statement to that effect is all that is needed. You cannot decline but still reserve the right to apply later. If a sole executor-nominate declines, the family may have to apply to the court for another executor to be appointed. In this case, it is quicker and cheaper for the nominated executor to bring someone else in as co-executor and then decline, leaving the co-executor to be confirmed and act alone. For a person who dies intestate, the court appoints an 'executor-dative'. In this case a member of the family, often the surviving spouse, normally (except for small estates, whose value before deduction of debts does not exceed £25,000) has to petition the court in the place where the deceased was domiciled for appointment as executor-dative. Such petitions are best put in the hands of a solicitor. The court normally handles them within two weeks.

All executors, whether nominate or dative, have to be officially 'confirmed' by the sheriff court before they can start collecting in the estate. However, confirmation of assets is not always needed. The rules for payments of smaller balances by organisations such as the National Savings and Investments are the same in Scotland as in England and Wales. If the only item in the estate is a bank account, it is worth asking the bank for details of its own small estates procedure. Most will pay up to about £10,000 against a formal receipt and indemnity. Confirmation is also unnecessary in the case of property held in common by the deceased and another on a title which contains a survivorship destination. On death, the deceased's share of the property passes to the other automatically, bypassing the executor.

If confirmation is required for even one item, all assets (cash, personal effects, furniture, car and similar items) have to be entered in an inventory for confirmation. They do not need to be professionally valued, however, and may be valued by the executor. Unless the title to the property contains a survivorship destination (when the share is disclosed for tax purposes only), the deceased's share of property held in common with another person must also be confirmed.

First formalities for executors
Executors, whether nominated in the will or appointed by the court, have limited powers before confirmation. In this period, they should confine themselves to safeguarding and investigating the

estate. They should not hand over any items to beneficiaries. Any person who interferes with the deceased's property may be held personally liable for all the deceased's debts, however large. This liability of confirmed executors for debts is limited to the overall value of the estate, providing they acted prudently and within their legal authority before confirmation.

If an executor discovers that the estate is insolvent, he or she should not continue with the administration but should take advice immediately from an insolvency adviser or from a Citizens Advice Bureau, an accountant or a solicitor. It may be necessary to petition the court immediately for a trustee to be appointed to administer the estate – otherwise, the executor may become personally liable for the debts.

Confirmation forms

In 2000 new forms, including C1 for confirmation of assets and liabilities, were introduced. They can be downloaded from the Inland Revenue website★ and are interactive, but require some skill. They can also be downloaded, printed out and completed in ink. Also, printed copies can be obtained from the Capital Taxes Office or the Commissary Department of the Sheriff Clerks' Office★. There are no special forms for lay applicants.

Once you, the executor, have all the information regarding the valuation of the assets in the estate and the deceased's debts, you are ready to fill in the appropriate form for obtaining confirmation. When there is more than one executor, one of them applies on behalf of all. If there is disagreement among the persons entitled to apply, the sheriff can be asked to make a ruling. An executor appointed by the will who does not wish to act must sign a statement to this effect. This accompanies the application for confirmation. Estates under £25,000 before debts are deducted – small estates – have special procedures you use to obtain confirmation.

Procedure for larger estates

If it is likely that there is IHT to pay, the Inland Revenue requires a return on form IHT 200. For the tax year 2003/4, where tax starts on estates over £255,000, a return is required for estates with a gross value over £240,000 and in cases where there have been lifetime gifts or trusts established by the deceased. The procedure is virtually identical in Scotland and England. Form IHT 200 can also be downloaded from the Inland Revenue website* along with detailed guidance.

Since 2000 the steps involved in completing IHT 200 where necessary and applying for confirmation are now quite distinct. This has made the confirmation process simpler than before. IHT due by the executors must be paid before confirmation is sought. Since the estate's funds are in effect frozen at this stage, the executors must ask a bank for temporary overdraft facilities to pay the tax.

Completing form C1

You first fill in details of the deceased and the appointment of executors. You have to make formal statements and complete and sign a declaration. Any document referred to, such as the will, should be marked up as relating to the declaration and signed. In the pages of form C1 which follow, you list, asset by asset together with their value, all the estate in the United Kingdom and moveable estate abroad. This ensures that everyone holding an asset hands it over.

Assets should be listed in the following order.

- **Heritable estate (that is, land or buildings) in Scotland** A typical example is the deceased's house if he or she was sole or part-owner. While the postal address of a house is normally a good enough description, for land you need to use the formal wording in the title deeds. Include the Title Number if the property is registered in the Land Register of Scotland. Do not include here property whose title contains a survivorship destination but use the space later in the form.

- **Moveable estate in Scotland** This includes cash, furniture and personal effects, car, bank or building society accounts where the branch is in Scotland, National Savings investments and government stock, shares in Scottish companies, income tax refunds, arrears of pay or pension and all other debts due to the deceased.

- **Real and personal estate in England and Wales** Real estate (land or buildings) is put first. Personal estate is other types of property, such as shares in English companies.
- **Real and personal estate in Northern Ireland** As for England and Wales.
- **Real estate outside the United Kingdom** This should be listed in a separate will made in the country concerned.

Summary for confirmation

At this point you summarise the value of the estate under the above headings, giving you the total amount for confirmation. There is a set way in which the summary is prepared for the sheriff clerk. *Note*: moveable property outside the United Kingdom such as shares in foreign companies is listed separately.

Lodging the form

You can now lodge the form (usually by post but you can do it personally) with the sheriff court for the place where the deceased was domiciled at the time of death. If you are in any doubt, ask your local sheriff court to advise you. At the same time as you lodge the will, you pay the fee for confirmation. For estates between £5,000 and £50,000, the fee is currently £81; for estates larger than £50,000 the fee is £114. Please note that these fees are liable to be increased without warning.

For an estate with a range of assets, ask for certificates of confirmation for individual items of estate. These cost £3 each if ordered when you apply for confirmation. You can collect the assets simultaneously, using the appropriate certificate of confirmation as evidence of your right to demand and receive them.

After a week or so, if everything is in order, the confirmation is sent to you by post and the will is returned, the court keeping a copy for its records. The confirmation itself is a photocopy of parts of the form you lodged showing details of the deceased, the executors and all the assets of the estate in the United Kingdom together with a page in which the sheriff court 'in Her Majesty's name and authority approves of and confirms' the named executor(s) and 'gives and commits to the said executor(s) full power' in relation to the estate.

Confirmation

Your name and address

Your reference

IR CT reference

About the person who has died

Surname

Title

Forenames

Occupation

Date of birth

Date of death

Place of death

Address

Testate/Intestate
(delete as appropriate)

**Total estate for
Confirmation**

£

Executors

Full name(s) and address(es). If nominate, list in order shown in the will, etc.

| 19 | Recorded in the Court Books of the |
| | along with relative Deeds. |

C1 **(PDF)** Version 2.0.0.1

1

144628062000DTP

Declaration by

Griselda Scott, residing at 999 Waverley Street, Glasgow G43 9ZZ

1. who declares that the deceased (full name)

Jeannie Scott or Deans

died on the date and at the place shown on page 1

domiciled in

the Sheriffdom of Glasgow and Strathkelvin in Scotland.

2. That I am

the sole surviving executor nominate of the said deceased appointed by a Will of the said deceased dated 1 April 1999 which is produced, docquetted and signed as relative hereto. In the said Will I am designed as "my sister"; Robert Burns, who resided at The Cottage, Alloway, Ayrshire, who was also nominated as executor in the said Will, predeceased the said deceased.

3. That I/   have entered or am/are about to enter, upon possession and management of the deceased.s estate as Execut   foresaid along with the said

4. That I do not know of any testamentary settlement or writing relating to the disposal of the deceased's estate or any part of the deceased.s estate other than that mentioned in paragraph 2.

5. That the Inventory (on pages 3 -) is a full and complete Inventory of the

   - heritable estate in Scotland belonging to the deceased or the destination of which (s)he had the power to and did evacuate,
   - moveable estate of the deceased in Scotland,
   - real and personal estate of the deceased in England and Wales and in Northern Ireland,
   - estate of the deceased situated elsewhere

   including property, other than settled property over which (s)he had and exercised an absolute power of disposal.
6. That confirmation of the estate in Scotland, England and Wales and Northern Ireland amounting in

   value to £ 155,208   is required

   All of which is true to the best of my knowledge and belief

   Signature   Date

   Griselda Scott   10 May 2001

Warning to Executors

You may be liable to penalties or prosecution if you fail to make full enquiries and to include all property on which Inheritance Tax is payable.

2

Inventory

Inventory of

- the heritable estate in Scotland belonging to the deceased or the destination of which (s)he had power to and did evacuate,

- the moveable estate of the deceased in Scotland

- the real and personal estate of the deceased in England, Wales and Northern Ireland

- the estate of the deceased situated elsewhere

Include property, other than settled property, over which the deceased had and exercised an absolute power of disposal.

List the estate under these headings and in this order

Estate in Scotland (heritable property first)
Estate in England and Wales
Estate in Northern Ireland
Summary for confirmation
Estate elsewhere (say in which country)

Item No	Description	Price of shares	£
	Estate in Scotland Heritable property		
1	Dwellinghouse at 999 Waverley Street, Glasgow G43 9ZZ, registered in the Land Register of Scotland under Title Number GLA 999999999, valued by executor at		65,000
	Moveable property		
2	Household furniture and personal effects, valued by the executor at		2,500
3	Partick Bank plc, 123 Somewhere Street, Glasgow G0 9ZZ on account 123456, interest nil		7,589
4	Wonderful Building Society, PO Box 1, Glasgow G0 1AA on account 1234.98765, and interest £9.50		75,009
5	National Savings Income Bonds £5,000 bonds Interest for 20 days		5,000 20
	Premium Savings Bonds		5
6	Department of Social Security balance on retirement pension		85
7	Summary for Confirmation Heritable Estate in Scotland £65,000 Moveable Estate in Scotland £90,208 Estate in England and Wales nil Estate in Northern Ireland nil Total for Confirmation £155,208 Estate Elsewhere nil		90,208
		Carried forward	

3

Summary of amounts to be paid on this form

Tax and interest being paid now which may not be paid by instalments *(J11 on IHT200)*

Tax and interest being paid now which may be paid by instalments *(J18 on IHT200)*

Tax and interest being paid now on this form *(J19 on IHT200)* | £0.00

For IR CT use only

IR CT Cashiers

Received this day the sum of

£

for Inheritance Tax and interest thereon

_____
for Commissioners of Inland Revenue

The stamp and receipt are provisional.
The Inventory will be examined after it has been recorded and the amount of tax adjusted if necessary.

Additional information required for Commissary purposes

Joint property

Was the deceased a "joint owner" of any property Heritable or Moveable passing by survivorship? If so, identify the property, state the share and appropriate reason below.　**No** ✔　**Yes**

Value of share

Descendants surviving the deceased

State the number of any children or grandchildren who survived the deceased　Children `0`　Grandchildren `0`

Aggregate chargeable transfer

Enter the aggregate chargeable transfer *(box H15 on IHT200)*　£ 0

Enter the total liabilities at the death　£ 0

Is the estate an excepted/small estate?　**No**　**Yes** ✔

Your telephone number　0141 221 4667

Bond of caution

If you are an executor-dative appointed by the court, you are required to supply a guarantee that you will carry out your duties as executor properly before confirmation is issued. This guarantee is called a 'bond of caution' (pronounced 'kayshun') and is usually provided by an insurance company. In recent years the insurance companies have become more difficult about issuing these bonds and the premiums quoted can be quite high. This is an area where almost certainly an executor will require professional help, as the insurers are reluctant to issue bonds to inexperienced executors. Instead of an insurance company, you can in theory have an individual as a cautioner but the court would need to be satisfied that, if called upon to do so, the individual is rich enough to pay the sum due. In practice this course is not an option.

Losses caused by the negligence or fraud of an executor are made good by the cautioner in the first instance, with the cautioner then seeking to recover the money from the executor personally.

A bond of caution is not required if you are a surviving spouse and you inherit the whole estate by virtue of your prior rights.

Procedure for small estates

To reduce the expense of obtaining confirmation, special procedures apply to small estates which, before deduction of debts, have a gross value of less than £25,000. For a small estate with no will, you do not have to petition the court for appointment of an executor, and the necessary forms are completed for you by the staff at the sheriff court.

Whether or not a will exists, you apply to any convenient sheriff court by post or in person. You take (or send) to the court:

- a list of all assets and their values
- a list of debts (including the funeral account)
- the deceased's full name and address, date of birth and date and place of death
- the will, if there is one.

The sheriff clerk then prepares the appropriate form for you to sign then and there or to return in a few days' time. The fee for confirmation is payable on signing the form. No fee is charged if the estate is below £5,000. Above that figure, the fee is currently £81. A few days after you have signed the form, confirmation is sent to you by post or to the executor-dative appointed by the court. The will is returned, with the court keeping a copy for its records.

Paying debts

Now that you are confirmed as executor, you first pay the deceased's debts. Some of these may be secured against specific assets, for example a building society loan where the building society has a security on the deceased's home or an overdraft for which the bank holds a life policy as security. Other debts, such as medical and funeral expenses, the cost of obtaining confirmation, tax bills and ordinary accounts, can be paid as soon as it is clear that there are sufficient funds. If funds seem insufficient, the executors must take immediate advice, as suggested above.

Ordinary creditors are expected to claim within a reasonable period, usually taken to be within six months of the deceased's death. It is now not very common to advertise for claims in the press, but whether or not to do so depends on the circumstances. If the deceased had complicated or confused business affairs it would be advisable to advertise. After six months from the date of death or such longer period as executors decide (there is no written rule about this and practice varies among law firms), executors can pay all known creditors and distribute the balance of the estate to the beneficiaries. Creditors who claim later are paid if the executors still have estate in their hands. Executors who have no estate left do not have to pay such creditors out of their own pockets unless it can be claimed they should have known of their existence.

Problems can arise if the deceased was claiming social security benefits to which he or she was not entitled. The Department of Work and Pensions checks inventories lodged at court and is entitled to claim back any overpayment from an estate. If this is a possibility, it is prudent to send the department an enquiry.

Legal rights

You must not forget about legal rights. You should write to every person who could claim, telling them how much their legal rights

227

are worth and suggesting they take legal advice before deciding what to do.

Children can present a particular problem. If they are under 16, they cannot legally decide whether to renounce or claim and, since the surviving spouse has a conflicting interest, he or she cannot renounce on their behalf as guardian. Children aged 16 and 17 can renounce but the court should be asked to ratify their decision. Unless this happens, children can apply to the court later if they feel they renounced wrongly. Where the legal rights are under £5,000, the executors may hand over the money to the surviving parent (or guardian) who should invest it for the children. Alternatively, the executors may open a building society account or buy National Savings certificates in the child's name and hand over the passbook or certificates to the parent. A parent (or guardian) who misappropriates the money may be sued for its return. For sums over £20,000, the executors should contact the Accountant of Court*, and for sums between £5,000 and £20,000 they may contact him or her. The Accountant of Court is a government official based in Edinburgh who, after considering the circumstances, decides how the money is to be best managed. The options are:

- a court-appointed manager (for large sums only)
- the Accountant of Court to be manager
- the parent (or guardian) to be manager but supervised by the Accountant of Court.

Transfer of the house

If the title deed contained a survivorship destination, the executor is not involved in transferring the house of the person who died. The deceased's share of the house is automatically transferred to the surviving co-owner. In other cases, the house must be transferred to a beneficiary under the will or the rules of intestacy.

The procedure for this involves, in simple cases, the preparation of a form of transfer attached to the confirmation and, in more complicated cases, a 'disposition' – which is a formal conveyancing document. The documents are lodged in the public registers in Edinburgh. If the titles are already registered, the procedures are different from unregistered property. In either case, this work should be done by a solicitor. At the same time as the title is transferred, and if money is available, any building society loan can be discharged. Otherwise, arrangements need to be made for the loan to continue under the new owner's name or for a new loan.

Paying legacies

Wills usually provide that no interest is due on a legacy but that it is clear of tax. However, the actual wording must be checked. Otherwise interest at an appropriate rate can be claimed if the executor has delayed unreasonably in paying out. The executor should take care to get a receipt.

Settling the residue

Once the executor has paid the debts and legacies and complied with bequests and any other instructions, the remainder of the estate, the residue, can be divided according to the will. As in England and Wales, the executor should provide the beneficiaries with a draft set of accounts for approval before settling with them. Payment should be made against receipts from them.

Chapter 12

Wills and probate in Northern Ireland

The law on wills and probate in Northern Ireland is similar to that in England and Wales. In fact, the law relating to wills is almost identical, following legislation passed on 1 January 1995. This legislation generally applies to wills made both before and after this date, regardless of when the testator died.

The Administration of Estates Act 1925 does not apply in Northern Ireland. The equivalent legislation is the Administration of Estates Act (Northern Ireland) 1955. Likewise, the Trustee Act 2000 does not apply in Northern Ireland. However, the Trustee Act (NI) 2001, which is very similar to the Trustee Act 2000, came into force on 29 July 2002.

One major difference between England and Wales and Northern Ireland has been created by the 1995 legislation. In Northern Ireland, provided the will is actually signed after 1 January 1995, a married minor or minors who have been married can now make a valid will. It is not possible for a married minor in England and Wales to make a valid will.

After someone dies and probate has been obtained, anyone can apply to see it or obtain a copy of it at the Probate and Matrimonial Office, Royal Courts of Justice★. If it is more than five years since the grant was obtained, application should be made to the Public Record Office of Northern Ireland★.

Differences between England and Wales and Northern Ireland

Use the basic information already given for England and Wales in Chapters 1 to 10, but take into account the special conditions in Northern Ireland relating to the issues discussed below.

Death of husband and wife
In Northern Ireland, the common-law presumption of simultaneous deaths in cases where it is not certain who died first still applies.

Solicitors' fees
There is no recommended scale of fees for solicitors. However, the profession in Northern Ireland tends to follow these guidelines:

- on the first £10,000 of the gross value of the estate – 2½ per cent
- on the next £20,000 – 2 per cent
- on the next £220,000 – 1½ per cent.

Where the gross value of the estate includes the principal private dwellinghouse, the house's value is normally reduced by 50 per cent for the purpose of calculating fees. In addition to these 'standard' fees, the time spent by various members of staff in the solicitor's office is also costed and charged.

Executor not wishing to act
Only if the executor resides outside Northern Ireland or is incapable of managing his or her own affairs and a controller has been appointed by the Office of Care and Protection, can a person named as an executor in a will appoint an attorney. So, when you make your will, make sure that your nominated executors are willing to serve.

Advertising for creditors
The special procedure for formally advertising for creditors in Northern Ireland requires both an advertisement in the *Belfast Gazette* and an advertisement twice in each of any two daily newspapers printed and published in Northern Ireland. If the assets

include land, the advertisements should be in the *Belfast Gazette* and in any two newspapers circulating in the district where the land is situated.

Applying for probate forms

Personal applications should be made to the Probate and Matrimonial Office, Royal Courts of Justice★ in Belfast or the District Probate Registry★ in Londonderry. If the deceased had a fixed place of abode within the counties of Fermanagh, Londonderry or Tyrone, application may be made to either address. If the deceased resided elsewhere in Northern Ireland, the application must be made to the Belfast office.

The fees in all applications are based on the net value of the estate. They are:

- net estate under £10,000 – nil
- net estate between £10,000 and £25,000 – £75
- net estate between £25,000 and £40,000 – £145
- net estate between £40,000 and £70,000 – £260
- net estate between £70,000 and £100,000 – £330
- net estate between £100,000 and £200,000 – £410
- for each additional £100,000 thereafter – £65.

There is currently no additional fee to be paid for a personal application. Personal applications must be made in person – that is, not by post. The fees are increased from time to time with little prior warning, so it is best to check with the appropriate Probate Office before writing the cheque.

Inheritance tax payments

The cheque for inheritance tax (IHT) due should be made out to the 'Inland Revenue' and the cheque for the Probate Office fees should be made out to 'The Supreme Court Fees Account'.

Form PA1

In Northern Ireland, it is not necessary to serve a notice on an executor who is not acting and who has not renounced. It is therefore possible for one executor to obtain probate, without another executor even being aware that he or she is an executor.

Transfer of the house

While property is registered or unregistered as in England and Wales, land law legislation generally in Northern Ireland is very different from that in England and Wales.

Registered property

In the case of registered land, the executors or administrators complete an assent (Form 17, see sample form later in this chapter). The completed Form 17 (see later in this chapter for instructions on how to complete the form) is then sent to the Land Registers of Northern Ireland* in Belfast, together with the land certificate, the original grant of probate or letters of administration and Form 100A, *Application for Registration* (see sample form later in this chapter). Both Form 17 and Form 100A are available from the Land Registers. The fee is £50. If the property is subject to a mortgage, the certificate of charge with the 'vacate' or receipt sealed by the bank or building society should be lodged at the same time, together with an additional fee of £25. Cheques should be made payable to 'DOE General Account'.

Unregistered property

Unregistered land is in fact registered in the Registry of Deeds, held at the Land Registers. Although no particular form of words is required in order to vest property in a beneficiary, the wording varies both as to whether the title to the property is freehold, 'fee farm grant' or leasehold, and as to whether the property has been specifically bequeathed or forms part of the residue. In these cases, ask a solicitor to prepare an assent for unregistered land. The solicitor can arrange for a memorial of the assent to be registered in the Registry of Deeds, for which the Registry charges a fee of £14. The memorial is an extract of the assent giving the date, names of the parties executing the deed, the address of the property and whether the property is freehold or leasehold.

Distribution on intestacy

The main difference between English and Northern Irish law about wills and probate relates to the rules on intestacy. In Northern Ireland, unlike in England and Wales, no life interests are created on intestacy. As in England, the nearest relatives in a fixed order are entitled to apply for the grant of letters of administration and, if the nearest relative does not wish to be administrator, he or she can renounce the right to do so, in favour of the next nearest.

The surviving spouse normally becomes the administrator. Where there is a surviving spouse, he or she is always entitled to the deceased's personal effects, no matter how great their value. If there is only one child, the surviving spouse is entitled to the first £125,000 of the estate. In addition, the spouse is entitled to interest at 6 per cent from the date of death to the date of payment and, after payment of all debts and administration expenses, to half the residue. The remaining half-share of the residue passes to the child, either absolutely if the child is over 18 or in trust until the child becomes 18.

If there are two or more children, the surviving spouse only receives a third of the residue, with two-thirds divided between the remaining children. This rule applies no matter how many children there are.

If there is no surviving spouse, the entire estate is divided equally between the children. If any child has died before the intestate, the children of the deceased child divide their parent's share between them. As in England, no distinction is made between natural or adopted children.

Where someone dies intestate without children but with one or both parents still alive, the surviving spouse (if any) receives the first £200,000 of the estate, plus interest at 6 per cent per annum from the date of death until payment, together with half the residue. The other half of the residue passes to the parents of the intestate equally or, if only one parent is still alive, to that parent in its entirety. If there is no surviving spouse, the parents inherit the entire estate equally or, if only one parent survives, that parent inherits the entire estate.

Where someone dies without children and parents but with brothers or sisters or children of predeceased brothers and sisters, the surviving spouse (if any) takes the first £200,000, plus interest at 6 per cent from the date of death to the date of payment, and half of the residue. The other half of the residue is divided between the surviving brothers and sisters. The children of a predeceased brother or sister divide their parent's share equally between them. If there is no surviving spouse, the entire estate is divided between the brothers and sisters, with the issue of any predeceased brother or sister taking their parent's share.

There is a second major difference between English and Northern Irish law. In Northern Ireland, in the case of there being no spouse, issue, parents, siblings, grandparents or uncles or aunts or their issue, there is a special order of precedence to determine the next of kin. Consult a solicitor.

The following examples relate to those given in Chapter 10, but assume that the deceased had died while domiciled in Northern Ireland.

Case study A

Deceased's family
Wife and three children.

Net estate
Personal effects (that is, strictly, 'personal chattels', including a car because it was not used for business purposes, furniture, clothing, jewellery and all goods and other chattels) and £9,500 (in savings bank and savings certificates). The family lived in rented accommodation.

Division of estate under intestacy rules
All to wife.

Explanation
The entire estate passes to the wife, as the surviving spouse takes the personal effects no matter how great their value and the first £125,000 of the rest of the net estate.

Case study B

Deceased's family
Wife and three adult children.

Net estate
Personal effects and £185,000 including investments and house, owned solely by the deceased husband.

Division of estate under intestacy rules
Wife gets:
a) personal effects
b) £125,000 plus interest thereon at 6 per cent per annum from the date of death until payment
c) £20,000 absolutely.

The three children get £40,000 divided between them equally: that is, £13,333.33 each.

Explanation
The intestacy rules give the widow all the personal effects, £125,000 (plus interest at 6 per cent from the date of death to the date of payment) and a third of the remainder. The children share the remaining two-thirds equally.

If one of the children had died before the father, leaving any children, then those grandchildren of the deceased share their parent's portion of their grandfather's estate. As in England, it makes no difference whether the widow is not the mother of some or all of the children.

Case study C

Deceased's family
Wife and four children; two of them are over 18 years old at the deceased's death, two of them are younger.

Net estate
Personal effects and £219,000, made up of £129,000 of investments and half the value of the house, worth £180,000 in total, which was owned as tenants in common in equal shares by husband and wife.

Division of estate under intestacy rules
Wife gets:
a) personal effects
b) £125,000 plus interest at 6 per cent per annum from date of death until payment
c) £31,333.33 absolutely.

The four children receive £62,666.66 between them: that is, £15,666.66 each.

Explanation

The explanation for case study C is similar to that for case study B. As the wife already owns half the house, only the remaining half is distributed. The widow may take it as part of her legacy of £125,000. The administrator invests the money for the two minor children until their respective eighteenth birthdays. During that time, the administrator has discretion to apply some of the income to their maintenance.

Case study D

The situation is as for case study C, but the house was owned by husband and wife as joint tenants. Therefore, regardless of the intestacy rules, the wife acquires the rest of the house automatically and becomes the sole owner. The intestacy rules only apply to the rest of the estate, so the wife gets:

a) personal effects
b) £125,000 plus interest thereon at 6 per cent per annum from date of death until payment
c) £1,333,33 absolutely.

The children divide £2,666.66 between them (that is, they each receive £666.66 absolutely). There is no life interest under the intestacy rules in Northern Ireland, so the surviving spouse receives a third of the residue, with two-thirds divided between the children.

Case studies E, F, G and H

These are the same in Northern Ireland as in England and Wales.

Case study I

Deceased's family
Two brothers.

Net estate
£3,000 including personal effects.

Division of estate under intestacy rules
£1,500 to each brother.

Explanation

If the parents of a bachelor or a spinster (or widow or widower without descendants) are both dead, the whole estate is shared between brothers and sisters equally. The share of a deceased brother or sister goes to his or her children. If one parent is still alive, he or she gets everything. If both parents are alive, they share the estate equally.

Unlike in England, relatives of the whole blood and the half-blood are treated equally in Northern Ireland. If, for example, a bachelor whose parents are dead has one brother and one half-brother, the estate is divided equally between the brother and the half-brother. If there is no brother of the whole blood, a half-brother receives everything in priority to grandparents, or aunts, uncles or cousins. In these complex cases, seek a solicitor's advice.

Case study J

This case study has the same result in Northern Ireland as in England. However, the statutory advertisement should be placed in the *Belfast Gazette* and also on two separate occasions in two different local newspapers.

Case study K

Deceased's family

Five second cousins (relatives who have the same great-grandparents as the deceased).

Net estate

£10,000.

Division of estate under intestacy rules

Each second cousin will receive £2,000.

Explanation

Unlike in England, second cousins inherit and, where they are all related in the same degree, they inherit equally.

The legislation concerning possible claims by next of kin is contained in the Inheritance (Provision for Family and Dependants) (Northern Ireland) Order 1977. The legislation is similar to the 1975 English Act. Anyone considering making a claim should consult a solicitor.

Land Registry assent form – instructions for completion

(1) General
Complete all relevant panels and schedules. If the space is insufficient, continuation sheet(s) (size A4) should be securely attached. Each continuation sheet must be headed with the appropriate folio number(s) and county, and reference to the panel or schedule to which it relates. A cross-reference note should also be included in the panel or schedule (e.g. 'continued on attached sheet').

(2) The deceased
Insert appropriate details and have the Certificate of Identity on page 4 completed.

(3) The personal representatives
(i)   Insert full name(s) and address(es) and description(s). If the details differ from those in the grant include explanatory words (e.g. 'formerly of/known as ...'). If a name has changed or a personal representative has died since the grant, furnish appropriate evidence.
(ii) Where there is a chain of executorship, furnish appropriate evidence.

(4) Settlements
(i)   The entire panel should be deleted if a settlement has not been created.
(ii) The reference to trustees may be deleted if there are no trustees of the settlement for the purpose of the Settled Land Acts.

(5) The property
(i)   Identify the land or estate as the subject of the Assent. If all the land in a folio is being vested in the Assentee(s), this must be made clear.
(ii) If part only of the land in a folio is being vested, insert a description referring to colours on an attached map.
(iii) The part being vested should be defined on an extract from the latest available Ordnance Survey (OS) plan drawn to the

largest published scale. (In cases of a very small plot, or for an area of complex OS detail, the location map must be supplemented by a larger-scale plan.)

(iv) All maps/plans must be securely fastened to the Assent.

(v) If the Assent deals with two or more separate pieces of land, it may be necessary to number the entries in this column.

(6) The assentee

(i) Enter the full name(s), postal address(es) in the UK for service of notices and descriptions(s) of the Assentee(s) for entry in the register.

(ii) If an assentee is an existing owner of an estate in the land, or a minor, that fact must be stated.

(7) Assentees' share

If the Assent is to two or more persons who are to hold as tenants in common, that fact must be stated, and the precise fractional shares which pass to each person must also be stated (*e.g. if the Assent is of an undivided half-share to two tenants in common who take equally, the appropriate entry in the 'share' column opposite each person would be 'one-quarter' **not** 'one-half' or 'equal'*). If no shares are specified, any co-assentees will be taken to be joint tenants *inter se*.

(8) Class of ownership

State whether the Assentee is to be registered as 'FULL OWNER' or (where a settlement has been created) as 'LIMITED OWNER' of the land.

(9) The burdens

(i) Give precise details of the burden.

(ii) Identify which folio or part of a folio and, where necessary, whose estate or interest therein is subject to the burden. (Where the burden does not affect all the Land in this Assent make this clear – *e.g. 'affecting only the land in entry 1 of the First Schedule/the land shown coloured ... on the attached map/the dwelling house on the land in Folio ...'*).

(iii) If a burden is a charge for payment of money, identify it as such and state whether interest is payable.

(iv) If two or more burdens are to be registered, their priority *inter se* should be clarified.

(10) Person entitled to burden

Where the burden is a charge or right of residence, maintenance or support, state the name, address in the UK for the service of notices and description of any person entitled to the benefit of the burden.

(11) Execution

Unless witnessed by a solicitor the Assent must be witnessed by two people neither of whom is a party to the Assent. Witnesses must subscribe their names, addresses and descriptions.

(12) Certificate of identity

(i) The relevant details should be completed and the certificate should be signed by the solicitor handling the deceased's estate or, if none, by an independent person having knowledge of the facts.

(ii) Add any other certificate of identity which may be necessary to prove that the personal representative is entitled to make the Assent.

LAND REGISTRY FORM 17

ASSENT BY PERSONAL REPRESENTATIVE

COMPLETE PANELS AS PER ATTACHED INSTRUCTIONS

Note 1

County: XXX	Date: 1 November 2001
All Folio(s) affected: FOLIO NO. YYY	**Registered Owner(s):** OONAGH MARY O'BRIEN

Note 2

Deceased Registered Owner: OONAGH MARY O'BRIEN
who died on: 12 MAY 2001

Note 3

> **The Personal Representative(s) of the said deceased:**
>
> 1. Patricia Helen Partridge, 3 Lower Street, Belfast – Teacher
> 2. Norman Bruce Martin, 28 Paul Avenue, Belfast – Radiographer

I/We the above named personal representative(s), for the purpose of administering the estate of the deceased Registered Owner, assent to the vesting of the property described in the First Schedule in the Assentee(s) as set out in the said Schedule and request registration accordingly, subject as appears in the folio(s) and also subject to registration of the burden(s)(if any) set out in the Second Schedule.

Note 4

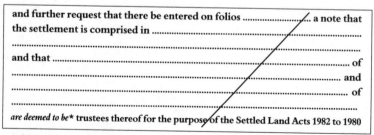

and further request that there be entered on folios .... **a note that the settlement is comprised in** ....

....

and that .... **of**

.... **and**

.... **of**

....

are deemed to be★ **trustees thereof for the purpose of the Settled Land Acts 1982 to 1980**

★ *delete if inappropriate*

THE FIRST SCHEDULE

The Property (Note 5)	The Assentee(s) (Note 6)	Assentees' Share (Note7)	Class of ownership (Note 8)
All the land in Folio YYY County XXX	Peter Morris Eltham Park House Beech Avenue Marbleton Co. Antrim	All	Fee Simple

THE SECOND SCHEDULE

Burdens (Note 9)	Person(s) entitled to benefit of burden (Note 10)
None	None

Note 11

SIGNED SEALED AND DELIVERED
by the said PATRICIA HELEN PARTRIDGE
in the presence of:

SIGNED SEALED AND DELIVERED
by the said NORMAN BRUCE MARTIN
in the presence of:

Certificate of Identity – Note 12

I NORMAN BRUCE MARTIN

of 28 Paul Avenue, Belfast

hereby certify that OONAGH MARY O'BRIEN

named in a Grant of Probate of the Will

issued on 9 July 2001 **is one and the same person as** OONAGH MARY O'BRIEN
the registered owner of the within mentioned folio(s)

Dated this   **day of**   **200**

Signed ....

Application Number

Day Code

New Folio Number

Received

NIHE DEV

Mark Off

Application for Registration

Form 100A

Please complete the white boxes on pages 1 & 2 using typescript or BLOCK CAPITALS

For Official Use
Map Ref:

1. County: X X X

Folio(s) affected

FOLIO No. YYY

If unsufficient space continue on a separate sheet and enter 'See list'

2. Queries to be sent and documents returned to:–

NORMAN BRUCE MARTIN
28 PAUL AVENUE
BELFAST

Postcode__________ **DX**__________

Telephone (code)__________

Fax__________

Applicant's Land Registry Code_/_/_

Applicant's Reference
_/_/_/_/_/_/_/_/_/_/_/_/_/_/

3. Clients PATRICIA HELEN PARTRIDGE AND NORMAN BRUCE MARTIN

4. Fees and Priority (Describe each dealing concisely and indicate whether it affects the **Whole** or **Part** of the Folio.)

List applications in **priority** order	Current Market Value (£)	Fee Paid (£)	Fee Impression
RELEASE OF CHARGE	25,000	25.00	
ASSENT	125,000	50.00	
	Tick if required	Fee Paid (£)	
Certificate of Charge			
New Land Certificate (new folio)			
Uncertified Copy Map (new folio)			
Certified Copy Map (new folio)			

I/We enclose a crossed cheque/postal order payable to DOE General Account for

Total Fee	£75.00

For official use only
Fee due £
Fee received
Overpayment refunded ☐
Underpayment requested ☐

5. Documents lodged – list all documents lodged (attach a continuation sheet if necessary)

Date	Document	Parties	Checked
—	FOLIO YYY	LAND CERTIFICATE	
—	CERTIFICATE OF CHARGE	OONAGH MARY O'BRIEN TO BUILDING SOCIETY	
9 JULY 1999	PROBATE	OONAGH MARY O'BRIEN DECEASED	**Date**
	ASSENT	PERS REPS O'BRIEN TO ELTHAM	

6. Special directions
Complete where any document is to be returned to a person or firm **not** mentioned in panel 2.

Description of document _____ NONE _____

Addressee_____

_____

_____

_____Postcode_____

7. Change of address
This panel should be completed if the address of any person named (or to be named) on the folio is to be updated.

Please update the address of _____

to read _____

_____

_____Postcode_____

8. Checklist

a. Have you enclosed the appropriate fee and signed the cheque? ☐

b. Have all deeds been executed dated and witnessed? ☐

c. Have deeds been presented to the Stamp Office or has a PD1 Form been enclosed? ☐

d. Where the application refers to a map is the map enclosed and does it meet the current requirements? ☐

e. Have all the necessary Land Certificates and Certificates of Charge been lodged? If not have you lodged a request for an order to produce/dispense with production and appropriate fee? ☐

If you have any query about the completion of this form please ring our Customer Information Unit on 01232 251515

9. Declaration by applicant or solicitor

I/We certify that the information supplied is correct.

Signature of applicant or solicitor_____

Date_____

Glossary

Lay executors need to understand clearly the meaning of legal terminology and expressions used in connection with wills and probate. Some of them are obscure or unusual. Always check if you are uncertain. The most commonly used words and expressions are listed below.

administrator the person who administers the estate of a person who has died intestate

bequest a gift of a particular object or cash (as opposed to 'devise', which means land or buildings)

chattels personal belongings: for example, jewellery, furniture, wine, pictures, books, even cars and horses not used for business. Does not include money or investments

child (referred to in a will or intestacy) child of the deceased including adopted and illegitimate children but, unless specifically included in a will, not stepchildren

co-habitee a partner of the deceased who may be able to claim a share of the estate. The term 'common law wife' has no legal force

confirmation the document issued to executors by the sheriff court in Scotland to authorise them to administer the estate

demise a grant of a lease

devise a gift of house or land

disposition a formal conveyancing document in Scotland

estate all the assets and property of the deceased, including houses, cars, investments, money and personal belongings

executor the person appointed in the will to administer the estate of a deceased person

heritable estate land and buildings in Scotland

inheritance tax the tax which may be payable when the total estate of the deceased person exceeds a set threshold (subject to various exemptions and adjustments)

intestate a person who dies without making a will

issue all the lineal descendants of a person, that is, children, grand-children, great-grandchildren and so on

legacy a gift of money

life interest a gift which gives someone the right to income or occupation of an investment or property for life only after which the asset goes to the remaindermen (*q.v.*)

life tenant the person who enjoys the benefit for life

minor a person under 18 years of age

moveable estate property other than land and buildings in Scotland

next of kin the person entitled to the estate when a person dies intestate

letters of administration the document issued to administrators by a probate registry to authorise them to administer the estate of an intestate

personal estate or personalty all the investments and belongings of a person apart from land and buildings

personal representative a general term for both administrators and executors

probate of the will the document issued to executors by a probate registry in England, Wales and Northern Ireland to authorise them to administer the estate

proving the will making the application for probate to a probate registry

probate registry the government office which deals with probate matters. The Principal Probate Registry is in London with district registries in cities and some large towns

real estate or realty land and buildings owned by a person

remaindermen the persons who get an asset on the death of the life tenant

residue what is left of the estate to share out after all the debts and specific bequests and legacies have been paid

specific bequests particular items gifted by will. They may be referred to as 'specific legacies'

testator a person who makes a will

will the document in which you say what is to happen to your possessions on your death

Useful addresses

Accountant of Court
Parliament House
2 Parliament Square
Edinburgh EH1 IRQ
Tel: 0131-240 6758
Email: enquiries@scotcourts.gov.uk
Website: www.scotcourts.gov.uk

Age Concern England
Astral House
1268 London Road
London SW16 4ER
Tel: (0800) 009966
Website: www.ageconcern.org.uk

Belfast Gazette
The Stationery Office
16 Arthur Street
Belfast BT1 4GD
Tel: 028-9089 5135
Email: belfast.gazette@tso.co.uk
Website: www.gazettes-online.co.uk

District Probate Registry
Court House
Bishop Street
Londonderry BT48 7PY
Tel: 028-7126 1832
*for people living in Londonderry (Derry),
Fermanagh and Tyrone*
*For free booklet: 'Step by step guide to
personal probate applications'*

Edinburgh Gazette
73 Lothian Road
Edinburgh EH3 9AW
Tel: 0131-622 1342
Email: edinburgh.gazette@tso.co.uk
Website: www.gazettes-online.co.uk

FT Interactive Data
Fitzroy House
Epworth Street
London EC2A 4DL
Tel: 020-7825 8642/8672
Website: www.ftid.com
*For back copies of the Stock Exchange
Daily Official List*

Inland Revenue Capital Taxes Office
Ferrers House
PO Box 38
Castle Meadow Road
Nottingham NG2 1BB
Helpline: (0845) 302 0900
Inheritance tax helpline
Websites:
www.inlandrevenue.gov.uk
www.inlandrevenue.gov.uk/cto/iht.
htm *(inheritance tax)*

Inland Revenue Capital Taxes Office (Northern Ireland)
Level 3 Dorchester House
52-58 Great Victoria Street
Belfast BT2 7QL
Tel: 028-9050 5353
Websites:
www.inlandrevenue.gov.uk
www.inlandrevenue.gov.uk/cto/iht.
htm *(inheritance tax)*

Inland Revenue Capital Taxes Office (Scotland)
Meldrum House
15 Drumsheugh Gardens
Edinburgh EH3 UG
Tel: 0131-777 4293
Websites:
www.inlandrevenue.gov.uk
www.inlandrevenue.gov.uk/cto/iht.
htm *(inheritance tax)*

Institute of Professional Will Writers
Wiske Farm House
Great Smeaton
Northallerton
North Yorkshire DL6 3HQ
Tel: (01609) 881332

Land Registers of Northern Ireland
Lincoln Building
27-45 Great Victoria Street
Belfast BT2 7SL
Tel: 028-9025 1555
Website: www.lrni.gov.uk

Land Registry
32 Lincoln's Inn Fields
London WC2A 3PH
Tel: 020-7917 8888
Website: www.landregistry.gov.uk

Law Society of England and Wales
Correspondence Team
Ipsley Court
Berrington Close
Redditch
Worcestershire B98 0TD
Tel: (0870) 606 6575
For public information including solicitors who specialise in wills and probate
Tel: 020-7242 1222 *(switchboard)*
Email:
info.services@lawsociety.org.uk
Websites: www.lawsociety.org.uk
www.solicitors-online.com

Law Society of Northern Ireland
Law Society House
98 Victoria Street
Belfast BT1 3JZ
Tel: 028-9023 1614
Email: info@lawsoc-ni.org
Website: www.lawsoc-ni.org

Law Society of Scotland
26 Drumsheugh Gardens
Edinburgh EH3 7YR
Tel: 0131-226 7411
Email: lawscot@lawscot.org.uk
Website: www.lawscot.org.uk

London Gazette
PO Box 7923
London SW8 5WF
Tel: 020-7394 4580
Email: london.gazette@tso.co.uk
Website: www.gazettes-online.co.uk

National Savings and Investments
Glasgow G58 1SB
Use this office for enquiries about Capital Bonds, Children's Bonus Bonds, FIRST Option Bonds, Fixed Rate Savings Bonds, Ordinary Accounts and Investment Accounts

National Savings and Investments
Durham DH99 1NS
*Enquiries about Deposit Bonds, Cash
mini-ISAs, TESSA ISAs, Savings
Certificates, SAYE Contracts and Yearly
Plan Agreements*

National Savings and Investments
Blackpool FY3 9YP
*Enquiries about Premium Bonds, Income
Bonds, Pensioners'
Guaranteed Bonds, Guaranteed Equity
Bonds*
Tel: (0845) 964 5000
*Central helpline for enquiries about
National Savings products,
including advice on filling in form NSA
904 'Death of a Holder of
National Savings'*
Email:
customerenquiries@nsandi.com
Website: www.nsandi.com

Office for the Supervision of Solicitors
Victoria Court
8 Dormer Place
Leamington Spa
Warwickshire CV32 5AE
Helpline: (0845) 608 6565
Tel: (01926) 820082
Email: enquiries@lawsociety.org.uk
Websites: www.solicitors-online.com
www.oss.lawsociety.org.uk
*For information on solicitors specialising in
wills and probate*

Oyez Straker
Oyez House, 16 Third Avenue
Denbigh West Industrial Estate
Bletchley
Milton Keynes MK1 1TG
Tel: (01908) 361166
Website: www.oyezformslink.co.uk
*Telesales for probate forms and other
stationery*

The Pension Service
Tyne View Park
Whitley Road
Newcastle upon Tyne NE98 1YJ
Tel: (0845) 606 0265
Textphone: (0845) 606 0285
For pensions enquiries
Tel: 0191-213 5000
Websites: www.dwp.gov.uk
www.thepensionservice.gov.uk

Principal Probate Registry
First Avenue House
42-49 High Holborn
London WC1V 6NP
Tel: 020-7947 6939 *(information and
advice)*
Minicom: 020-7947 7602
Helpline: (0845) 302 0900 *(for IHT
and probate information, and for probate
packs)*
Email:
ade.ojo@courtservice.gsi.gov.uk
Website: www.courtservice.gov.uk

*Principal Registry of the Family
Division*
see Principal Probate Registry

Probate and Matrimonial Office
Royal Courts of Justice
PO Box 410
Chichester Street
Belfast BT1 3JF
Tel: 028-9023 5111
Email:
probateandmatrimonial@courtsni.
gov.uk
Website: www.courtsni.gov.uk

*Public Record Office of Northern
Ireland*
66 Balmoral Avenue
Belfast BT9 6NY
Tel: 028-9025 5905
Email: proni@dcalni.gov.uk
Website: www.proni.gov.uk

Registers of Scotland
Customer Service Centre
Erskine House
68 Queen Street
Edinburgh EH2 4NF
Tel: (0845) 6070161
OR
Customer Service Centre
9 George Square
Glasgow G2 1DY
Tel: (0845) 6070164
Email:
customer.services@ros.gov.uk
Website: www.ros.gov.uk

Royal Courts of Justice
Strand
London WC2A 2LL
Tel: 020-7947 6000
Website: www.courtservice.gov.uk

Sheriff Clerks' Office
Commissary Department
27 Chambers Street
Edinburgh EH1 1LB
Tel: 0131-225 2525
Website: www.scotcourts.gov.uk
*Ask for the commissary department for
documents and advice on wills and
confirmation*

Society of Will Writers
First Floor Chambers
Roe House
Boundary Lane
South Hykeham
Lincoln LN6 9NQ
Tel: (01522) 687888
Email: society.willwriters@virgin.net
Website: www.willwriters.com

Terence Higgins Trust
52 –54 Grays Inn Road,
London WC1X 8JU
Tel: 020-7831 0330
Email: info@tht.org.uk
Website: www.tht.org.uk

Index

administration of an estate 90, 156–85
  accounting to the Inland Revenue 92,
      125–7, 140–51, 164–6, 184
  accounts 181–4
  completion point 165
  distribution 167–81
  gathering the assets 156–62
  paying off creditors 162–4
  process 96–7
  Scotland 217–29
  without grant of probate 88
administrators 10, 48–9, 50, 90, 189, 193
alterations to a will 81–6
  codicils 72, 81–3
  deed of variation 44, 46, 83–4, 188
assent 176–7, 179–80, 239–44
assets
  abroad 22, 59, 60, 191
  business assets 173
  gathering 156–67
  joint assets 10–11, 21–2, 32, 45, 66,
      111–12, 191
  Scotland 220–1
  valuation 53–4, 105–21, 129–33, 160,
      161, 167

bank accounts 107–9
  executorship account 95, 158, 167
  freezing 107, 129
  Girobank account 107, 136
  joint bank accounts 108–9
          Scotland 211–12
  overdrafts 102, 157
banks
  depositing a will with 63, 64, 99
  as executors 49, 51–2, 94
  and share sales 161
beneficiaries
  bankrupt beneficiaries 28, 189
  predeceasing 25–6, 28–9, 209
  tracing 93, 189, 203

under-18s 25, 60, 93, 169–70
  as witnesses 62
bona vacantia 204
bond of caution (Scotland) 226
building society accounts 88, 109–10, 211
businesses 16, 20–1

capital gains tax (CGT) 98, 165, 166,
      173–4
  and the home 45, 111, 175
  indexation allowance 173
  taper relief 173
Capital Taxes Office 98, 126, 135, 136,
      137, 160
capital transfer tax (CTT) 35
  see also inheritance tax
cars 102, 125, 168
cash 127
charge certificate 174, 175–6
charities, gifts to 26, 38, 55, 73, 161
children
  adopted children 14, 25, 55, 194
  disinheriting 59, 207, 212
  drug addiction and profligacy 28, 34
  guardians see guardians
  illegitimate children 14, 25, 53, 55, 194
  and intestacy law 13–14
  legacies to 25, 60, 93, 169–70
  minority interests 93
  predeceasing the testator 25–6, 29
  and Scottish law 205, 208, 228
  stepchildren 14, 25, 32, 33–4, 55
  trusts for 24, 28, 49, 74–5
claims against the estate 12, 27, 28, 59,
      88–9, 93, 185, 188–9, 190–1, 204
codicils 72, 81–3
cohabitees
  and intestacy law 11–12
  joint bank accounts 109
  provision, application for 204
  Scotland 213

wills 79–80, 85
confirmation (Scotland) 217–18, 219,
    221, 222–5
Court of Protection 47, 65–6, 191
creditors
    advertising for 129, 158–9, 190, 227,
        231–2
    creditor priorities 128
    Northern Ireland 231–2
    paying off 162–4
    Scotland 227
Crown, estate passing to the 14, 194, 204,
    215

death certificates 101, 102–3
debts 95, 127–30
    due from the deceased 27–8, 127
    payment of 56, 128–9
    Scotland 227
    shortfall 128–9
    see also creditors
deeds 175, 176, 178, 179
deeds of family arrangement 44, 46
deeds of variation 44, 46, 83–4
destroying a will 84–5
disabled people, trusts and 25
disinheritance 59, 188, 190
    in Scotland 207–8, 212
District Valuers 110, 111, 112, 160,
    167
divorce *see* separation/divorce

enduring power of attorney 65–6
estate
    administration of *see* administration of
        an estate
    distribution of 167–81
    held in trust 46
    insolvency 27–8, 94, 128
    residue 43, 47–8, 55–7, 73, 129, 181,
        185, 229
    see also assets; property
estate duty *see* inheritance tax
executors 48–52, 60, 90–1
    appointing 10, 47, 48, 50–1
    banks as 49, 51–2
    directions to 58–9, 64
    expenses 51, 103, 167–8
    guardians as 53, 75
    legacies to 62
    liabilities 50, 89, 93, 190, 219, 226
    negligence 189–90
    Northern Ireland 231, 232
    powers and duties 48, 50, 103
    professional executors 51

renouncement of
    appointment/removal 49, 73, 91,
        189
    Scotland 209, 217–19, 226
    solicitors 51, 189
    substitutes 52, 73, 91
    as trustees 49, 50, 73–4

farms and agricultural land 16, 20–1, 38
foreign domicile 16, 22, 192
foreign property and land 22, 59, 60, 191
funeral expenses 101, 127
funeral wishes 10, 59, 66

gilts 161, 174
guardians 10, 13, 47, 52–3, 60, 64, 73, 75,
    82

hire purchase loans 125, 126–7, 164
home
    CGT 45, 111, 174
    IHT 45, 111, 133
    joint tenancy 10–11, 21–2, 32, 45, 66,
        111–13, 122, 191
    life interest 176
    making a gift of 44–5
    registered property 175–8, 233
    Scotland 212, 215–16
    tenancy in common 21, 33, 45, 66,
        111, 112, 191
    transferring 174, 175–81
        assent 176–7, 179–80, 239–44
        leasehold property 177, 179, 180
        Northern Ireland 233
        Scotland 228–9
    unregistered property 178–81, 233
    valuation 110–13, 160
household and personal goods 122–5, 168

income tax 125–7, 164–6, 184
income tax return 126, 127, 164–6
inheritance tax (IHT) 35–46, 167
    calculation 39–40, 41–4
    form IHT 200 135, 136, 137, 140–51
    grossing-up 43, 44, 79
    IHT mitigation 17, 20, 38–9, 45–6, 79,
        83–4
    and intestacy 194–5
    lifetime gifts 36–7, 43
    nil-rate band 36, 84
    PETs (potentially exempt transfers)
        23, 37, 60
    raising finance to pay 95, 133–5, 165
    rates 36, 37, 43
    rectification 160–1

seven-year rule 36, 37
tapered relief 37–8
Inland Revenue
  accounting to 92, 125–7, 140–51,
    164–6, 184
  income tax return 126, 127, 164–6
insurance
  house insurance 102
  life insurance 110
intestacy 9, 89, 193–204
  administrators 10, 48–9, 50, 90, 189, 193
  distribution on 10–14, 93, 193–204
    Northern Ireland 233, 234–8
    Scotland 212–17
  IHT and 194–5
  partial intestacy 29, 212

jewellery 125

land certificate 174
Land Registry 174, 175, 176
leasehold property 177, 179, 180
legacies 47, 54–5, 168–70
  free-of-tax legacies 43, 73
  interest on 169–70
  pecuniary legacies 29, 54–5, 129
  postponed legacies 74, 169–70
  tax-bearing legacies 44, 73
Legal Help scheme 17
legal rights (Scotland) 207–8, 216–17,
    227–8
letters of administration 10, 49, 87–8, 89,
    90, 153, 193–4
life interest 11, 16, 36, 56–7, 78, 80, 176,
    185
living wills 66–7
Lloyd's underwriting syndicates 16, 38

mail redirection service 102
marriage, revocation of a will by 48, 85–6
married couples 29–30
  deaths close together/simultaneous
    deaths 12, 13, 30, 40
  disinheritance 59, 207
  inheritance tax 7, 29, 30, 40–1
  and intestacy 10–11, 12
  married minors (Northern Ireland)
    230
  remarriage 12, 32–4
  sample wills 68–76, 78–9
medical research, use of body for 59, 66
mental incapacity 19, 65, 191
mortgages 28, 54, 101, 113–14, 128–30,
    175
moveable estate (Scotland) 207, 216, 220

nation, gifts to the 38
National Savings 22, 88, 92, 106–7,
    134–5, 157
nomination 22, 92
Northern Ireland, wills and probate in
    230–46
nursing and residential homes 26–7, 29,
    31–2, 47

organ donation 66

paintings 125–6
partnerships, business 16, 21, 38
PAYE 125
pensions 119–21
  occupational pension schemes 119–20
  in Scotland 208
  state retirement pension 121
personal representatives
  duties and responsibilities 95, 98, 159
  removal 189
  see also administrators; executors
pets and animals 27
political parties, gifts to 38
Premium Bonds 106–7, 134, 157
prior rights (Scotland) 215–16
probate 87–155
  application forms 135–7, 139
  caveats and citations 188, 192
  confirmation (Scotland) 217–18, 219,
    221, 222–5
  disputes 188, 192
  do-it-yourself 95
  fees 135, 136, 139
  grant of probate 87, 90, 153–4, 155
  Northern Ireland 230, 232
  process 96–7, 138
  when no grant is needed 88
probate oath 139, 152
Probate Registry 98, 135, 137, 139, 152,
    153, 188
property
  automatic transfer of 11, 21, 45, 60, 66,
    88, 92
  foreign property and land 22, 59, 60,
    191
  joint ownership 92, 111–13, 122
  life interest 11, 13, 16, 36, 56–7, 78, 80,
    176, 185
  see also assets; home

relatives
  tracing 93, 203
  whole blood and half-blood 202
reservation of interest 44

residue/residuary estate 43, 47–8, 55–7, 73, 129, 181, 185, 229
revocation of a will 72, 84–6
　by destruction 84–5
　by marriage 48, 85–6
　divorce and 86
　revocation clauses 48
　in Scotland 211

Scotland, wills and confirmation in 205–29
separation/divorce 16, 27
　and claims upon the estate 27, 28, 77–8, 190
　and intestacy laws 12
　maintenance payments 27, 28, 77, 190
　wills 77–8, 86
shares 114–19, 127, 170–2
　dividing up 170–1
　lost share certificates 131–2, 159–60
　private companies 16, 21, 36, 118–19
　sale of 161–2
　taxation 126
　transferring 170, 171–2, 173
　unit trusts 118
　valuation 21, 115–16, 119
solicitors 15–17
　consulting 15–17, 92–5
　depositing wills with 99
　as executors 51, 99, 189
　fees 15, 94–5, 99, 231
Somerset House 64
state benefits 26–7, 101, 121, 159, 227
survivorship destination 212, 228
survivorship provision 40–1, 73, 80

testators 19
　blind testators 19, 62, 210
　testamentary capacity 19, 30–1, 47, 188
　undue influence on 19, 31, 188
Title Information Document (TID) 174, 175, 176, 178
Treasury stock 166, 174
trustees 23, 49–50
　beneficiaries 49
　charges and expenses 57
　dismissing 49
　executors as 49, 50, 73–4
　guardians as 53, 74
　investment responsibilities 58, 74, 75
　powers and obligations 23, 24, 57–8
　professional trustees 57

trusts 22–5, 60
　accumulation and maintenance trusts 24
　children and 24, 28, 49, 74–5
　for disabled beneficiaries 25
　discretionary trusts 24, 27, 28, 33, 34, 37, 79
　fixed trusts 24
　life interest 11, 36, 78, 185
　lifetime gifts to 22, 23, 37
　power of appointment 16
　protective trusts 24
　taxation 23–4, 25
　'trust for sale' 74
　two-year discretionary trust 46
　will trusts 22, 23, 60

unit trusts 118, 170, 171
unmarried people
　and intestacy 11–12
　wills 79–80
　see also cohabitees

will-writing services 15
wills
　alterations 44, 46, 72, 81–6, 188
　ambiguous language 19–20
　attestation clause 18, 19, 61, 62
　challenging 19, 188
　in contemplation of marriage 82, 85–6
　contents 47–67
　examples 68–80
　formal reading 100–1
　home-made will 8, 14–15, 93
　layout 47–8
　living wills 66–7
　lost wills 187
　more than one will 48, 187
　in Northern Ireland 230
　problems 8, 20, 186–7
　reasons for making a will 9–17
　reviewing 65
　revocation 48, 72, 84–6, 211
　safekeeping 63–5, 210
　in Scotland 205–7
　signing and dating 18, 62–3, 187, 209–10
　validity 18–20
　variation of 188–9
witnesses 18, 61, 62, 82, 187
　Scotland 209–10